NEW PERSPECTIVES
ON ANCIENT JUDAISM

VOLUME THREE

NEW PERSPECTIVES
ON ANCIENT JUDAISM

VOLUME THREE

JUDAIC AND CHRISTIAN INTERPRETATION
OF TEXTS:
CONTENTS AND CONTEXTS

Edited by
Jacob Neusner
and
Ernest S. Frerichs

UNIVERSITY
PRESS OF
AMERICA

Lanham • New York • London

Copyright © 1987 by

University Press of America,® Inc.

4720 Boston Way
Lanham, MD 20706

3 Henrietta Street
London WC2E 8LU England

British Cataloging in Publication Information Available

Library of Congress Cataloging-in-Publication Data

Judaic and Christian interpretation of texts.

(New perspectives on ancient Judaism ; v. 3)
Bibliography: p.
1. Bible. O.T. Pentateuch. Aramaic—Criticism,
interpretation, etc. 2. Talmud Yerushalmi—Criticism,
interpretation, etc. 3. Talmud—Sources. 4. Aggada—
History and criticism. I. Neusner, Jacob, 1932-   .
II. Frerichs, Ernest S. III. Series.
BM177.N485   vol. 3   296'.09'01 s   87-16129
[BS1225.2]   [296.1]
ISBN 0-8191-6562-X (alk. paper)
ISBN 0-8191-6563-8 (pbk. : alk. paper)

All University Press of America books are produced on acid-free
paper which exceeds the minimum standards set by the National
Historical Publication and Records Commission.

For

George Landow

Professor of English
Brown University

The editors value his learning and
benefit from his scholarship.

They treasure his human gifts and enjoy them.

We pay our honor to the scholar and our tribute to the man.

CONTENTS

Chapter I. Galatians (1:1-5): Paul and Greco-Roman Rhetoric...................... 1
Robert M. Berchman
University of Virginia

Chpater II. Text as Interpretation: Paul and Ancient Readings of Paul........... 17
Stanley Stowers
Brown University

Chapter III. Translation and Exegetical Augmentation in the Targums to the Pentateuch... 29
Paul Virgil Flesher
Brown University

Chapter IV. Topic, Rhetoric, Logic: Analysis of a Syllogistic Passage in the Yerushalmi.. 87
i.   Logical Discourse 87
ii.   Three Maps: Topic, Rhetoric and Logic.................................... 89
iii.   The Sample Passage... 92
iv.   Translation 93
v.   Topical Analysis... 97
vi.   Rhetorical Analysis... 99
vii.   Logical Analysis..103
viii.   Classification of Rhetorical Forms According to Syllogistic Patterns..106
ix.   Conclusion 122
Richard E. Cohen
Brown University

Chapter V. System or Tradition? The Bavli and its Sources......................127
i.   Tradition or System..127
ii.   The Bavli as Tradition or System 128
iii.   The State of the Question in Prior Research 130
iv.   The Literary Context of Judaic Tradition...............................134
v.   The Literary Corpus and its Cogency: Criteria of Systemic Composition..137
vi.   The Bavli in Relationship to the Yerushalmi...........................140
vii.   The Bavli in Relationship to Other Extant Documents: A Brief Sample..161
viii.   System or Tradition in Light of Literary Facts.......................176
Jacob Neusner
Brown University

Chapter VI. Literary Studies of Aggadic Narrative: A Bibliography.............185
    i.   Bibliographies and Surveys of Secondary Literature 187
    ii.   Aggadah with Reference to Narrative......................................188
    iii.   Folk-Narrative with Reference to Aggadah 190
    iv.   Aggadic Narrative in General..191
    v.   Personalities and Events...194
    vi.   Themes and Motifs..200
    vii.   Aggadic Retellings of Biblical Narratives..............................206
    viii.   Parables and Fables 209
    ix.   Court Cases and Legal Precedents...210
    x.   Sources and Parallels of Aggadic Narratives..........................211
    xi.   Interpretations and Retellings of Aggadic Narratives..............216

Joseph M. Davis
Harvard University

Chapter One

Galatians (1:1-5):
Paul and Greco-Roman Rhetoric[1]

Robert M. Berchman
University of Virginia

I

In this essay I shall attempt to clarify some issues concerning New Testament interpretation through rhetorical criticism.[2] My approach will be based on the assumption, shared by many students of the New Testament, that to see how a text is formed and to assess how it functions, we must view it from the vantage point of Greco-Roman rhetoric.[3] Two of the better known exponents of this approach to the study of the New Testament are Hans Dieter Betz[4] and George Kennedy.[5]

On a very general level rhetorical critics begin with the assumption that the forms of Greco-Roman rhetoric are employed by New Testament writers.[6] Identifying these forms is a simple task. They are extant in the rhetorical handbooks and doxographies of Aristotle, Anaximenes, Cicero, Quintilian, and

---

[1]Versions of this paper were read before the New England Regional *SBL*, the University of Minnesota's Classics faculty, the Religious Studies Section of the Michigan Academy of Arts and Sciences, and the Early Christianity Colloquium at the University of Virginia. I am grateful for helpful discussion on these occasions, especially to Karen King, Stanley Stowers, John Tracey Greene, Robert Anderson, Harry Gamble, and Robert Wilken.

[2]These issues are raised by G. Kennedy, cf. *New Testament Interpretation Through Rhetorical Criticism*, Chapel Hill: 1984, 3-38.

[3]Cf. e.g., A. Wilder, *The Language of the Gospel: Early Christian Rhetoric*, New York, 1964. Also E. Koenig, *Stilistik, Rhetorik, Poetik in Bezug auf die biblische Literatur*, Leipzig: 1900; T.Y. Mullins, "TOPOS as a New Testament Form," *JBL* 99 (1980), 541-547.

[4]H.D. Betz, *Galatians: A Commentary on Paul's Letter to the Churches in Galatia*, Philadelphia: 1979.

[5]G. Kennedy, *New Testament Interpretation Through Rhetorical Criticism*, Chapel Hill: 1984.

[6]Cf. e.g., F.F. Church, "Rhetorical Structure and Design in Paul's Letter to Philemon," *HTR* 61 (1978), 17-33. Also J. Weiss, "Beiträge zur paulinischen Rhetorik," *ThS* (1897). *Festschrift für Bernhard Weiss*, ed. C.R. Gregory, Göttingen: 1897.

Theon of Smyrna.[7] Once the topics *(topoi, loci)*, genres *(genê, genera)*, parts of speech *(moria logou, partes orationis)*, and syllogisms *(enthymêmê, epicheirêmê, epagôgê)* are identified, the more difficult task begins. Working as a form-critic, the rhetorical critic describes the form and defines its function in a New Testament text.[8] A good example of this method is its application to the letters of Paul, specifically Galatians.[9]

Although this type of rhetorical criticism is theoretically sound, it does exhibit exegetical shortcomings. This is clear from the results of rhetorical criticism on Galatians. According to Betz's interpretation, Paul's letter is forensic.[10] It is composed according to the forms of forensic rhetoric and functions to defend Paul's character and defame his opponent's character. Kennedy, on the other hand, tries to show that Paul's letter is deliberative and exhortatory.[11] The letter functions not to defend Paul's character, but to exhort the Galatians to specific actions.

The problem exemplified in these interpretations of Galatians is that if it is not clear what genre of rhetoric Paul employed, then surely the more complex aspects of rhetorical criticism such as the definition of Paul's mode of topical arrangement, his forms of syllogistic argumentation, and the speech parts employed to frame his speech act, appear beyond description and definition. Furthermore, if these questions cannot be answered, then those concerning the meaning of the speech act and its function cannot be addressed at all.

An inability to settle such basic questions does not beset the literary critic in an analysis of Paul's epistolography.[12] Indeed, a healthy skepsis concerning the applicability of rhetorical criticism to an analysis of Paul is warranted. Its application to Galatians appears wrecked on the shoals of formal description.[13] This suggests either some flaws in the method of rhetorical criticism, or a mistake in the claim that Paul was a rhetorician.

---

[7]For a description of rhetorical theory in antiquity, cf. R. Volkman, *Die Rhetorik der Griechen und Römer in systematischen bersicht,* Leipzig: 1885; G. Kennedy, *The Art of Rhetoric in the Roman World,* Princeton: 1972 and *Greek Rhetoric Under Roman Emperors,* Princeton: 1983. Also H. Lausberg, *Handbuch der literarischen Rhetorik: Eine Grundlegung der Literaturwissenschaft,* München: 1960; J. Martin, *Antike Rhetorik: Technik und Methode, Handbuch der Altertumswissenschaft,* ii. 3, München: 1974.

[8]Cf. e.g., W. Wuellner, "Paul's Rhetoric of Argumentation in Romans," *CBQ* 38 (1976), 330-351; D.G. Bradley, "The TOPOS as a Form in the Pauline Paraensis," *JBL* 72 (1953), 238-246; J.C. Brunt, "More on the TOPOS as a New Testament Form," *JBL* 104/3 (1985), 495-500.

[9]Cf. e.g., H.D. Betz, *Galatians,* Philadelphia: 1979; G. Kennedy, *New Testament Interpretation,* Chapel Hill: 1984, 144-152.

[10]*Galatians,* ch. 1.

[11]*New Testament Interpretation,* 144-152.

[12]Cf. e.g., R. Bultmann, *Der Stil der paulinischen Predigt und die kynistischstoische Diatribe,* Göttingen: 1910; S.K. Stowers, *The Diatribe and Paul's Letter to the Romans,* Chico: 1981; R. Jewett, "Romans as an Ambassadorial Letter," *Interpretation* 36 (1982), 5-20.

[13]This criticism is raised by N. Lund in his *Chiasmus in the New Testament,* Chapel Hill: 1942, esp. 8, 23. New Testament texts do not display any of the formal characteristics common to Attic rhetoric.

This negative conclusion leads directly to the central issue of this essay: How ought we understand the relationship between Greco-Roman rhetorical forms and the rhetorical composition of Galatians? I will try to show that there are important formal parallels between Greco-Roman and Pauline rhetoric. However, it is confusing to suggest that these forms exist in pure form in Galatians.[14]

The confusion arises from the assumption by rhetorical critics of a mimetic relationship between the theory and practice of rhetoric.[15] According to the handbooks, rhetorical forms are self-contained constructs that are employed in a regular, indeed almost mechanistic, way. Functionally, these forms fit strictly defined persuasive situations. Certain topics are associated with specific genres of rhetoric. There are forensic, deliberative, and laudatory places of argument. A rhetorical composition is framed in one genre and its corresponding parts of speech. Never is there a mixture of genres, topics, and parts of speech in a single speech act. Finally, specific topics and types of syllogism are associated. Deductive proofs complement certain topics, inductive proofs others.[16]

Although these rhetorical forms had the meaning ascribed to them by the theoreticians for Paul, they had a quite different application. His art of rhetoric is not stereotyped.[17] He moves between different genres of rhetoric and topics in a single speech act. His parts of speech are equally flexible and his mode of syllogistic argumentation is connected with a wide range of commonplaces. As Paul sees it, rhetorical forms are adjusted to fit the persuasive context his letter(s) address. Thus the inventive and not the mimetic aspects of rhetoric are what interest him.[18]

This gap between rhetorical *theôria* and *praxis* explains why rhetorical critics dispute the genre of Galatians, argue over its parts of speech, disagree on its topical arrangement, and contest its syllogist structure.[19] Paul combines

---

[14]Following G. Kennedy, *New Testament Interpretation*, 12.

[15]This is particularly true in regard to New Testament composition. This is partially due to the logography of its rhetoric, cf. K. Burke, *The Rhetoric of Religion: Studies in Logography*, Berkeley-Los Angeles: 1970. Also R. Funk, *Language, Hermeneutic, and Word of God: The Problem of Language in the New Testament and Contemporary Theology*, New York: 1966. It is also due to the distinct nature of the *koine* rhetoric found in the New Testament, cf. J.C. Brunt, "More on the TOPOS as a New Testament Form," *JBL* 104/3 (1985), 495-500.

[16]The basic theoretical concepts underlying classical rhetoric are enunciated by Aristotle in his *Rhetoric*, in the *Rhetoric to Alexander*, and in Cicero's and Quintilian's handbooks on rhetoric. For a complete portrayal of ancient rhetorical theory see the works by Kennedy, Lausberg, and Martin, cf. n. 6.

[17]This is clear from his use of the *topos*, cf. J.C. Brunt, "More on the TOPOS as a New Testament Form," *JBL* 104/3 (1985), 495-500.

[18]This is brought out well by T.Y. Mullins, "TOPOS as a New Testament Form," *JBL* 99 (1980), 541-547.

[19]Cf. e.g., "The TOPOS as Rhetorical Form in the Pauline Paraensis," *JBL* 72 (1953), 238-246; V.P. Furnish, *The Love Command in the New Testament*, Nashville: 1972, 90; J.E. Crouch, *The Origin and Intention of the Colossian Hauftafel*, Göttingen: 1972, 10, n. 1. This

elements of forensic and deliberative oratory in Galatians, and occasionally complements both with the use of the epideictic genre. He moves from judicial narrative to paraensis and back again without breaking stride, and often amplifies both with a panygeric *lalia.*

Adaptability and flexibility are the hallmarks of Pauline rhetoric. The recognition of this basic fact forces the rhetorical critic to align handbook *apriora* with Pauline *praxis.* There are profound discontinuities between the accounts of how rhetoric ought to be practiced and how Paul practices rhetoric. Therefore, to undertake a rhetorical exegesis of Galatians requires one to bracket theoretical assumptions and observe rhetoric in practice.

Assuming this is the correct way of approaching and understanding Pauline rhetoric, we have a basis for examining how it works in Galatians. I now want to turn to the purely formal dimensions of rhetorical patterning characteristic of persuasive composition.[20]

We can recognize the structure of Paul's rhetoric at least in Galatians by reference to its (1) logic, (2) topic, and (3) genre. These three aspects of the speech act, when combined, provide the foundations for a rhetorical exegesis of Galatians.[21]

(1) A speech is built upon external and internal proofs. The first type of proof relies on facts while the second is the product of invention. These proofs refer to a series of basic issues which are fact, definition, quality, and jurisdiction. Proofs are formed logically. There is the deductive proof *(enthymêmê or epicheirêmê)* which takes the form of a statement with a supporting reason. The statement can be categorical, hypothetical, conjunctive, or disjunctive. It is often supported by a maxim. There is also the inductive proof *(paradeigma)* which uses a series of examples to demonstrate a general conclusion. Examples are drawn from the sources of external and internal proofs.

(2) In constructing a speech, topics are used. These are places of argument. Topics of *enthymemes* may be opposites, comparisons, considerations of time, different meanings of a word, consequences, advantages and disadvantages, to mention but a few. They function as places from which exhortation, dissuasion,

---

debate on *topos* circles on the issue whether rhetorical topics in Paul have any relation to the problems and needs the apostle is facing. The genre issue is debated by H.D. Betz, *Galatians,* Philadelphia: 1979, and G. Kennedy, *New Testament Interpretation,* Chapel Hill: 1984.

[20]This entails a description of rhetorical theory alone. Once the forms of rhetoric are identified, the exegete has a form-critical apparatus which can be applied to the exegesis of a text. This process of formal description and identification brackets the question whether or not these forms appear in their pure form in the text to be exegeted. This form-critical method of rhetorical exegesis has been applied to Origen of Alexandria's *Periarchon* and *Mishnah Tosefta Tohorot,* cf. R.M. Berchman, *From Philo to Origen: Middle Platonism in Transition,* Chico, 1984, 215-293; "Rabbinic Syllogistic: The Case of Mishnah Tosefta Tohorot," *Approaches to Ancient Judaism* v, Atlanta: 1985, 81-98.

[21]For a description and definition of these forms of rhetoric, see no. 6.

praise, and blame arise and end. They touch on things possible and impossible, past and future fact, and degree. There are material and strategical headings under which these topics are arranged.

(3) A speech is composed according to three modes of internal or artistic proof. There is the character which inheres in the speaker, the emotion that inheres in the audience, and the logic that inheres within the discourse. Once the proof is introduced, it is argued through one or more of the three rhetorical genres. In the genre of forensic oratory, the aim is to defend one's character by manipulating the emotions of the audience through discourse. In deliberative rhetoric, the aim is to exhort an audience to particular actions. This is done through an appeal to the emotions of the audience through the speech act. With epideictic oratory, the aim is to extol virtues the rhetor wishes to cultivate. This strengthening of audience adherence to values is effected through an emotional appeal to the audience on behalf of these values.

With these general rules in hand we move to the prologue or proem of Galatians (1:1-5). The goal of this section of the essay is to see how Paul crafts the opening of his letter. First, the logical, topical, and generic characteristics of the proem will be outlined. This will permit a rhetorical exegesis of the pericope.

The goal of form-critical exegesis is to identify the formal structure of Paul's proem. This description of the proem's rhetoric permits us to reconstruct the strategy of composition reflected in a text, and the rhetorical situation it reflects. No claim is made that these forms appear in pure form in Galatians. Thus the rhetorical exegesis that follows functions as a hermeneutical experiment.[22]

II

The proem (1:1-5) is a linear speech that exhibits the characteristics of the topical and inductive syllogism. The syllogistic structure of Galatians (1:1-5) is:

(1) *Pisteis*

    A. Proem

1:1 *lysis, ergasia*	1:1 *paradeigma*, conclusion
1:2 *ergasia*	1:2 *auxêsis* (amplification)
1:3 *ergasia*	1:3 *paradeigma*
1:4 *epicheirêmê*	1:4 conclusion
1:5 *epenthymeme*	1:5 *auxêsis* (amplification)

---

[22]This type of rhetorical exegesis was carried out on Origen's *Periarchon, Praef.* 1-4 and *De Deo* 1:1-9 by R.M. Berchman, *From Philo to Origen*, 215-293. For a description of this method and its limitations, see 320-321, n. 14.

Each of the topics within a part of speech is logically arranged to make an intelligible sentence. A series of sentences constitutes a proposition. (1:1-5) is the initial subproposition of the proem (1:1-10).

In this pericope, the common topics are fact, and the impossible; the material topic is the question of apostleship; and the strategical topics are from opposites, from authority, from relation, from the more and the less, and from parallel cases.

The topical arrangement of Galatians (1:1-5) is:

(2) *Topoi (Loci)*

A. Proem: *Common Topic,* Past Fact, the Impossible; *Material Topic,* Apostle

1:1 from opposites *(ek tôn enantiôn);* from authority *(ek kriseôs)*

1:2 from relation *(ek tôn pros allêla);* from the more and the less *(mallon kai êtton)*

1:3 from authority *(ek kriseôs);* from relation *(ek tôn pros allêla)*

1:4 from parallel cases *(ex epagôgê);* from authority *(ek kriseôs)*

1:5 from authority *(ek kriseôs)*

From an examination of the topics used in a speech, it is possible to define the species of rhetoric employed in composition. The internal evidence of (1:1-5) suggests that the pericope was composed under the genres of forensic, deliberative, and epideictic oratory. The genres of (1:1-5) are:

(3) *Genera Causarum*

A. Proem	Topics	Genre
1:1	from opposites; from authority	forensic
1:2	from relation; from the more and less	forensic
1:3	from authority; from relation	deliberative
1:4	from parallel cases; from authority	deliberative
1:5	from authority (panegyric)	epideictic

This outline, in short, suggests that the proem of Galatians reflects an adaptation by Paul of Greco-Roman rhetorical forms. In the remainder of the essay I will try to illustrate in greater detail what is involved in this suggestion, and at the same time attempt to give it the sort of exegetical support it needs.

Let us look at (1:1-5) moving from its logical to its topical and general aspects.

1:1

> **Paul an apostle,** not from men nor through man, but through Jesus Christ and God the Father having raised him from the dead.

The syllogistic structure of the pericope is the following. The bold words are the statement *(lysis)* and the remainder of the pericope is the initial working out *(ergasia)* of this statement. Paul argues inductively. He begins with an example *(paradeigma):*

> Paul an apostle

The conclusion from this example is:

> Not from men nor through men, but through Jesus Christ and God the Father having raised him from the dead.

The example results in a conclusion which makes an intelligible sentence. This sentence is the initial building block of Paul's proposition that his apostolic claim is sound.

The topics make up the smallest unit of rhetorical discourse. The topical arrangement is twofold. The underlined words constitute the topic from authority *(ek kriseôs).* The other words make up the topic from opposites *(ek tôn enantiôn).*[23]

This topical sentence is a rhetorical argument. First, Paul establishes his authority as an apostle. Second, he bases it upon the opposites of:

> not from men nor through man

and:

> but through Jesus Christ and God the Father having raised him from the dead.

Paul's apostolic claim is valid because it stands in opposition to any anthropological origin, but in connection with a divine origin. The truth of his claim is sound, at least rhetorically, because of the topical arrangement and logical structure of his argument.

Colpe states:

> in the thesis *ek tôn enantiôn*...see if the contrary of the one follows from the contrary of the other, either directly or conversely, both when you are establishing or demolishing a view.[24]

Since Paul has the authority of an apostle on divine grounds, it is contrary to argue that his apostleship rests on anthropological bases. It would be contrary if

---

[23]Cf. Aristotle, *Rhetoric,* 2.23.12; 2.23.1.

[24]Cf. Aristotle, *Topics,* 2.8 ed. Colpe. Cambridge: 1877.

Paul's authority as an apostle came from men or through man. Hence it comes from God the Father and Jesus Christ. This is clear from the example and its conclusion.

(1:1) establishes the fact of his apostolic claims. It establishes Paul's view that he is a true apostle. Paul amplifies this fact topically and syllogistically. His rhetorical argument leaves little room for either his opponents in Galatia, or the Galatians themselves, to reject his claims, or as Paul will argue later, to ignore the course of conduct he advocates.

Since Paul argues from the topics of authority and opposites, the species of rhetoric is either forensic or deliberative. These topics are commonly used for defense and attack as well as for advice. In this pericope it appears that Paul employs judicial oratory. There are two grounds for this assessment. First, he argues from a past fact to establish a present fact. This means that he wants to defend his authority as an apostle, and refute the charge that it is invalid. Second, he establishes this fact by illustrating that which is impossible. Once he has established his claim, he can advise a course of action, but not before.

1:2

And all the brothers with me, to the churches of Galatia.

This pericope is a continuation of the *ergasia* that supports the *lysis* of (1:1). It is an amplification *(auxêsis)* of the *paradeigma* of (1:1). Logically, Paul adds to the sentence which began his speech. This extended sentence has the following syllogistic structure:

lysis: paradeigma	Paul an apostle,
ergasia:	not from men nor through man, but through Jesus Christ and God the Father having raised him from
auxêsis:	the dead. And all the brothers with me to the churches of Galatia.

The word "and" *(kai)* ties together the topics which make up the working out *(ergasia)* of Paul's argument. This addition is called an amplification *(auxêsis)*, and constitutes another building block of the first subproposition (1:1-5).

The topical arrangement of (1:2) is bipartite. The italicized words are the topic from relation *(ek tôn pros allêla)* and the other words constitute the argument from the more and the less *(mallon kai êtton)*.[25]

The topic from relation identifies the attributes of a doer and his deed and holds each party responsible for a transaction. The topic from the more and the less is a critique that establishes a view.

---

[25]Op. cit., 2.23.3; 2.23.4.

The argument from relation permits Paul to assert that all the brothers (fellow Christians) accept the apostolic claim he postulates in (1:1). Using the construct *(tais ekklêsiais galatias)* he argues comparatively. This permits him to place the Galatians in relation to their brothers. This suggests they have broken with Paul and his Christian community, are in opposition to the authority of Jesus Christ and God the Father, and are less in their eyes.

This topical arrangement functions to isolate the Galatians emotionally and strengthen Paul's character *(ethos)*. By manipulating the emotions of his audience, Paul's argument has an ethical end. The argument from relation identifies the attributes of the Galatians as less than Paul and the brothers. Since each party is responsible for their actions, the inference is the Galatians by their actions place themselves in opposition to divine authority.

The species of rhetoric is forensic. Paul's use of topics suggests this genre of composition. He argues from relation to defend his apostolic claim, and from comparison to criticize his opponents in the churches of Galatia.

In (1:1) Paul established the fact of his apostleship. In (1:2) he establishes the fact of opposition to his apostleship among the Galatians. Once he has established this second datum he can advocate a course of action the Galatians should follow. Since his apostolic claims were authoritatively demonstrated from contraries, and their brothers accept this claim, Paul opens the issue, why not the Galatians?

1:3

> Grace to you and peace from our God the Father and from the Lord Jesus Christ.

Topically, this pericope is a continuation of the *ergasia* which supports the *lysis* postulated at (1:1). Paul is adding to the *auxêsis* concluded at (1:2). (1:3) is also the beginning of a second inductive syllogism. It is the example *(paradeigma)* whose conclusion unfolds at (1:4).

(1:3) is an addition to the extended sentence (1:1-2). This sentence has the following syllogistic structure:

lysis: paradeigma	Paul an apostle,
ergasia:	not from men nor through man, but through Jesus Christ and God the Father having raised
auxêsis:	him from the dead. And all the brothers with
ergasia:	me to the churches of Galatia. Grace to you
paradeigma:	and peace from our God the Father and from the Lord Jesus Christ.

The new argument constitutes another building block of the subproposition (1:1-5).

The topical scheme of (1:3) is twofold. Paul argues from the topics of authority *(ek kriseôs)* and relation *(ek tôn pros allêla).*[26] Since this sentence is a salutation in the form of a prayer, it is authoritative. Paul, as the sender of this salutation-prayer, strengthens his relation to Jesus Christ and God the Father and establishes his jurisdiction as an apostle. He is mediator for the Galatians to Jesus Christ and God the Father. That is, Paul opens a new issue *(stasis).*[27] The first issue was one of fact. This issue is one of jurisdiction. Paul rejects the right of the Galatians to make a judgment on the validity of his apostolic claims.

Paul sets up the conditions for the re-establishment of a correct relationship between the Galatians and divine authority. He is the bridge for the Galatians to their savior and God. In order to be associated with Jesus Christ and God the Father the Galatians must accept Paul as their apostle. The key word in (1:3) is "our" *(hêmon).*

When Paul used these topics in (1:1-2), he argued forensically to establish a *stasis* of fact. In this pericope he employs them to argue deliberately to establish a *stasis* of jurisdiction. Paul reminds them of the fact of his apostleship, and then advises them to follow a definite course of action. They cannot be the judges of his authority.

This genre shift is self-conscious. Under a new issue, Paul advises the Galatians of their correct relationship to him and divine authority, and of the advantages *(viz.,* grace and peace) which come with their recognition of his jurisdiction.

1:4

The one having given himself on behalf of our sins so that he might deliver us out of this present evil age according to the will of our God and Father.

The logical structure of (1:4) is manifold. Paul's formula is an amplification *(auxêsis)* of the salutation at (1:3). As an amplification of an example, the pericope is the working out *(ergasia)* of the topical argument of the preceding verse. It is a conclusion inferred from an example. (1:3-4) has the following syllogistic structure:

paradeigma	Grace and peace to you from God our Father and the Lord Jesus Christ
auxêsis	having given himself on behalf of our sins so as he might deliver us out of the present evil age according to the will of our God and Father.

---

[26]Ibid., 2.23.12; 2.23.3.

[27]A *stasis* is the basic issue of a case. There are four main issues that can be addressed. They are fact, definition, quality, and jurisdiction, cf. Quintilian, *In. Or.,* 3.6. Classical theorists thought that *stasis* theory was applicable to deliberative rhetoric, although its categories had their origin for use in forensic oratory in the law courts.

(1:4) is also the authoritative statement which concludes the topical argument of (1:1-3). (1:1-4) constitutes a topical syllogism, or an *epicheirêmê.*[28] It is a list of topics worked out *(ergasia)* to support a statement *(lysis).* The syllogistic structure of this extended argument is:

lysis: (1:1)	Statement
ergasia: (1:1-3)	Apostolic Formula, Salutation, Prayer
epicheirêmê: (1:4)	Supporting Statement

Paul attaches this authoritative christological formula to the salutation which preceded it in order to conclude the initial subproposition of his proem. This extended subproposition has the following architectonic:

lysis: paradeigma:	Paul an apostle,
ergasia:	not from men nor through man, but through Jesus Christ and God the Father having raised
auxêsis:	him from the dead. And all the brothers with me
ergasia:	to the churches of Galatia. Grace to you and
paradeigma:	peace from our God the Father and from the Lord
ergasia:	Jesus Christ. The one having given himself on behalf of our sins so that he might deliver us
auxêsis:	out of this present evil age according to the will of our God and Father.

The topical arrangement of (1:4) is bipartite. Paul argues from parallel cases *(ex epagôgê)* and from authority *(ek kriseôs).*[29] The topic from parallel cases works in the following manner. In the salutation-prayer of (1:3) Paul proclaims that grace and peace come from God the Father and the Lord Jesus Christ. This example is Paul's general case. From this general statement he infers a particular case. The particular statement is (1:4), "The one having given himself on behalf of our sins so that he might deliver us out of this present evil age." The topic from authority begins with the clause, "according to the will of our God and Father." The *kata*-clause validates Paul's argument from parallel cases.

The argument is from the general to the particular. Paul's goal is to outline

---

[28]The ancient rhetoricians maintained that topics were the source of a rhetorical system, cf. *Rhetores Graeci* (ed. Spengel), Leipzig: 1853-56, vol. 1., p. 447. According to this definition, a rhetorical syllogism *(epicheirêmê)* is a list of topics with a concluding authoritative statement. Hermogenes places the rhetorical syllogism under the category of *stasis.* A syllogism *(epicheirêmê)* is a topically ordered statement that supports a speaker's answer to what an opponent claims. An *epicheirêmê* is a supporting statement to a *lysis*, cf. *On Invention* (ed. Rabe), 140-154.

[29]Aristotle, *Rhetoric*, 2.23.11; 2.23.12.

to the Galatians the advantages gained if they are in an association with Paul. The content of the good is told in order that he may advise them on how they should act.

Logically and topically (1:4) is linked to (1:3). The species of rhetoric in the specific example is identical to the species of rhetoric in the general example. That is to say, the genre of oratory in (1:4) is deliberate or advisory. Arguing from authority, Paul reminds the Galatians of his *stasis* of fact. Arguing from parallel cases, he reminds them of his *stasis* of jurisdiction. In continuing in the advisory stance he assumed in (1:3), Paul can reaffirm the juridical stance he assumed in (1:1-2).

1:5

To whom the glory unto the ages of the ages, amen.[30]

The syllogistic structure of (1:5) is twofold. It is the concluding statement *(epenthymeme)* of the subproposition (1:1-5).[31] It functions to clinch the argument of the first half of the proem. It is also an amplification of the inductive syllogism (1:3-4). In both cases it is the concluding sentence of the extended set of sentences which runs from (1:1) to (1:4).

lysis: paradeigma	Paul an apostle,
ergasia:	not from men nor through man, but through Jesus Christ and God the Father having raised
auxêsis:	him from the dead. And all the brothers with me
ergasia:	to the churches of Galatia. Grace to you and
paradeigma:	peace from our God the Father and from the Lord
ergasia:	Jesus Christ. The one having given himself on behalf of our sins so that he
auxêsis:	might deliver us out of this present evil age according to the will of our God and
epenthymeme:	Father to whom the glory unto the ages of
auxêsis:	the ages, amen.

(1:1-5) constitutes a series of topical arguments in support of two issues *(stasis)*. The first issue addressed the fact of Paul's apostleship. The second issue focused on the jurisdiction of the Galatians to judge the efficacy of Paul's apostleship. Paul clinches the arguments in support of each issue by invoking a doxology. (1:5) functions to clinch the topical syllogism in support of Paul's apostolic statement (1:1-4).

---

[30]For the background to this doxology, see H.D. Betz, *Galatians,* Philadelphia: 1979, 43.

[31]The *epenthymêmê* is an extension of an *epicheirêmê*. It is an addition to the supporting statement that clinches the argument, cf. Hermogenes, *On Invention* (ed. Rabe), 140-154.

(1:5) is formed topically as an argument from authority *(ek kriseôs)*.[32] This argument from authority serves as a strengthening of audience adherence to a value, as the basis for a general policy of action. It strengthens Christian belief and induces the Galatians to follow Paul as their apostle.

Paul composed this doxological hymn[33] in the species of epideictic oratory. Since epideictic passages regularly occur in other genres of oratory (1:5) secures a favorable hearing for Paul's argument and moves the audience to take a course of action. The doxology is a bit of epideictic color added to Paul's juridical and advisory speech. Paul's shift into laudatory rhetoric at (1:5) is self-conscious. This hymn of praise gives attention to a belief which supports the argument of (1:1-4). The doxology is intended to be persuasive because it implies support of Paul's argument in the first part of the proem.

III

Thus we conclude that, in the initial subproposition of his proem, Paul utilizes all three species of rhetoric. The determination of the species brings out the emphases of the speech and the intent of the author. Paul argues judicially around the truth of his character, deliberately concerning the self-interest and future benefits of the Galatians, and epideictically to deepen the values of his audience concerning Christian faith and belief.

Paul arranges his speech topically. A determination of topical strategy informs us about the context of a speech. In (1:1-5) Paul seeks to obtain the good will and sympathy of the Galatians. He accomplishes this goal by arguing from authority, opposites, relation, and difference. Through the topics he amplifies his thesis, states the evidence for it, and develops his basic idea by relating it to the experience of the audience. The proem (1:1-5) is the working out *(ergasia)* of a series of inventional topics. Here Paul develops his authoritative ethos and lays an authoritative basis for his subsequent admonitions to the Galatians. Defense and advice are laid out syllogistically through examples. Paul's character is affirmed in two inductive arguments and the emotions of the audience are played with in his use of example and conclusion.

Paul organizes his speech through the three modes of artistic proof. His speech is argued in the three genres of rhetoric through common, material, and strategical topics that are arranged logically. The results of rhetorical criticism suggest that our view of the historical and religious situation in Galatia is Paul's inventive view. Nonetheless, working from Paul's speech we can mine some important information.

Since Paul argues forensically in (1:1-2), the central issue is the validity of Paul's apostleship and the allegiance of the Galatians to Paul. We do not know

---

[32]Aristotle, *Rhetoric*, 2.23.12.

[33]For an excellent synopsis of these formulae, see H.D. Betz, *Galatians*, Philadelphia: 1979, 37-43.

if (1:1) is the actual charge made against Paul by his opponents, but we do know that the Galatians have deserted him (1:2). We base these conclusions on the evidence of forensic rhetoric in these pericopae. Paul's character was at issue. This is clear from the fact that Paul opens his letter in defense of his apostleship and in attack against those no longer with him. The situation was serious in Galatia. Paul would not argue so forcefully if anything less than his credibility were at stake.

Paul argues deliberately in (1:3-4). The issue is the right of the Galatians to judge the validity of Paul's apostleship. Since advisory rhetoric suggests a relationship between speaker and audience, we assume that although Paul's character was at issue, he was convinced the situation was redeemable. This is clear from the fact that he advises the Galatians on a future course of action. The situation was serious in Galatia, but Paul and his church (or at least a part of it) were in a relationship that had not irrevocably broken down.

Paul's use of the prayer in salutation under the species of deliberate rhetoric is significant. It tells us that both Paul and the Galatians agree on the benefits and the significance of being Christian and following the gospel of Christ. Paul and the Galatians shared a common christological and soteriological matrix. Paul would not advise the Galatians from this position if this were not the case. He employs these ideas so that he can work on the emotions of his audience and persuade them to accept his two issues *(stasis)*.

Paul argues epideictically in (1:5). The doxology is introduced in support of his forensic and deliberative arguments. Since laudatory rhetoric suggests complete agreement between speaker and audience, we assume that Paul is reminding his audience of a past fact in order to affect their emotions. He argues epideictically in support of forensic and deliberative arguments. The situation may be grave in Galatia, but Paul and the Galatians share a common world-view expressed in praise of a God they believe in. He would not use the hymn if this were not the case. Paul argues epideictically to produce an impression concerning the ethos of both himself and the Galatians. This rhetorical device strengthens his character, disarms dissent, and permits him to introduce the *causa* (1:6-10).

The strategy of Paul's rhetoric is clear. Paul moves from confrontation (1:1-2), to advise (1:3-4), to praise (1:5). He scolds, advises, and then reminds the Galatians of the values they hold dear. Once he has manipulated their emotions in such a thorough manner, he can introduce the cause *(cause)*, which is the second part of the proem (1:6-10).

What all this shows is that, formally at least, Paul exhibits a knowledge and use of Greco-Roman rhetoric. He employs rhetorical forms independently of their prescribed use, but in practicing his own art of rhetoric he adapts these forms to suit his particular persuasive needs. He moves beyond handbook stereotypes and applications of rhetoric. He applies them to the persuasive situation that confronted him in Galatia.

Much more needs to be done on the study of Paul's rhetoric.[34] But perhaps we have at least shown that in this introductory section of Galatians, as in others, Paul owes much to sophistic. His debts are deep even though the study of Pauline rhetoric in this stage of expression remains fragmentary if not illusive. Given the nature of the sources and the problems they raise, this is not surprising. It is hoped that this study makes an obscure and difficult field of New Testament studies less obscure and difficult.

---

[34]Especially on the weak link in rhetorical criticism of the New Testament writings, i.e., the connection between the forms of Greco-Roman *haut-rhetorique* and the practice of rhetoric as exemplified in New Testament *bas-rhetorique*. Lund's challenge to rhetorical criticism still presents a formidable one, cf. *Chiasmus*, 8.

Chapter Two

Text as Interpretation: Paul and Ancient Readings of Paul

Stanley K. Stowers

Brown University

In this paper I will argue that modern scholars tend to treat critical editions and ancient manuscripts of the Pauline letters as if they represent "given" or non-interpreted texts. Furthermore, this blind spot supports readings of the letters which present the ancient church's appropriation of Paul as Paul. Scholars of early Christian literature always work with some implicit understanding or theory of text, language, and literature. Before going to the "data," I will make my assumptions about texts explicit.

Language is always prior to the individual speaker. A language belongs to a particular human community. Languages have their meanings because they are grounded in the social practices, shared meaningful activities, of particular communities.[1] Texts belong to languages and therefore also derive their meanings from social practices rather than, say, the intentions in the heads of authors, supposedly pre-linguistic experiences, or objects which words are supposed to name. The meanings of texts are constrained in both a wider and a more specific sense by the shared meaningful activities of particular communities. An author may extend the meaning of the word "tiger" to refer to a certain person but this extension is made possible by the fact that there is a deep "agreement" among speakers of English that "tiger" means a certain kind of large cat. That "agreement" has been formed by many centuries of an English and western tradition of communities which relate to animals in certain ways, e.g., domesticate some, hunt others, classify by species. Social practice also constrains meaning in a narrower sense. This narrower context of social practice includes what we often describe as historical situation, authorial intention, implied audience, and genre. The author who uses "tiger" for a person might be writing poetry, something meaningful to moderns in the context of aesthetic

---

[1] In a broad way I owe many debts for the view of language which I am presenting. Most specifically, my perspective is in debt to the work of the late Ludwig Wittgenstein.

appreciation, or the author might be teaching an English class about simile and metaphor. Practical contexts (e.g., worship, planting seed, eating food, playing games) seem to be almost limitless and each person in society participates in many of these "language games." Texts serve many different purposes–think of a hymn, a stop sign, a law, a grocery list–but depend for their meanings upon both a wider history of meaningful activity and the more specific practical context of the texts' composition.

In order to read a text, a person must understand both the wider language and a specific practical context of composition. Thus a text is not objective in the sense that it is ever "given" or non-interpreted. The markings on the paper are only meaningful because they are the conventions of a particular community. In different contexts of social activity the same markings might have different meanings. In another culture the same markings might mean something different or nothing at all. Texts are only objective in the sense that a community "agrees" deeply about a text's meaning. Their interpretation is relatively determinate most of the time because they play certain relatively stable roles in various social practices. Communities, however, are always changing and the shared meaningful activities which constrain the meanings of texts also change. From one perspective, a community can be understood as a group of people who carry on a conversation between the past, present, and anticipated future of their traditions (histories of shared meaningful activities). The traditions of communities consist of oral and written texts which have continued to be made meaningful by shared meaningful activities.

Since the practical contexts change as the communities change, the meanings of the texts change. The original practical context of Paul's letters is not the same as the practical contexts of the letters as scripture in the worship, moral instruction, and doctrinal controversy of the fourth century church. One way of describing the meaning given to a text by its context of social practice, is to speak of genre. In a real sense, the scriptural letters of the fourth century were read as a different genre than in the first century. In order for modern scholars to approximate the readings given to a text in the first or fourth centuries they must understand the codes of meaning belonging to the practical social activities of the particular time and place in question. The marks on the page do not magically jump into the mind and force a meaning upon the reader. The text is a set of socially agreed-upon cues from the wider language which the reader constructs into a particular pattern of meaning according to the codes (e.g., generic expectations, pre-understandings of words, webs of belief) of the corresponding practical social context.

The assumption of much scholarship is that there is a text out there which is objective in the strong sense and interpretations which are subjective.[2] This leads to treating the text as neutral or non-interpreted at certain levels.[3] What I wish to argue is that "the problem of interpretation" is acute even at what is often supposed to be the most basic level of the text, namely, word division, punctuation, indicators of sense units, transitions, and textual arrangement.

Paul composed his letters without punctuation, divisions between words, paragraphs, or chapter divisions.[4] He or his scribe wrote in *scriptio continua*, unbroken lines of capital letters from margin to margin. He may have assumed that the very specific social-historical contexts in which he anticipated that the letters would be read, would make their meanings clear. He may also have authorized the carriers of the letters to be the readers. In that case, the written scroll would have been the cue for someone who would know well both the writer's and hearer's side of the practical social context. The carrier of the letters might even have a memorized text to use in reading the scroll.

The oldest extant manuscripts of Paul's letters are already edited and have begun to take on a definite interpretive shape. As I have said, a change in the context of shared meaningful activity in which a text is used means a change in the codes of its interpretation, a change of genre. The most obvious change of genre for Paul's writings in the ancient church is that from occasional letters of various sorts to that of scripture addressed the universal church or to humanity rather than to particular congregations at specific times and places. One way the Church dealt with the problem was through the theory of seven letters to seven churches.[5] The theory held that Paul had written to seven churches because the sacred number seven was symbolic for the whole church. Romans was also generalized in much more violent ways. In the late first or early second centuries some person or persons excised the specific addresses to the Gentile believers in Rome (1:15, 17) and removed chapters 15 and 16 with their historically and

---

[2]For a good discussion of objectivity see Richard Bernstein, *Beyond Objectivism and Relativism: Science, Hermeneutics, and Praxis* (Philadelphia: University of Pennsylvania, 1983).

[3]The widely used metaphor of levels or layers of the text is itself revealing. The image supposes that there is some bedrock or foundation of textual fact and that the interpreter's task is to get past the subjective interpretations to the neutral layer of fact.

[4]The bibliography on the punctuation and textual editing of New Testament manuscripts and ancient manuscripts in general is sparse. The following are helpful: F.C. Burkett, response to "The Punctuation of the New Testament Manuscripts" by C. Lattey in JTS 29 (1927-28), 397-98; Donatien DeBruyne, *Sommaires, divisions et rubriques de la .Bible latine* (Namur, 1914); Bruce Metzger, *The Text of the New Testament* (Oxford: Clarenden, 1964) 22-25; *Manuscripts of the Greek Bible* (Oxford: Oxford University, 1981), 32, 40-4.

[5]Nils A. Dahl, "The Particularity of the Pauline Epistles as a Problem in the Ancient Church" *Neotestamentica et Patristica*, NovT suppl. 5; (Leiden: E.J.Brill, 1962) 261-264; Harry Gamble, *The Textual History of the Letter to the Romans* (Studies and Documents 42; Grand Rapids, Mich.: Eerdmans, 1977), 117; Krister Stendahl, "The Apocalypse of John and the Epistles of Paul in the Muratorian Fragment," *Current Issues in New Testament Interpretation*, ed. W. Klassen and G.F. Snyder (New York: Harper & Row, 1962), esp. 243.

locally specific materials.[6] With this material removed, Romans could be read quite easily as a general letter to Christendom. The influence of this edited form of Romans was far-reaching and affected all branches of the textual tradition.[7] Romans became a theological treatise about Humanity and Christianity. Paul's situation of a Jewish "sectarian" who preached the redemption of the Gentiles became incomprehensible.

A more subtle and much more significant editing of the text took place with the introduction of paragraph divisions, chapter divisions, and punctuation.[8] Divisions always impose specific interpretations upon the text. Some criteria are necessary for the placement of paragraph and chapter divisions. Such criteria are necessarily related to what the editor believes about the genre of Romans. The division of Romans in this way is a kind of outlining according to a certain perception of the argumentation, rhetoric and contents of the letter. If the editor conceives of Romans as a document to instruct Christians in right doctrines, then that assumption will be reflected in the way that the letter is outlined or paragraphed. Moreover, the very concept of a paragraph or a chapter is foreign to Paul's way of writing and obscures his intended rhetoric. The effect of this obscuring on Romans was particularly radical. Paul composed Romans with dialogical exchanges, ring compositions, transitional false conclusions and rejections, various rhetorical figures, midrashic periods, etc. A poetic text arranged according to meter would read quite differently if edited into prose paragraphs and chapters. A scholar with a knowledge of poetic practices contemporary with the poem's writing might have to study it intensively in order to show that it should be read poetically. A similar editing has happened to Paul's letters, especially Romans.

It was also inevitable that, as part of a collection of sacred writings, homogenization should occur. Codex Vaticanus, for example, numbers the chapters of the whole collection of Pauline letters continuously as if the letters were one book. The homogenization of the letters into the "New Testament" is also illustrated by the use of colometry in many manuscripts.[9] Colometry is the division of a text into *kola* and *kommata* or clauses and phrases. A *comma* was usually said to have not more than eight syllables and a *colon* nine to sixteen syllables. Although the divisions were supposed to be made according to sense,

---

[6]Dahl, "Particularity," 261-7; Gamble, *Textual History*, 115-129.

[7]Gamble, *Textual History*, 129.

[8]Literary works do not seem to have been divided into chapters and paragraphs until the second century C.E. Their origin appears to have been in legal documents whose chapter and article divisions were used for reference. Reference was probably the major reason for their later use in the New Testament. See H.K. McArthur, "The Earliest Divisions of the Gospels," *Studia Evangelica*, III, Part 2, ed. F.L. Cross (Text Unters, 88; Berlin: Akademie, 1964) 266-72.

[9]J.A. Kleist, "Colometry and the New Testament," *Classical Bulletin* 4 (1928) 26; Albert Debrunner, "Grundsatzliches uber Kolemetrie im Neuen Testament," *Theologische Blatter* 5(1926) 231-33; Roland Schutz, "Die Bedeutung der Kolemetrie fur das Neuen Testament," ZNT 21(1922) 161-184; Metzger, *Manuscripts*, 39-40.

the arbitrariness of this kind of editing is obvious. When it is applied to the whole New Testament there is a mass homogenization of an extremely diverse body of literature. The final result of this process on the text of Romans was as if someone had taken a panel of deeply carved marble relief from an ancient Greek temple which depicted an epic scene of gods and heroes and had sanded the features, the emotions of the faces and bodies down to a flat outline of the scene. Now new details could be carved into the outline and a different scene would appear.

I will illustrate this process of levelling Paul's rhetoric and the appearance of another reading by the development of the chapter division at 2:1. There Paul suddenly shifts from his description of the vices into which the Gentile nations have fallen to a vocative address in the second person singular: "Therefore you have no excuse, O man, whoever you are, when you judge another...." As I have shown elsewhere, this device of a speaker or writer suddenly turning from the audience to an imaginary individual is important in the rhetoric of the diatribe and the literature influenced by its style.[10]

The teacher giving the diatribe speaks to an imaginary person who represents a certain vice. The apostrophe characterizes this type of person and the sharp censure of the teacher against this fictitious person is actually meant to be a censure for students in the audience who fit the type. The teacher who has been speaking abstractly of this vice or type of behavior uses the apostrophe to drive the message home in a sharp but indirect way which censures any of his hearers to whom the indictment is applicable. Such apostrophes are hortatory and were used in practical social contexts of teachers molding the characters of their disciples according to certain patterns.

Paul's use of this rhetoric in 2:1f is stylistically and rhetorically characteristic. The type depicted is the hypocritical judge or the pretentious moralist which is familiar from hellenistic philosophical literature. The whole point of the device is lost when 2:1 is understood to begin a "new section."[11] Among the vicious types of people which Paul lists in 1:29-31 are the insolent (*hubristes*), the arrogant (*huperephanos*), and the pretentious (*alazon*). The imaginary person whom Paul censures in 2:1f is one characterized by precisely these vices.

The intended effect must have been something like the effect of Nathan's parable to David about the poor shepherd in 2 Samuel 12:1-7, when at the parable's end Nathan says, "You are the man." Paul graphically describes the decline of the Gentile nations into sin (1:18-32). Just as the audience is at the point of saying, "Amen, the world is sinful brother Paul," he says, "when you

---

[10]Stanley Kent Stowers, *The Diatribe and Paul's Letter to the Romans* (SBLDS 57; Chico, CA: Scholars Press, 1981) 79-118.

[11]Jouette Bassler (*Divine Impartiality: Paul and a Theological Axiom* [SBLDS 59; Chico, California, Scholars Press, 1981]) also argues against the division at 2:1 but on other grounds.

judge another, mister, you judge yourself." The whole point of the apostrophe is lost when 2:1 is made into the beginning of a new chapter.

The oldest chapter divisions, the *kephalaia majora* and a system in Codex Vaticanus, have no break at 2:1. Both mark off 1:18-2:12 as a section. That division highlights what I take to be Paul's major theme: God judges both Jews and Gentiles impartially according to their works.[12] Patristic commentators gave various opinions about who was being addressed in 2:1ff, but there was not a strong emphasis on a break between 1:32 and 2:1 until Augustine. Origen thought that the apostrophe was especially meant for ministers of the church.[13] Chrysostom first says that the text applies to civil magistrates, then allows that its message is meant for all people.[14] Pelagius understood 2:1-5 to be addressed to morally arrogant Gentiles.[15]

On the other hand, another tradition eventually became dominant in the West. Codex Fuldensis, a manuscript of the Latin Vulgate copied between 541 and 546, has a major division at 2:1. Codex Amiatinus, regarded as the best Vulgate manuscript, also has the same system of chapter divisions.[16] The final version of chapter divisions which are standard today were introduced into the Vulgate early in the thirteenth century by Stephen Langton, later Archbishop of Canterbury. The theological reasons for reading the text with 2:1 understood as a new section are best illustrated by Augustine. In *The Spirit and the Letter* (44), Augustine gives the view which would become dominant. Speaking of 2:1-5 he says, "Then he passes to those who judge and yet do the things which they condemn. This no doubt refers to the Jews, who made their boast in the law of God; though he does not at first name them expressly.[17]

Augustine notes that Paul explicitly turns to the Jews only in 2:17 but he is nevertheless certain that the hypocritical judge in 2:1-5 refers to Jews. As we have already seen, Paul's diatribal rhetoric does not refer to a Jew but to those who fit a certain vice. Furthermore, the effect is to censure his Gentile audience. Paul's rhetoric can be amply illustrated from pagan literature. Plutarch certainly was not referring to Jews when he wrote the diatribal apostrophe in *de curiositate* 515D:

---

[12]The centrality of the theme has been demonstrated by Bassler, *Ibid.*.

[13]P.G. 14, col. 873f.

[14]P.G. 60, Col. 423.

[15]Alexander Souter, *Pelagius' Expositions of Thirteen Epistles of St. Paul* (Texts and Studies 9; Cambridge: University Press, 1931) II 24, on Romans 2:21.

[16]I would like to thank Professor Robert Mathiesen for allowing me to use his microfilm copy of Codex Amiatinus.

[17]Augustine, *Later Works*, ed. and transl. John Burnaby (LCC8; Philadelphia: Westminster, 1954), 227. In his much earlier *Propositions from the Epistles to the Romans*, 7-8, Augustine thinks that 2:1 refers both to Jews and Gentiles. See Paula Fredriksen Landes, *Augustine on Romans: Propositions from the Epistle to the Romans: Unfinished Commentary on the Epistle to the Romans* (SBLTT23, ECL6; Chico, California: Scholars Press, 1982), 5.

Why do you look so sharp on others' ills, malignant man (*anthrope baskanotate*), yet overlook your own? Shift your curiosity from things without and turn it inwards; if you enjoy dealing with the recital of your troubles, you have much occupation at home. Great as the water flowing down Alizon, many as the leaves around the oak, so great a quantity of transgressions will you find in your own soul, of oversights in the performance of your own obligations.

Nor does Seneca depict the hypocritical Jew when he turns the tables on those who criticize philosophers for inconsistency:

But as for you, have you the leisure to search out others' evils and to pass judgement upon anybody? "Why does this philosopher have such a spacious house?' 'Why does this one dine so sumptuously?" you say. You look at the pimples of others when you yourselves are covered with a mass of sores. This is just as if someone who was devoured by a foul itch should mock at the moles and warts on bodies that are most beautiful,... (vit.bea. 27.4)

There is no evidence that the character of the hypocritical and arrogant judge was ever applied to Jews until after Paul's time, and then by Christians. But then, why is Augustine so certain that Romans 2:1-5 is the depiction of a Jew?

First, long before Augustine's time, the relation between the Church and Judaism had radically altered. The situation of Paul's own time was no longer comprehensible. The normative Judaism of Augustine's time did not exist when Paul wrote.[18] When Paul wrote, the church was still fundamentally one of the "sects" within the diverse Judaisms of the second temple period. By Augustine's time, Christianity and Judaism were not only distinct religions but religions with a history of hostility toward one another. Second, the church had developed a theologically motivated stereotype of Judaism. The characterization of the Pharisees in the canonical gospels, especially the Gospel of Matthew, had become the stereotypical view of "the Jew." The Jews were legalists who rejected human mercy and God's grace. When combined with a view of the Jews as Christ-killers disinherited by God, this characterization often became powerfully anti-Jewish. Third, Augustine himself, especially in his anti-Pelagian writings, developed a way of understanding the gospel and of reading Romans which made "the Jew" the archetypical sinner and rebel against God's grace.

It is well known that Augustine internalized, individualized and generalized Pauline concepts such as justification, sin, law, works, salvation, and election. As Krister Stendahl, for example, says, "The Law, the Torah, with its specific

---

[18]Jacob Neusner, "Pharisaic-Rabbinic Judaism: A Clarification." *History of Religions* 12 (1973) 250-70; "The Formation of Rabbinic Judaism: Yavneh (Jamnia) from A.D.7 to 100", *Aufstieg und Niedergang der romischen Welt* (hereafter ANRW) ed. H. Temporini (Berlin: deGruyter, 1979) pt.2, vol. 19.2, 3-43; "The Use of the Mishnah for the History of Judaism prior to the time of the Mishnah," *JSJ* 11 (1980), 1-9.

requirements of circumcision and food restrictions becomes a general principle of 'legalism' in religious matters."[19] Whereas for Paul, the censure of pride or boasting is part of an attempt to respond to a specific historical situation, for Augustine pride becomes the fundamental sin of all men which is epitomized by the legalistic, self-asserting Jew. The aim, the very generic conception of Romans is thus transformed. Augustine says that, "the apostle's aim is to commend the grace which came through Jesus Christ to all peoples, lest the Jews exalt themselves above the rest on account of their possession of the law."[20]

For Augustine, to defend the gospel of God's grace means also to attack "the Jew." The arrogant pride epitomized by the Jew becomes a fundamental human problem with which all must wrestle.

> Paul...contends with such vigour and zeal on behalf of this grace of God, against the proud and arrogant presumers upon their own works.... Rightly then is he loud and eager above all in the defense of grace. ...and in this letter to the Romans this very matter is almost his sole concern – waging his fight with such manifold argument as to weary the reader's endeavour to follow: yet such weariness is profitable and wholesome, training rather than enfeebling the physique of the inward man.[21]

Augustine has partially individualized and psychologized the understanding of Romans as polemical and apologetical. Paul defends God's grace. The acceptance of grace crushes man's pride and he is justified by faith. Paul attacks human pride, epitomized by Jewish attempts to justify themselves by works.

The same understanding of Romans occurs in Luther. He also agrees with Augustine that 2:1-5 is an attack on the Jew. In his lectures on Romans, he cites the summary for 2:1 from his printed New Testament text which had been derived from the glosses of Nicholas of Lyra (d.1340): "The apostle refutes the faults of the Jews, saying that as far as their guilt is concerned they are the same as the Gentiles and in a certain respect even worse."[22] With regard to the arrogant and hypocritical judgement depicted in 2:1-5 he says: "With this sickness the Jews are afflicted more widely than all the Gentiles." Therefore he mentions at the very beginning of the chapter that he is directing his verbal attack against the Jews.[23]

---

[19]"The Apostle Paul and the Introspective Conscience of the West," *HTR* 6 (1963) 199-215; reprinted in *Paul Among Jews and Gentiles* (Philadelphia: Fortress, 1976).

[20]Burnaby, *Augustine*, 200 ("Letter and Spirit," Par. 9).

[21]*Ibid.*, 202 ("Spirit and Letter," 12).

[22]*Luther's Works: Vol. 25: Lectures on Romans, Glosses and Scholia*, ed. Hilton C. Oswald (Saint Louis: Concordia, 1972), 15. In contrast to Luther, Bullinger's view is interesting. He wrote that 2:1-5 was a response to pagan philosophers and moralists who could claim exemption from Paul's indictment in 1:18-32.

[23]*Ibid.*, 16.

About the purpose of the letter, Luther disagrees with Nichola of Lyra who said that the aim was "to recall them from the error of a sham faith" which had been reflected in discord within the Roman church.[24] Luther says, "I prefer to believe that he wanted to take advantage of this opportunity to write to the faithful so that they would have the witness of the great apostle for their faith and doctrine in their fight against the Jews and Gentiles of Rome who still did not believe and boasted of their flesh and opposed the humble wisdom of the faithful."[25] Luther also cites the text from Augustine given above concerning how Paul fights against the proud and profitably wearies the reader in Romans.[26] The chapter division at 2:1, then, reflects an understanding which not only obscures Paul's diatribal rhetoric but assumes a different understanding of Romans as a whole. Both Augustine and Luther view Romans as both an attack on human pride, epitomized by Jewish keeping of the law, and also a defense of the gospel of God's grace. Romans has become a polemical theological treatise about humanity in which Jews and Gentiles are only examples of human depravity. The chapter division at 2:1 is a way of arranging the text which reflects a certain reading of Romans, and that reading in turn supposes a generic conception of the letter.

If the chapter division at 2:1 first of all illustrates the later churches' understanding of Judaism, then, the division at 4:1 represents criteria for text arrangement which are foreign to Paul's rhetoric. I have elsewhere shown that 3:27-4:2 is a dialogue between Paul and the imaginary Jewish interlocutor who is introduced at 2:17.[27] I have suggested that it be read as follows:

A. Int.: What then becomes of boasting?
B. Paul: It is excluded.
C. Int.: By what sort of law? Of works?
D. Paul: No, but through the law of faith. For we consider a man to be justified by faith apart from works of law. Or is God the God of Jews only? Is he not the God of Gentiles also?
   Int.: Yes of the Gentiles also.
   Paul: If he really is, he is the one God who will justify the circumcised by faith and the uncircumcised through faith.
   Int.: Do we then overthrow the law through faith?
   Paul: By no means! On the contrary we uphold the law.
   Int.: What then shall we say that Abraham our forefather according to the flesh found? For if Abraham was justified by works he has something to boast about.
   Paul: But not before God. For what does the scripture say? —

---

[24]*Ibid.*, 138, n.9.
[25]*Ibid.*, 138.
[26]*Ibid.*, 136.
[27]*The Diatribe and Romans*, Chap. 4.

If my reading is correct, what has come to be the standard textual arrangement has completely obscured Paul's rhetoric. The division at 4:1 cuts the dialogue in half. Moreover, the choice of prose paragraphs has hidden the dialogue. What happened? Some understanding of Paul's diatribal rhetoric persisted among well-educated Christians. Origen and John Chrysostom both note that Paul discusses with a fictitious interlocutor in Romans.[28] At the same time they have little grasp of Paul as a Jew before 70 and find it difficult to understand the substance of Paul's discussions about Jews and Gentiles. *Codex Ephraemi rescriptus* (C) employs capitals set into the margins and stops in 3:27-4:2.[29] This gives the sense of a dialogue. In the West, Codex Amiatinus has a new chapter beginning at 3:31 rather than 4:1. Considerations of rhetorical form and not just content are clearly reflected in the text's arrangement. Amiatinus uses sense lines, stops, and marks which indicate that lines A and B are a question and its answer.

If these traditions of text arrangement persist so late, why did the division at 4:1 and the prose paragraph become standard? The answer is to be found in the contexts of practical activity which gave meaning to the text. In the later churches' moral and doctrinal instruction, the Biblical texts were more and more treated as information. Information occurs when the reader is already supposed to have accepted the truth of the text before it is read.[30] The ruling criterion for textual division and arrangement became content. Rhetorical form was unimportant, only moral and theological ideas were significant. Argumentation was subordinated to an outline of the letter based on theological topics about sin and salvation. Thus 4:1 introduces Abraham, who is an example of justification by faith. The dialogue disappears and a new topic, Abraham, appears. The genre of the text ceases to be diatribal exhortation and becomes doctrinal information. It is not surprising that even today some scholars persist in describing Romans as a theological treatise.

The theory of text which I sketched at the beginning of this paper suggests that it is misleading to think of the church transmitting a text in which Paul's meaning was fully and objectively present and that in a secondary step the church appropriated and applied that meaning in light of their own circumstances. That some of Paul's meaning was understood is clear. What is called "interpretation," however, occurred at every level. To have a meaningful text at all is a constructive activity, and practical social context determines the generic pattens for making a text meaningful.

---

[28] See for example Origen on Rom. 3:1-8; 7:14f, and 9:14-19: P.G. 14, 839-1291; *Le Commentaire d'Origène sur Rom.III.5-V.7 d'après les extraits du papyrus No. 88748 du Museé du Caire et les fragments de la Philocalie et du Vaticanus Gr. 762*. Ed. Jean Schèrer (Cairo: Inst. Franc. d'Arch. Orient., 1957); Chrysostom on Rom. 7:7; *Hom. in Rom.* 12-4 (500).

[29] *Codex Ephraemi Syri Rescriptus* ed. Constantine Tischendorf (Lipsiae: 1843).

[30] Thomas H. Olbricht, "The Historical Awareness of Informative Communication" (an unpublished paper presented at the Colloquium in Philosophy and Rhetoric at the Pennsylvania State University, February, 1964). Argumentation recedes.

I have chosen examples of text editing to illustrate my point because the text seems hardest and most objective on that level. Objectivity, however, really means that there is broad tacit agreement that the editing presented in critical editions, which is based largely on manuscript traditions, represents Paul's meaning. If my position is correct, text editing is not just a matter of punctuating sentences. It has larger generic implications. The way a text is edited corresponds to the editor's larger generic conception of the work, whether that conception be explicit or an unrecognized set of assumptions. Without diminishing the helpfulness of critical editions, I suggest that scholars ought to also work with a text in *scriptio continua*. Then it will be more difficult to forget that to have a text at all is an act of interpretation.

Chapter Three

Translation and Exegetical Augmentation in the Targums to the Pentateuch[1]

Paul V. Flesher

The problem of dating the different versions of the Palestinian Targum (PT) to the Pentateuch is closely bound to the problem of the relationship between these versions.[2] The various texts that make up the PT – Targum Neofiti, Targum Pseudo-Jonathan, Fragmentary Targum mss. P and V, as well as fragments of targums from the Cairo Geniza and other sources – have many features in common but diverge in significant ways. The similarities point to a common background while the differences have so far prevented scholars from forming a consensus about that background's exact nature. This article provides the foundation for a new approach to understanding the relationships among the different targums. It argues that the complete targum texts of the PT are based on identifiable sources – a synoptic core and other sources that function in a manner very similar to the relationships among the gospels of Matthew, Mark and Luke. This new approach requires us to re-evaluate the set of questions and modes of analysis currently used to study the targums. In doing so, we will find that the questions and methods have grown out of scholars' initial desire to assign a date of composition to each targum. The search for dates of course no longer constitutes the main goal of scholarly investigation, but the modes of analysis developed in that quest are still being used today. There has been little discussion of whether these modes can solve the new questions to which they are being addressed. To accomplish this reevaluation, we must start at the beginning, with the issue of dating.

Dating the Palestinian Targum as a whole, indeed dating each individual text, is not straightforward. The crux of the difficulty is that research on each

---

[1]This article constitutes a revised version of the dissertation for my Masters of Philosophy at Oxford University. The dissertation was directed by Dr. Geza Vermes, to whom I would like to express my heartfelt appreciation. I also want to thank Professor Jacob Neusner for agreeing to publish this article under his editorship.
[2]See the list of abbreviations at the end of the article.

document must deal with two sets of dates. The first is that of each individual tradition in the targum, the second is the date of the whole *recension* which has come down to modern times. Therefore, dating worked out for a single tradition does not necessarily apply to the text as a whole.

This is most evident from the statements made by various scholars about the dating of the two targums to the entire Pentateuch, Targum Neofiti (TN) and Pseudo-Jonathan (PJ). Professor Alexandro Diez-Macho argues that although the present recension of TN stems from the first or second century AD, it represents on the whole a pre-Christian version of the PT.[3] Dr. M. McNamara is more cautious; he suggests that TN is from "talmudic times," but he too argues that the aggadic material as a whole is pre-Christian.[4] The situation for PJ is similar. In its present form, PJ appears to be post sixth century AD, for it contains mention of the wife an daughter of Muhammed. Despite this, it "has also preserved intact many early, sometimes pre-Christian traditions."[5]

A number of arguments for dating the different versions of the PT have been put forth over the past decades. They can be divided into six different types. First, there is an argument based on the identification of historical allusions in the targum. Dr. A. Geiger argued that the mention of the high priest Jonathan in Dt. 33:11 pointed to a second century BC data for PJ.[6] Dr. M. Klein has discussed two passages which, he argues, indicate that some elements of the Fragmentary Targums (FT) date from after the destruction of the temple.[7]

Second, Professor P. Kahle argued that when a passage is found in the targum which portrays a legal position which is contrary to one found in the Mishnah, it must have been propounded before the Mishnah became authoritative.[8] Third, Diez-Macho has argued that the "comparative-midrash"

---

[3]The Recently Discovered Palestinian Targum: Its Antiquity and Relationship with other Targumim." *NTS* Congress Volume (1959), pp. 245ff.

[4]*The New Testament and the Palestinian Targum to the Pentateuch*, Rome: 1966, p. 63.

[5]Schürer, Emil, *The History of the Jewish People in the Age of Jesus Christ*, ed. G. Vermes and F. Millar, Edinburgh: 1973, p. 104.

[6]A. Geiger in Excursus II of his *Urschrift und Übersetzungen der Bibel*, 2nd. ed. Frankfurt: 1928, reported via Theodor Nöldeke (*Die Alttestamentlich Literatur...*, Leipzig: 1868, p. 256) in P. Kahle, The Cairo Geniza, 2nd ed. Oxford: 1959, p. 202.

[7]Klein, *The Fragment-Targums of the Pentateuch*, Rome: 1980, pp. 24-25. There are two problems with this type of argument. First, it indicates only a time before which something could *not* have been written. Second, the identification of the allusion is only tentative since our knowledge of events in antiquity is extremely sparse. A case in point is the Bar Kochba War.

[8]Kahle, op.cit. pp. 205-207. For a discussion of the problems with this argument, see A. D. York, "The Dating of Targumic Literature", *JSJ* 1974, pp. 52-3. The most telling fault of this argument is that it assumes that no halakah existed at the time of the Mishnah which did not agree with it – an assumption that patently false. It further assumes that the influence of the rabbinic movement was all pervasive in Jewish society at the time. This assumption cannot be demonstrated.

method – first suggested by Dr. R. Bloch[9] and applied by Dr. G. Vermes[10] – indicates that some of the traditions found in TN are early.[11] This is said to show that TN itself is early. Bloch's suggested method is to compare traditions found in undated texts with those in dated Jewish texts of the Greco-Roman Period. This facilitates the tracing of the development of a tradition's different facets.

Fourth, Professor Diez-Macho has argued that the theological and messianic interpretation of Num. 24:17 prefigures the understanding of it found in the New Testament.[12] Fifth, he argues that geographical terms, proper names and the use of Greek and Latin loanwords in TN indicate that it is early.[13] Six, Professor Diez-Macho has attempted to reconstruct the *Vorlage* of the targumic translation and then argue that it is based on a pre-massoretic text.[14]

The soundness of each of these arguments has been discussed in the footnotes, but a few general observations can be made. Firstly, except for number six, the arguments are based on the comparison of selected portions of the targum with external information, and such a comparison always runs the risk of "parallelomania"[15] – the questionable argument that instances of an idea (a "tradition") are directly related because they evidence literary, thematic, or contextual parallels. The use of this type of comparison as a means of dating a "tradition" is made more unsatisfactory by the fact that it is unevenly applicable. Since outside texts do not follow the same interests as the targum, the appearance of parallels is arbitrary and unpredictable. Furthermore, the attitude that the targum is a document into which forays can be made to obtain material suitable for dating is highly suspect. It does not attempt to understand the targum as a document in its own right but treats it superficially as a document whose value lies in what it can reveal about other topics.

Secondly, even if the above arguments, again excepting the sixth, could indicate a date for the material they examine, this would not indicate a date for the targum. Although the proponents of the above concepts readily admit that the dating only applies to the individual idea, the formulation of the arguments gives a strong impression that such generalizations are being made. The generalization from the expansion to the targum cannot be made because modern scholars have not yet understood the relationship of the individual traditions of

---

[9]R. Bloch, "Note methodoligique pour l'étude de la littérature rabbinique" *RSR* 43(1955) pp. 194-227.

[10]See the relevant articles in *Post-Biblical Jewish Studies*, Leiden: 1975 and in *Scripture and Tradition in Judaism*, Leiden: 1973.

[11]Diez-Macho, op.cit., pp. 227. Cf. York, op.cit., p. 56.

[12]Diez-Macho, op.cit., pp. 226. Cf. York, op.cit., p. 54-55.

[13]Diez-Macho, op.cit., pp. 227ff. Cf. York, op.cit., p. 56.

[14]Diez-Macho, loc. cit., This argument is shown to be untenable by P. Wernberg-Møller, "An Inquiry into the Validity of the Text-Critical Argument for an Early Dating of the Recently Discovered Palestinian Targum," VT 12 (1962) pp. 312-30.

[15]A term attributed to Samuel Sandmel.

the targums to the targums as a whole.[16]

Now that the problems of the dating of the PT have been seen, the question of the interrelationships of the texts of the PT needs to be explored. TN has been welcomed as the first complete PT.[17] But why TN? Is not PJ also a complete PT? There are two characteristics which set off PJ from the other PT texts, its linguistic peculiarities and its special relationship to TO. More than any other PT, PJ agrees with the translation of TO and occasionally follows its choice of words, against the other PTs. Three possible reasons for this have been put forward; one, that PJ is a combination of TO with the expansive material of the PT; two, it is suggested that it is a PT which has been revised according to TO; three, TO and PJ are said to be derived from the same source.[18]

The positions of the FTs are also uncertain. It has been postulated by some authorities that they are collections of variations to TO, and by others that they are variations to the PT. It has also been suggested that they are attempts to preserve the expansive material of the PT after TO became authoritative.[19] Dr. Klein has suggested that some of them, particularly ms. P, may have liturgical links.[20] None of these explanations of the FTs has been given general credence by scholars. Instead of discussing the *raison d'être* of the FTs, as these suggestions have done, the problem has been studied from a different angle; what – not why – are the FTs? Two possibilities have been put forward, neither has yet gained scholarly support. The first is that they are the remainder of a complete targum which may been cut back. The second is that they are a collection of glosses and variant readings to a full targum.[21]

There are three other groups of mss. which are part of the PT but their exact relationship to the other texts is unknown. The first group comprises the fragments from the Cairo Geniza, which Professor Kahle has argued are the earliest extant mss. of the PT.[22] The second is made up of the glosses found in the margin of TN. Their relationship to TN and to the other texts of the PT is still a matter of speculation. The third group is the targumic tosafot, most frequently found in printed editions of TO but also in manuscripts. They show some connections with expansions from the PT, but this has not been studied in recent decades.

The problems which have been mentioned concerning the dating and the interrelationships of the different texts of the PT point toward the need for an

---

[16]See York, op. cit., p. 60.

[17]Cf. Joseph Heinemann, "Early Halakah in the Palestinian Targum" *JJS* special issue, 1974, p. 114; also John Bowker, *The Targums and Rabbinic LIterature*, Cambridge: 1969, p. 16.

[18]Schürer, loc. cit.

[19]For a survey of the literature, see Klein op. cit., pp. 12-19.

[20]Ibid., pp. 19-23.

[21]R. Le Deaut, "The Current State of Targumic Studies," *Biblical Theology Bulletin*, 4 (1974) pp. 3-32, especially p. 31.

[22]See York, op. cit., pp. 50-52.

understanding of the process by which the different texts of the PT were created. Are they the product of sporadic attachment of traditions to a translation text over the course of many centuries? Perhaps they developed as a single text for a time, and then each targum split off and accumulated different material. On the other hand, they may be the result of redaction. The actual manner of this redaction could have taken many forms. It could be the combination of a pre-existing translation with a number of traditions which circulated wither individually or as a collection, it could be the result of the traditions being combined with a translation as it was being written. The difference between these two ideas is important, for in the latter the targum as a whole document is constructed by a single person. This means that the impetus for including the expansive material is likely to be the same as for the translation. The former possibility, the process of redaction is separated from that of translation, thereby lessening the probability that the motivation and rationale of the translation is the same as that for the selection of the additional material.

Furthermore, one might inquire whether each targum was the product of one redaction or several. Perhaps the targum was redacted initially and then later, when it was already an expansive targum, acquired further material. What role did the translator have in creating expansive material alongside the translation?

These few explanations – which are by no means exhaustive – are possible solutions of the unexplored problem which underlies many of the present discussions in targum studies. Since the publication of the second edition of Professor Kahle's book, *The Cairo Geniza*, in 1959, there has been little headway made on the issues mentioned in the previous pages. This is due to the fact that the question of the formation of the PT has not been raised in a thorough and comprehensive manner. What is needed is an extended inquiry into the interrelationships among the different texts of the PT and the extent and strength of these connections. An analysis must be made not only of the common material but also of that which is not shared by all the targums.

The problem of the formation of the PT should be addressed by a protracted, two-part study. The first part would comprise a comprehensive and systematic source-critical inquiry into the formation of the PT. Such a study would attempt to delineate the material shared by the different targums of the PT and to identify different collections which are used in them. Since the arguments based on external factors have proved inconclusive, source criticism is a prerequisite to any further attempt to date the texts of the PT, and it is the means by which a detailed analysis of their interrelationships may be accomplished.

The analysis of the Synoptic Gospels may provide an example of the benefits realizable from this type of study. Source critical analysis set the stage for later analysis of them, particularly form and redaction criticism. It was found that Matthew and Luke had two common sources, Mark and Q. This realization allowed the delineation of the different thematic and theological emphases of the evangelists and provided the first stage for the accurate dating both of sources and of the evangelists' work.

However, source criticism can only identify the area where common material is found. It is unable to separate if from later encrustations. This is the goal of the second part of the study, for, in the words of Norman Perrin, it uses redactional criticism to "trace the form and content of material used by the author concerned" and to try "to determine the nature and extent of his activity in collecting, editing and composing."[23] This will allow the specification of the original PT, if there ever was one. If there was not, it will allow scholars to determine, at any rate, the content and form of the sources which underlie different versions of the PT which we now possess.

The central problem of a source critical inquiry is to locate the divisions in the text(s) which indicate possible divergence of source material. Once such signs are found, the texts which they outline are analyzed to determine whether they do indicate different sources or some literary phenomenon not related to the question of sources. In the targums, the obvious place to begin the inquiry is the division between the translation and the expansive material. There are three factors which indicate why the division should be sought here. One, the persons responsible for the extraction of the FTs were aware of the difference, for they often extracted additional material only a word or a few words long. Two, anyone who knew Hebrew and was familiar with the Pentateuch would have been aware of the insertion of extensive expansions. Three, although PJ and TN have many expansions which are similar, their translations often differ. This shows that even though the expansions were parallel, the translation was not.

Obviously, this short paper cannot even begin such an extensive and comprehensive study of the PT. However, it can attempt two preliminary tasks. The first section will explore the character of the translation and of the expansions. By attempting to illustrate the techniques used to translate the HT, as well as the changes which the expansions undergo, the feasibility of a division being drawn between them will be explored. The discussion of the expansion will also provide an example of the manner in which redaction-critical analysis should be undertaken.

Assuming that the inquiry in the first section is successful, the second section will separate the expansions from the translation text and search out any parallel expansions in other targums. The most straightforward way to do this would be to delineate the expansive material in one of the full targums, TN or PJ, and then collate with it the parallels to it found in other targums. TN is the most suitable because of its unquestioned Palestinian character. PJ would be less appropriate because of its differing linguistic nature and its suspected ties to TO. Such an exercise is not beyond the confines of this thesis. It involves the compilation of a list which contains all the expansions found in TN, with the

---

[23]*What is Redaction Criticism?* Philadelphia, Fortress Press: 1970, p. 2.

parallels found in all the different texts of the PT recorded.

The expansive material from all the texts of the PT is needed in order to provide the fullest information possible about the sources. But the parallels of the four complete targums are the most significant for they can be systematically analyzed for the whole of the pentateuch. This allows a comprehensive evaluation of their parallels. The four "complete" targums referred to are TN and PJ, which have translation and expansions covering the whole of the Pentateuch, and P and V, which although they lack translation, do contain expansions which cover the whole of the Pentateuch.[24] These four texts allow the complete and balanced investigation of sources to be undertaken for the whole of the Pentateuch and prevent the inquiry from being spoiled by the rogue influence of the chance preservation of partial texts.

The Literary Character of Translation in the Palestinian Targum

Targum Neofiti is predominately translation. On the average, there are less than two verses per chapter which are elaborated. Therefore, in order to understand the literary nature of the targum, it is necessary to investigate the characteristics of the translation text. In the following pages, I shall attempt to shed light on the translation techniques used in the production of the targum and the manner in which they represent the source text in the target text.[25]

Often, the first question asked about a translation is, is it "literal" or "free"? This dichotomy is inexact at best and is rarely, if ever, connected with a set of criteria which enable the evaluation of a translation's status. Professor James Barr has pointed out that

> The modern "free" ideal, the idea that one should take a complete sentence or even a longer complex, picture to oneself the meaning of this entirety, and then restate this in a new language in words having no necessary detailed links with the words of the original, then scarcely existed. A sophisticated study of the LXX, at least in many books, rather than dealing with the contrast between free and literal, has to concern itself much of the time with variations, diverse levels of literal connection, and various kinds of departure from the literal. For this reason the idea of literality, rather than the idea of free translation, can properly form our base line of definition. It is the various kinds of literalism that we seek to analyze and define: for each of them "free" means that which is opposite to this particular literalism.[26]

---

[24]As published by M. Klein, op. cit.; in this article, when V (i.e. ms. V) is referred to, the composite text printed by Klein is meant, which contains V, N, and L.

[25]I do not intend to deal with the problem of *Vorlage*; it has been addressed by A. Sperber in his editions of the targumim (Brill, Leiden) and by others.

[26]James Barr, "The typology of literalism in ancient biblical translations" p. 281. My argument in this section depends heavily on ideas in this article and in the article by Sebastian Brock, "Aspects of Translation Technique in Antiquity," *Greek, Roman, and Byzantine Studies*, 10 (1979) 1, pp. 69-87.

Professor Barr's observation, made in the context of the Septuagint, provides a helpful guide for the study of translation in TN and the other targums. The study of "different kinds of literality," through the analysis of the translation techniques applied to the HT, should reveal much about the literary character of the targum.

In addition to the importance of such techniques, both Professor Barr and Dr. S.P. Brock attempt to elucidate the motives of the translator and the social attitudes towards scripture which influenced him. Dr. Brock distinguished three areas of influence. The first was the nature of the source text. Was it legal, literary, poetry, sacred text, etc.? The second concerned the relative prestige of the two languages. The third dealt with the extent to which the source language was known in the intended audience of the translation.

The administrative documents of the eastern Roman Republic provide a good example of the interaction of these three factors. While those who translated works of literature attempted to translate by sense, those who worked with legal documents were required to compose their translation so that it conformed as closely as possible not only to the meaning but also to the form of the original text. Unfortunately this often made the translation ungrammatical and distorted the meaning. The Greek version of an official document pointed the reader to the original in Latin. "Obscurities resulting from excessive literalism (including the dating formulae) could be explained by Roman officials on the spot."[27]

The attitude towards the translation of scripture is similar to that of legal documents. In fact, the Hebrew Scriptures actually fulfilled the role of a law code in Judaism. The formula for quoting scripture, "as it is written...," derives from a legal context.[28]

Another parallel of scripture with legal documents is the effect caused by the knowledge of the source language. In Palestine, where many Jews were bilingual in Hebrew and Greek,[29] the ultraliteral technique of translation could be applied (e.g. Aquila). In Alexandria, where few Jews could read Hebrew, they "chose to regard the Septuagint as inspired rather than to correct it and thus render it virtually unintelligible."[30]

Literal translation often distorts the syntax – and consequently the meaning – of the language of the target text by the unnatural adherence to the syntax and word order of the source text. This adherence was found both in legal documents and in inspired scripture, because the form of the original was considered as

---

[27]Brock, op. cit., p. 74.

[28]Ibid. p. 72.

[29]The question of what language was dominant in Palestine during this period is a matter of debate. The presence of Greek, Hebrew, and Aramaic are all attested to, but the extent of their usage and the exact dates they were used is uncertain. I follow Dr. Brock on this matter (see p. 74).

[30]Ibid. p. 72 and p. 74.

important as the meaning. The trade-off between accurate rendering of the meaning of the source document and the retention of its formal characteristics could result in a translation decipherable only by someone familiar with the source language and who could refer to the original document. Professor Barr points out that "The 'free' books [of the LXX] had already used the literalist methods in considerable measure: what literalism did was to seek to use these methods more consistently."[31]

A discussion of the techniques of literal translation in antiquity, and the problems faced by the ancient translator which guided their use, will portray the range of options available to him. The first problem concerned the deciphering of the meaning of the source text and where the meaning was located. Was it based in a sentence or phrase, or in smaller units such as a "word"?[32] In biblical translation, the latter was chosen. This choice emphasizes not the meaning of a whole phrase/sentence but rather focuses on the word as the bearer of the necessary semantic information. In Hebrew this approach also necessitates the attribution of semantic importance to sub-word particles, particularly suffixes. This approach results in two distinct techniques of translation, both of which are commonly associated with literal translation but are often confused with each other. The first is the effort to translate each word in the source text with a corresponding word in the target text. Or, in Dr. Brock's words, "to render as far as possible each vocable with one that corresponds to it in grammatical function."[33] The other technique is adherence to the word order of the source text.

These two techniques attempt to transmit into the target language the semantic and formal relationships found in the original language. A segmentation of the text by phrase or sentence allows the translator leeway to reconstruct these relationships with a range of linguistic options found in the target language. But if the important semantic information is deemed to lie in the word, then each word's relationship with the surrounding text must serve as the indicator of the relationships. This results in the representation of both words and word order in the translation.

There is a second consideration which interacts with the one above, that of the level of meaning attributed to a word. This concern explains a number of translation techniques. The most important one is the translation of metaphor in the source text. The translator is faced with the problem of deciding to translate the actual word or the metaphor. The problem is more acute if in the target language the base word is not associated with the metaphorical meaning. He must then choose between clarity of meaning and the representation of the form

---

[31]Barr, op. cit., p. 281.

[32]The exact meaning of "word" is a matter of extensive linguistic disagreement. I use it merely to designate a continuous series of letters, which we as moderns separate by spaces, that expresses meaning.

[33]Brock, op. cit., p. 81.

of the text.

Other problems of this type are the rendering of "etymological" associations and homonyms, the translation of technical terms and idioms. The problem of technical terms is a common one and is generally solved in one of three ways; transcription, etymological translation or by a cultural equivalent. The first two are strictly literal, while the third is affected by cultural differences. The problem of idioms forces the translator to decide between representing the meaning of the original or its form. Barr provides an apt example of an "etymological association." In Aquila's translation, the first word of Genesis is BR'S, "head." The Greek translation for this word is not "beginning" but one related to the Greek word for "head."[34]

The final translation problem to come under this umbrella is that of homonyms, words which are spelled the same but have different meanings. Again the translator is faced with the problem of whether to translate meaning and thereby lose the formal associations of the word, or to use the same word throughout in order to preserve the form of the text, but thereby lose the semantic accuracy.

It is a feature of many literal texts that they solved the problem by deciding to do just that, always representing a particular word of the source text by the same word in the translation. This removed the decisions which confronted the translator in the case of metaphors, homonyms and idioms, but produced a translation which was often garbled and unreadable.

All these techniques are an attempt to represent the features of the original text; syntactical and contextual as well as semantic. However, there are a number of techniques, not strictly literal, which can be found in the targums. The most frequent of these are "interpretive" translation, double translation and circumlocation. The "interpretive" technique is the representation in the targum of a word of the HT with a different word interpretation. Often, the sentence in which such a word is found is translated in a strictly literal manner and only the single word is different.[35] A good example of this is TO's translation of Dt. 3:25; HT – "that goodly mountain and *Lebanon*," TO – "that goodly mountain and the *Temple*."[36] Double translation occurs when the HT is translated twice. This can be in the form of two literal translations as in the case of a homonym in the HT, two different "interpretive" translations, or one of each. The problem of circumlocations and anti-anthropomorphisms, although usually dealt with on a theological level, can be dealt with on the level of translation, for it usually

---

[34]Barr, op. cit., p. 320.

[35]The question of "interpretive translation" is a thorny problem, for it is intertwined with the question of the simple meaning that a translator intended to convey. The issues involved are too extensive for this paper and must be left for further analysis.

[36]Vermes, *Scripture and Tradition in Judaism*, p. 28.

takes terse, repetitive forms which, in the targum text at least, appear to be traditional circumlocutions devoid of meaning.[37]

The different techniques discussed above give an idea of the ways in which a translator can choose to represent the source text. But, as Professor Barr observes,

> Ancient biblical translations are seldom pure exponents of either the literal or the free mode of operation: generally speaking, they are compromises, in which different proportions of the literal and the free are to be found.[38]

But how are these techniques used in the targum? A definitive answer to this question cannot be determined within the confines of this thesis. However, two examples of TN's translation text, Gen. 38:5-15 and Ex. 2:5-15, will be examined and some tentative answers suggested. In them, the words which are not part of the exact formal correspondence of the HT are underlined. In the notes following each, these, and other features will be mentioned.

TN Genesis 38:5-15

5. And she (conceived) again and bore a son and she called his name Selah and it happened that she stopped[a] (bearing) after she bore him.
6. And Judah took a wife for Er, his first-born and her name was Tamar.
7. And Er, the first-born of Judah was *doing*[a] *evil*[b] *deeds*[a] before the Lord and (he)[c] was killed *by a word from before*[d] the Lord.
8. And Judah said to Onan, "Go into the wife of your brother and marry her and raise up seed of *sons*[a] for the *name*[b] of your brother."
9. And Onan knew that *his sons*[a] would not *be called by*[b] his *name*[c] and it happened that when he went in to the wife of his brother[d] he destroyed[e] his *works*[f] upon the ground so that he would not *raise sons*[g] for the *name*[h] of his brother.
10. And what he did was wicked *before*[a] the Lord and he[b] also was killed *by a word from before the Lord.*[c]
11. And Judah said to Tamar his daughter-in-law, "Dwell as a widow *in*[a] the house of your father until *the time*[b] when Selah my son has grown."[c] For he said, "lest he also die like is brothers." And Tamar went and dwelt *herself in*[a] the house of her father.
12. And many[a] days (passed) and the daughter of Shua, the wife of Judah died, and Judah was comforted and he went up *to*[b] Timnah to shear the flock, he and Hira his friend, the Adulamite.

---

[37]See C. T. R. Hayward "The Memra of YHWH and the Development of its Use in Targum Neofiti I" *JJS*, 25 (1974), pp. 412-418 and "The Use and Religious Significance of the Term Memra in Targum Neofiti I in the Light of the Other Targumim." D.Phil. thesis, Oxford, 1975. See also M. Klein, "The Preposition ('Before'): A Pseudo-Anti-Anthropomorphism in the Targums," *Journal of Theological Studies*, 30 (1979) 2, pp. 502-507.
[38]Barr, op. cit., p. 324.

13. And it was reported to Tamar saying, "Behold your father-in-law has gone up to[a] Timnah to shear the sheep."

14. And she took off her widows garments from upon her and she covered herself with a veil and wrapped herself in it[a] and she sat herself[b] in the crossroads of the paths[c] by the path towards Timnah. For she saw that Selah had grown and she had not been taken to him for a wife.

15. And Judah saw[a] her and Judah[b] thought[a] her to be a whore for she had covered her face (when) she was in the house of Judah and Judah did not recognize her.[c]

Notes

5. [a]HT BKZYB, "in Chezib."

6. Straight translation.

7. [a]added in TN; [b]change in number; [c]third masculine singular suffix is missing; [d]circumlocation.

8. [a]added in TN; [b]added in TN.

9. [a]"his" – added, "sons" – HT "seed"; [b]added in TN; [c]addition comes between two parts of a Hebrew word; [d]HT W-missing, HWH added, resulting in a tense change; [e]added in TN; [f]added in TN; [g]addition comes between two parts of a Hebrew word.

10. [a]circumlocation; [b]object in HT becomes nominative in TN; [c]circumlocution.

11. [a]added for syntactical reasons; [b]added in TN; [c]verb changed to passive in TN.

12. [a]verb changed to participle in TN; [b]TN adds L-, sign of dative.

13. [a]TN adds L-, sign of dative.

14. [a]added in TN; [b]added for syntactical reasons; [c]"crossroads in the paths" is an interpretation of HT "in the gate of eyes" (BPTH 'YNYM).

15. [a]TN adds YT; [b]added in TN; [c]added phrase in TN, cf. list number 223.

TN Exodus 2:5-15

5. And the daughter of Pharaoh came down to cool[a] herself by the river and the girl was walking by the side of the river and she saw the box in the midst of the meadow[b] and she sent out her servant girl and she took it.[c]

6. And she opened it and she saw the child and the child cried and she was filled with affection for it and she said, "From the sons of the Hebrews is he,[a] this one." (HW' DYN)

7. And his sister said to the daughter of Pharaoh, "Shall I go and call for you a woman, a wetnurse, from the Hebrews and she will nurse the child for you?"

8. And the daughter of Pharaoh said to her, "Go," and the girl went and she called the mother of the child.

9. And the daughter of Pharaoh said to her, "Take this child and nurse him[a] for me and I will give you your wages." And the woman took the child[a] and nursed him.[a]

10. And the child grew and she brought him[a] to the daughter of Pharaoh and (he) was to her like a son and she called his name Moses and she said, "For from the water I saved[b] him."[a]

11. And it was in those days that Moses grew and he went out to his brothers and he saw their servitude and he saw a man of the Egyptians strike[a] a man of the Hebrews, (one) of his brothers.

12. And he looked[a] this way and that and he saw that *there*[b] *was*[c] no man and he killed the Egyptian and he buried him in the sand.

13. And he went out a second day and behold two Hebrew men were fighting[a] and he said to the guilty one, "Why *now*[b] did *you*[b] strike[c] your companion?"[b]

14. [a]"Who set you[b] as a great man and judge over us. Will you kill me"[b] he said, "as you killed the Egyptian?" and Moses was afraid and he said, "Behold, now the matter has become known."

15. And Pharaoh heard of this matter and he sought to kill Moses and Moses fled from before Pharaoh and he dwelt in the land of Midian and he sat himself[a] upon a well.

Notes

5. [a]HT "to bathe"; [b]HT "the sea"; [c]TN adds YT
6. [a]TN adds "he"
7. straight translation
8. straight translation
9. [a]TN adds YT
10. [a]TN adds YT; [b]change in tense
11. [a]TN adds L-, sign of direct object
12. [a]HT is PNH "to turn," TN is a metaphorical translation; [b]TN adds TMN; [c]TN adds HWWH
13. [a]passive verb in TN; [b]added in TN; [c]TN adds L- to indicate direct object
14. [a]HT W'MR missing; [b]TN adds YT to indicate object
15. [a]added for syntactical reasons

At verse 15 in the Genesis passage there is an additional phrase which expands on the translation. Of the other changes, three of them are circumlocations and a large number of the rest are due to the syntactical requirements of Aramaic. This leaves eleven actual additions to the translation text of these ten verses, eight being in verses 8 and 9. It is interesting to note that two of the additional words in verse 9 are actually between a Hebrew word and its suffix, and that TN preserves the translation of both items. Only at one place, in verse 9, is any of the Hebrew text missing and then only a *waw*.

The Exodus passage is very literal, surprisingly so considering that it concerns the finding of Moses in the river and his slaying of the Egyptian. There are only five additional words in the ten verses, not including the markers of the object, YT and L-, which occur a number of times. There are a few metaphorical translations and in vs. 5 there is the translation of a Hebrew idiom by an Aramaic one. These differences indicate that the translator allows some leeway for the requirements of Aramaic syntax and attempts to provide the meaning of the text as well as its form. The only word of the HT that is missing is W'MR in vs. 14 and this is probably due to a copyist's error.

The most significant feature about the targum translation is that it is literal, not to the point of misrepresenting the semantics of the HT, but rather a literal translation with additional words to ensure comprehensibility. These are placed to fit with the actual translation and do not interrupt the flow of the narrative. The translation follows the word order of the HT very closely, and there is a one-to-one formal correspondence at the level of the word and the suffix. The translation does not rearrange the source material to represent it but takes pains to ensure that all of it is transmitted in the correct order. The Targumist's response to the conflicting problems of an inspired text versus the audience's need to understand, is to imitate the form of the HT exactly and where he thinks that the meaning is unclear, to clarify it with an additional word or two which he adds unobtrusively to the translation text. It is a misnomer to call the targum here paraphrastic.

Having observed TN's manner of translation, it must be asked whether it is peculiar to TN or do other targums translate in the same manner. This question can be tentatively answered by examining the witnesses to Gen. 38:17-24, to which there are five extant targumim: TN, PJ, TO, ms. D and ms. E. An examination performed in the manner just used for TN would be too cumbersome with so many targums, so instead the five targums and the HT have been arranged in parallel.

הצאן	מן	עזים		גדי	אשלח	אנכי	ויאמר	HT
ענה	מן	עזין	בר	גדי	אשלח	הא אנה	ואמר	TN
ענא	מן	ע]זין[	בר	גדי	א]שלח[	אנה כען	ואמר	D
ענה	מן	עזין	בר	גדי	משלח	אנה	ואמר	E
ענא	מן	עיזי	בר	גדי	אשדר	אנא	ואמר	PJ
ענא	מן	עיזי	בר	גדי	אשדר	אנא	ואמר	TO

שלחך			עד	ערבון	תתן	אם	ותאמר HT
דתשלח		זמן	עד	ערבון	תתן	אן	ואמרת TN
תשלח	די	זמן	עד	ערבון	תתין לי	אן	ואמרת D
תשלח לווחי	די	זמן	עד	ערבון	תתן	אין	ואמרת E
דתשלח			עד	משכונא	תתן	אין	ואמרת PJ
דתשלח			עד	משכונא	תתין	אם	ואמרת TO

לך	אתן	אשר	ערבון	מה	ויאמר HT
ליך	אתן	די	ערבון	מה	ואמר TN
ליך	אתן	די	ערבונה	מא	ואמר D
לך	אתן	די	ערבונה	מה	ואמר E

PJ ואמר	מה	משכונה		דאחן	לך
TO ואמר	מא	משכונה		דאיחין	ליך

HT ותאמר	חחמך	ופתילך	ומטך	אשר	בידך
TN ואמרת	עזקתך	ושושפך	וחוטרך	די	בידך
D ואמרת	עזקתך	ושושפך	וחוטרך	דאית	בידך
E ואמרת	עזקתך	ושושפך	וחוטרך	דאית	בידך
PJ ואמרת	סיטומתך	וחוטייך	וחוטרך		דבידך
TO ואמרת	עזקתך	ושושיפך	וחוטרל		דבידך

HT ויתן	לה	ויבא	אליה	וחהר	לו
TN ויהב	לוותה	ועל	לוותה	ועברת	מיניה
D ויהב	לה	ועאל	לוחה	ועברת	מינה
E ויהב	לה	ואזדמן	לוותה	ועברת	ליה
PJ ויהב	לה	ועל	לוחה	ואיתעברת ליה	
TO ויהב	לה	ועל	לוחה	ועדיאת	ליה

HT ותקם	ותלך	וחסר	צעיפה	מעליה	ותלבש	בגדי אלמנותה
TN וקמת	ואזלת	ועברת	רדידה	מעילוווה	ולבשת	לבושי ארמלוותה
D וקמת	ואזלת	ועברת	רדידה	מן עלוייה	ולבשת	לבושי ארמלוותה
E וקמת	ואזלת	ועברת	רדידה	מן עלוי	ולבשת	לבושי ארמלוותה
PJ וקמת	ואזלת	ועדת	רדידה	מיניה	ולביש	לבושי ארמלוותה
TO וקמת	ואזלת	ו עדיאת	עיפה	מינה	ולבישת	לבושי ארמלוותה

HT וישלח	יהודה	את	גדי	העזים	ביד	רעהו העדלמי
TN ושלח	יהודה	ית	גדייה בר	עזייא	ביד	רחמה עדולמייה
D ושלח	יהודה	ית	גדי בר	עזין	ביד	חבריה עדולמיא
E ושלח	יהודה	ית	גדייה בר	עזוינה	ביד	חברה עדולמיה
PJ ושדר	יהודה	ית	גדי בר	עיזי	ביד	רחמיה עדולמיה
TO ושלח	יהודה	ית	גדי בר	עיזי	ביד	רחמיה עדולמאה

HT לקחת		הערבון	מיד	האשה	ולא	מצאה
TN למיסב	ית	ערבונה	מן ידא	דאתתא	ולא	אשכח יתי
D למיסב		ערבונא	מן ידה	דאחתא	ולא	אשכח יתה
E למסב		ערבונה	מן ידיה	דאנתתה	ולא	אשכח יתה

PJ למיסב משכונא מידא דאיתחא ולא אשכחה

TO למסב משכונא מידא דאיתחא ולא אשכחה

HT וישאל את אנשי מקום לאמר

TN ושאל ית עמא דאתרא למימר

D ושאל ית עמא דאתרא למימר

E ושאיל ית עמא דאתרא למימר

PJ ושאיל ית אינשי אחרא למימר

TO ושאל ית אנשי אחרא למימר

HT איה הקדשא הוא בעינין על הדרך

TN אן היא נפקת בר דיתבה בפרשות אורחתאאל ארחא

D [הן] ' היא אתתא נפקת בר דהוא יתבא בפרשת אורחתאאל ארחא

E הן היא נפשת בר די יתבא בפרשת אורחתא

PJ האן מטעיא דהיא בסכות עייניך על ארחא

TO אן מקדשתא דהיא בעינין על ארחא

HT ויאמרו לא היתה בזה קדשא

TN ואצרין לית הכא אחה נפקת בר

D ואצרין לא הכא הוות אי[חא] נפקת בר

E ואמרין לית הכא לן נפקת בר

PJ ואמרו לא הכא הות מטעיתא

TO ואמרו לית הכא מקדשא

HT וישב אל יהודה ויאמר לא מצאתיה

TN וחזר לוות יהודה ואמר לא אשכחית יתה

D וחזר לות יהודה ואמר לא אש[כח]ת יתה

E וחזר לוות יהודה ואמר לא אשכחה יתה

PJ תב לות יהודה ואמר לא אשכחתה

TO ותב לות יהודה ואמר לא אשכחתה

HT וגם אנשי המקום אמרו לא היתה בזה קדשה

TN ולחוד עמה דאתרא אמרו לית נפקת בר אחא הכא

D ולחוד [עמא דאתרא] אמרו לא הות [הכה] איתא נפ]קת ב[ר

E ולחוד עמא דאתרא אמרין לית לן הכה נפקת בר

PJ ואוף אינשי אתרא אמרו לית הות הכא מטעיתא

TO ואף אנשי אתרא אמרו לית הכא מקדשתא

HT ויאמר יהודה תקן לה פן נהיה לביז

TN ואמר יהודה תסב לה דלא נהווי לביזיין

D ואמר יהודה תסב לה דלא נהוי לבזיון

E ואמר יהודה תסב לה דלא נהויה לבזזין

PJ ואמר יהודה תיסב לה משכונייה דילמא נהו לגחוך

TO ואמר יהודה תסב לה דילמא נהי חוך

HT הנה שלחתי הגדי הזה ואתא לא מצאתה

TN הא שלחית גדייה הדין והא כדון לא אשכחיתחה

D הא שלחית [גדה] הדין ואת לא אשכחתה

E ארום שלחית גדייה הדין ואת לא אשכחתה

PJ הא שדרית ית גדיא הדין ואנח לא אשבחתה

TO הא שדרית גדיא הדין ואת לא אשכחתה

HT ויהי כמשלש חפשים

TN והוה היך בתר תלתא ירחין

D והוה לסוף [תלתא] ירחין]

E והווה לסוף תלתה ירחין

PJ והוה בזמן תלתה ירחין אשתמודעה במעברא היא

TO והוה כתלתות ירחין

HT ויגר ליהודה לאמר זנתה תמר כלתך

TN ואתני ליהודה למימר זנית תמר כלתך

D ואתני [ליהודה] למימר זנית [תמר] כלתך]

E ואתני ליהודה למימר זניית תמר כלתך

PJ ואתני ליהודה למימר זניית תמר כלתך

TO ותחוה ליודה למימר זניאת תמר כלתך

HT וגם הנה הרה לזנונים

TN ולחוד הא היא מעברה בגין דזנן

דזנן	בנין	מעברה	היא	הא	ולחוד	D
דזנן	בנין	מעברה	היא	הא	ולהוד	E
לזנן		מעברא		הא	ואוף	PJ
מזנותה		מעדיא		הא	ואף	TO

ותשרף		הוציאות			יהודה	ויאמר HT
ותתוקד	יתה	אפיקו			יהודה	ואמר TN
ותתוקד	יתה	[אפקו]			יהודה	ואמר D
ותת[וקד]	יתה	אפקו			יהודה	ואמר E
ותיחוקד		כהין היא הנפקוהא	הלא בת		יהודה	ואמר PJ
ותיחוקד		אפקותא			יהודה	ואמר TO

With a few exceptions, all five targums translate the HT, following both the word order and the formal aspects of the HT. The most significant exception is in the second line of vs. 21. The Hebrew of this line is very difficult to understand and the targums echo this problem. There are three different translations; that of TN, D and E, that of PJ and that of TO. The HT is literally "the prostitute who (was) in the eyes upon the way." TN and D interpret this as "the prostitute who sat in the crossroads of the paths upon the path," whereas E is the same but leaves out "upon the path." PJ has a different understanding, "the prostitute who (was) in the booths of eyes upon the path." TO translates the HT in a strictly literal manner. Another exception is that PJ adds two short phrases in vs. 24. These aside, the translation of all five targums can be characterized as taking great care to represent the syntactic feature of the HT as well as the semantic.

The Literary Character of Expansions in the Palestinian Targum

Now that the nature of targumic translation has been discussed and a few examples studied, the next step is to investigate the characteristics of the expansions. Genesis chapter 38 is the story of Judah and his daughter-in-law Tamar. In TN, there is a large expansion at the climax of the story, verse 25, which readily lends itself to such a study. The analysis of the literary units which constitute the different versions and the delineation of the redactional elements from the source material, should show the changes they underwent and demonstrate their interrelationships.

In addition, the following study may also be likened to the *Internal Comparison* proposed by Dr. R. Bloch. Although my analysis is limited to the mss. of the PT, it "essentially traces a single tradition through the various stages represented by the different documents. It tries to distinguish the most primitive elements and variants, the developments, the additions and the revisions..."[39] But rather than proposing to trace the "evolution of the observed tradition" as in Bloch's proposal, this study attempts to illustrate the differences among the versions, show the composition of the source material and portray the types of treatment by redactors. In this way, the redactional history of the expansion may be set forth.

There are eleven different versions of this expansion. Six are in the language of the PT and five in that of TO. The Palestinian texts are TN, PJ, Kahle's ms. D and ms. E,[40] and ms. P and ms. V from Klein's edition of the Fragmentary Targums.[41] The other five are all targumic tosafot: three are from manuscript fragments and two from Rabbinic Bibles. One of the fragments is in the Bodleian Library and is published by Ginsburger.[42] Of the other two fragments, both from the Cairo Geniza, one is in the Bodleian and the other in the Taylor-Schechter Collection at Cambridge.[43] One of the Rabbinic Bibles is *Biblia Hebraica* published in Lisbon in 1491. The other is also *Biblia Hebraica* but published in Ixar in 1490.

Before beginning the literary analysis, it is necessary to outline the linguistic relationships among the targumim. On the basis of the language used, the eleven targumim can be separated easily into three distinct groups. The first is made up of P, V, D, E, and TN. The second consists of the five targumic tosefot in the language of TO. The third is PJ. The second group is fairly uniform in matters of word choice and arrangement but these criteria further divide the first group. Ms. P and ms. D parallel each other in arrangement and word choice with few important differences. Ms. V follows these two except that it has been rearranged slightly. Ms. E differs from these three in that most of the second part of the expansion is lacking. TN's arrangement follows that of PJ in many places against the others. This division results in three single targums, E, TN and PJ, and two groups, PDV and the tosafot. To simplify the discussion, P will be used to represent the former group and Lisbon will be used for the latter.

The expansion under study is based on the Hebrew text of Gen. 38: 25-26. In order to facilitate discussion, it is given here.

Verse 25

1. She was being brought out (MWST)
2. and she sent to her father-in-law saying,

---

[39]Note methodoloque pour l'étude de la littérature rabbinique" *RSR*, 43 (1955), pp. 194-227, translated as "Methodological Note for the Study of Rabbinic Literature" by W. S. Green, in W. S. Green, *Approaches to Ancient Judaism*, Atlanta, GA: Scholars Press for Brown Judaic Studies, 1978, p. 60.

[40]Published in *Masoreten des Westens II*, Stuttgart: 1930.

[41]*The Fragment-Targums of the Pentateuch*, Rome: 1980.

[42]Cod. Ox. 2305, published in *Das Fragmententhargum*, Berlin: 1899, p. 71.

[43]Published in Dr. Klein's edition of the Cairo Geniza fragments, New York: KTAV, 1986.

3. "By the man to whom these belong, by him am I pregnant."
4. And she said, "Recognize please (HKR N') for me, (whose) signet-ring, cords, and staff are these?"

Verse 26

5. And Judah recognized (WYKR) and said,
6. "She is more righteous than I (SDQH MMNY)
7. "because I did not give her to Selah my son."
8. And he did not know her again.

The analysis will be done in two parts. In the first part, each targum will be discussed in turn and compared with those which preceded it. The versions are discussed in the order in which I shall argue they were created. The second part is a step-by-step treatment of each literary unit of the expansion which draws together all the different versions for comparison and contrast. The analysis will begin with ms. E.

Ms. E (Kahle)

1. (HT, vs. 25; E, vs. 25) And *She, Tamar, was brought out* (NPQT) to be burned,
2. and she sought (B'T) her three witnesses (SHDYYH)
3. and she did not find them.
4. She raised her eyes to the heights and said,
5. "I pray in the mercies from before you Lord,
6. "Answer me in this hour for it is the hour of my distress.
7. "And I will raise up for you three righteous men in the valley of Dura, Hananiah, Mishael, and Azariah."
8. In that hour the Lord signaled to the angel Michael and said to him,
9. "Go down, give them to her."
10. When she saw them, her eyes were illumined,
11. and *she cast* (them) under the feet of the judges *and said,*
12. *"The man who owns these, by him am I pregnant.*
13. "Even if ('L MNT) I am burned I will not reveal him
14. "because the pledge is between me and him.
15. "It will put in his heart to recognize them, *for whose* Signet-ring ('ZQTH) cloak (SWSPH) and staff (HWTRH) are these?"
16. (E, vs. 26) When Judah saw them he said in his heart,

A. 17. "It is better for me to be ashamed in this world
A. 18. "and not be ashamed in the world to come.
A. 19. "It is better for me to be burned in the fire which is extinguished in this world
A. 20. "and not be burned in the fire which consumes fire in the world to come."
21. (HT, vs. 26) *And Judah recognized it and said,*
22. "She, Tamar is *justified.*
23. *"This happened because I did not give her to Selah my son."*
24. *And he did not again know her.*

Kahle's ms. E represents the earliest extant stratum of Genesis 38:25-26. The first half of the expansion (lines 1-15) has all the literary elements found in later texts and will change relatively little throughout the different occurrences. The second part (lines 16-24) is not as full as later versions.

The first section, lines 1-10, is based on a double translation of the Hebrew word MWS'T, found in HT line 1. El interprets it in a manner which fits with the context of the HT. It derives MWS'T from the root YS', "to go out," – the hiphil meaning "to bring out." The second interpretation, E2-10, derives it from MS' "to find." The expansion plays on this meaning by attaching a story about Tamar losing and finding the pledges.

The largest literary unit in this section is Tamar's prayer. Most of the items mentioned comprise standard rituals of prayer, the raising of one's eyes towards heaven, the polite introductory phrase, the request for the prayer to be answered. But in addition Tamar bargains with God and "offers" Him three righteous men. These are Hananiah, Mishael and Azariah, who in Daniel chapter three, are thrown into a roaring fire because they refuse to worship Nebuchadnezzar's idol. Tamar can offer them because they are/will be her descendants.[44] The connection in the mind of the Targumist between Tamar and the three men possibly is that both are to be cast into the fire. Perhaps the Babylonian Talmud in Sotah 10b reflects another relationship he considered. It draws a connection between the number of people in each instance to be thrown into the fire. Just as Hananiah, Mishael and Azariah are three, so are Tamar and her two unborn sons. "A Bat Kol issued forth and proclaimed, 'Thou didst rescue Tamar and her two sons from the fire. By thy life, I will rescue through thy merit three of thy descendants from the fire.'"[45]

God then signals to Michael and tells him to go down and give the pledges to her. (E8-9) She takes them and puts them before the judges. (E10-11) The scene in the targum is different from that in the HT (line 2), where Tamar sends the three items to Judah. Here there is a full court and she gives them to the judges. This is probably due to the change in social attitudes. Adultery and its punishment are no longer a family matter, but must be tried in a court.

Tamar's speech to the judges consists of four lines. Two of these are translations from the HT. E12 is a straight translation, while E15 adds a few words to the HT translation to alter the emphasis. E13-14 put the onus for action directly upon Judah, for Tamar states that she will not reveal the man.

At this, Judah considers "in his heart" how his confession would affect him both in this world and in the world to come (section A). Although I think that the idea of being burned in the fire is due to the association with Tamar, it is obvious that Judah considers both being burned and being ashamed to apply to

---

[44]They are all of the tribe of Judah, see Daniel 1:6.

[45]Bavli Sotah 10b. Translation by Rev. Dr. A. Cohen, in *Sotah*, The Soncino Talmud, London: 1936, p. 50.

him.[46] In fact, the major elements of the expansion, the reference to Hananiah, Mishael and Azariah and Judah's thoughts, are both based on a connection with fire.

The place of vs. 26 in this expansion is a problem. Although here it is little more than a straight translation, it is evident that the expansion depends on it to complete the story. Despite the fact that the translation of vs. 26 actually begins E21, the ms. marks it as E16. This probably is because the person responsible for placing the verse markings decided to indicate the start of vs. 26 at the end of vs. 25, E15 (HT line 4). This misplacing indicates that the verse markings were not put in by the person responsible for the original redaction.[47]

Pseudo-Jonathan (PJ)

1. (HT, vs. 25; PJ, vs. 25) Tamar *was being brought out* (MYT'PQ') to be burned.
2. And she sought (B'T) the three pledges (MSKWNY')
3. and she did not find them.
4. She raised her eyes to the heavens above and thus she said,
5. "I pray by the mercies from before you Lord,
6. "Answer me in this hour of my distress
7. "Illumine my eyes and I will find three witnesses
8. "And I will raise up for you from my loins three righteous men who will sanctify your name and go down to the fiery furnace in the valley of Dura."
9. In that hour the Holy One signaled to Michael
10. And he illumined her eyes and she found them.
11. And she took them and *cast* them before the feet of the judges *and said,*
12. *"The man to whom these pledges belong, by him am I pregnant.*
13. "Even though I be burned I will not reveal him,
14. "for the Lord of the world will put in his heart to remember them,
15. "and he will save me from this great judgment."
16. And as soon as Judah saw them, he recognized them and said thus in his heart,

A. 17. "It is better for me that I be ashamed in this world, for this world passes,
A. 18. "and not be ashamed before the righteous fathers in the world to come.
A. 19. "It is better for me to burn in this world in an extinguishable fire,
A. 20. "and not burn in the world to come in the fire which consumes fire.
B. 21. "For measure receives (QBL)[48] measure.
C. 22. "Thus, according to what I said to Jacob, my father,
C. 23. "'Recognize now, the cloak of your son,'
C. 24. "Thus I must hear in this court,

---

[46] I have translated the Aramaic, NBHWT, as if it was from BHT "to be ashamed," it is possible to understand it as a Hebraism of NBY "to blow ablaze; burst forth."

[47] Such is not the case in the other targums. In TN, vs. 26 starts after the expansion. In PJ, it begins at the translation of the HT, as it does in both P and Lisbon.

[48] Taking it as a Pael, "to receive," see Jastrow.

C. 25. "'To whom belong these, *the ring* (SYTWMT'), *the cord* (HWTY') *and the staff* (HWTR')?'"

26. (HT.vs.26; PT,vs.26) *And Judah recognized them and said,*

27. "She, Tamar, is *justified, by me* she is pregnant."

28. A Bat Qol came down from heaven and said,

29. "For from before me is this matter, both of them are redeemed from judgment."

30. And he said,

31. *"Because I did not give her to Selah, my son,* this has happened to me."

32. *And he did not again know her* sexually (lit. "in bed").

The targum of Pseudo-Jonathan follows the organization of ms. E, but it contains PJ parallels E10 and PJ10. PJ7 is not in ms. E, it appears to be derived from PJ10. PJ8 adds further detail concerning the three righteous men. Although it does not name them, it explicitly states that they will go into the fire and that they will praise God's name. In PJ, God does not speak to Michael as in ms. E (PJ9). As shall be seen later, PJ is similar in this respect to the targumic tosafot.

More significantly, PJ expands Judah's speech. The impetus for the expansion is based on Tamar's speech to him in HT line 4. The opening word of this speech is HKR N', "Recognize please...," which is paralleled by the words of Judah and his brothers when they ask Jacob to recognize the blood-stained coat of Joseph, in Gen. 37:32. "Recognize please (HKR N') is this the coat of your son or not?" This connection – made on the basis of a *gezerah sewa* – provides the basis for a moral lesson (section B), for an instance of "measure receives measure," the Golden Rule. Here the guilt for the deception of Jacob concerning the fate of Joseph his son implicitly is accepted by Judah (PJ22-23). But the punishment for this sin seems rather odd. The Targumist does not call down "Divine Retribution," nor does he have Judah struck blind, nor any number of other punishments often inflicted upon sinners. Instead, the punishment is that another of Judah's less than righteous deeds is revealed. Judah is not criticized for cohabiting with a whore (i.e. Tamar), his crime is that he is caught (PJ24-25).

The fact that PJ21-25, sections B and C, is distinct from section A, PJ17-20, along with the evidence of ms. E, indicates that it arose separately from sections B and C which were later combined with it in a targum. This is further confirmed by the fact that in the other targums, sections B and C are considered to be a unit and adhere to the present order but that the placement of section A is not constant.

The other significant addition is that of the Bat Qol in vs. 26, which acquits both Judah and Tamar from judgement. Not including the Bat Qol, PJ28-29, vs. 26 is only slight elaborated over the HT.

The secondary status of sections B & C is indicated also by the fact that they are concerned with a different problematic from the rest of the expansion.

The theme of the original pericope (= ms. E) is the saving of Tamar from the fire, but the additional literary units are concerned with the punishment and acquittal of Judah. The Targumist must have thought it improper that Judah and his brothers are never punished for their selling of Joseph and deceiving of their father. So he introduces that punishment here, against Judah. But the Bat Qol, PJ28-29, rescues him from judgment, thereby showing that it too is concerned with Judah, and not only the saving of Tamar.

One difference in word choice should be commented upon. PJ uses the word MSKWN', for "pledge," where E (and the other versions) use the word SHD', "witness." This usage is found elsewhere only in TO at Gen. 38:17-18. Although this may be an argument for the influence of TO on PJ, a closer study of the language of TO and PJ shows that the use of common language is inconsistent, for TO agrees with ms. E concerning the names of each of the three items, whereas PJ calls two of them by different names. The tosafot do not agree with PJ in either case, but use the same words found in TO & E.

Targum Neofiti

1. (HT,vs.25; TN,vs.25) And Tamar *was brought out* to be burned in the fire.
2. And she sought for the three witnesses
3. but she did not find them.
4. And she lifted up her eyes on high and said,
5. "I pray in the mercies from before you, Lord,
6. "You are He who answers the anguished in their hour of anguish,
7. "answer me in this hour for it is the hour of my distress, O God who answers my distress.
8. "Illumine my eyes and give to me the three witnesses,
9. "and I will raise up for you three righteous men in the valley of Dura, Hananiah, Mishael and Azariah,
10. "when they go down into the burning fire they will sanctify your Holy Name."
11. And immediately the Lord heard the voice of her prayer and said to Michael,
12. "Go down, give to her the three witnesses."
13. And he illumined her eyes and she saw them
14. and she gave them into the hands of the judges *and said* to him, (sic)
15. *"The man to whom these things belong, by him am I pregnant.*
16. "And I, even though I be burned, will no reveal him,
17. "because the witnesses are between me and him.
18. "He will put in his heart to see them in this hour,
19. "and he will redeem me from this great judgment."
20. (HT,vs.26?) Immediately Judah rose upon his feet and said,
21. "I beseech you, brothers and men of the house of my father, listen to me (QBYLW MYNY).

A. 22. "It is better for me to burn in this world in the fire which fades,

A. 23. "and not burn in the world to come, in the fire which consumes fire.

A. 24. "It is better for me to be ashamed in this world, for this world passes,

A. 25. "and not be ashamed before the righteous fathers in the world to come.
    26. "Listen to me (QBLYW MYNY), brothers and house of my father,
B. 27. "By the measure which a man measures, by it will he be measured,
B. 28. "whether it is a good measure or a bad measure.
B. 29. "Happy are all men who reveal their deeds.
C. 30. "For I took the cloak of my brother Joseph
C. 31. "and I dipped it in sheep's blood
C. 32. "and I said to Jacob,
C. 33. "'Recognize, recognize now, is this the cloak of your son or not?'
C. 34. "And I, it is said to me now,
C. 35. "'*For the one* to whom *these – the ring, the coat and the staff* – belong, *by him am I pregnant.*'
    36. "She is *justified,* Tamar my daughter-in-law, *by me* she is pregnant.
    37. "Far be it from Tamar my daughter-in-law to conceive sons of harlotry."
    38. A Bat Qol went out from heaven and said,
    39. "Both of you are justified, the affair is from before the Lord."

The major change between PJ and TN is that TN combines the two speeches of Judah – the one to himself and the one declaring Tamar's innocence – into one speech directed to the court. To accompany this change, the Targumist adds two lines in which Judah asks the assembled crowd to listen to him. One of the introductory lines is before section A and the other before section B. If it may be argued that these are introductory phrases to a speech and that they function as a part of a recognized speech formula, then they may serve as a further indication that Judah's speech is made up from two traditions which developed separately and have been combined here in TN, as in PJ.

Another result of this change is that the separate identity of vs. 26 has been lost and has become part of the expansion. So much so that TN actually has a translation of vs. 26 immediately after this expansion. This indicates that the expansion first existed separately from the surrounding translation text in TN. TN28 which emphasizes that the quality of the measure, good or bad, does not matter in the application of the rule. The second is due to the change in the audience addressed by the speech. Rather than addressing himself, Judah speaks to the crowd. This results in TN29 in which Judah mentions the benefits of revealing one's deeds. TN30-33 has been reworked so that it conforms to the HT of Gen. 37:31-32. Here is the HT with the material found in TN in boldface.

> **And they took Joseph's coat** and they killed a male goat **and dipped the coat in blood.** And they sent the colored coat and they brought it to their father and said, "We found this, **recognize please (HKR N')** **is it the coat of your son or not?"**

Despite this, in TN33, Judah's words to his father follow the HT less accurately than in PJ, and in TN35, the translation of HT line 4 lacks any mention of HKR N', just as in PJ.

Another feature not found in the previous targums occurs in TN, the addition of TN37 to TN36. TN36 is an expansion of HT line 6, SDQH MMNY. Rather than interpreting the Hebrew as is usually done today, TN agrees only in the interpretation of SDQH. The comparative (MMNY) is taken as part of Judah's confession that he is responsible for Tamar's pregnancy. This is emphasized in TN37 where Judah emphatically states that Tamar would never be pregnant with "sons of whoredom." These two phrases are found in both P and in an altered form in Lisbon.

There are two phrases in which TN is parallel to PJ not found in any other targum. The first PJ7 & TN8, are the duplication of the phrase originally found in PJ10 & TN13. The second are PJ8 & TN10 where Tamar says that the three men will sanctify God's name.

Ms. P (Klein)

1. (HT,vs.25; P,vs.25) Tamar, when *she was brought out* to be burned in the fire,
2. and she was seeking the witnesses
3. and she did not find them.
4. She raised her eyes to the heights and said,
5. "I pray (by the) mercies from before you Lord,
6. "Answer me in this hour for it is the hour of my distress (D ' NYNQY).
7. "And I will raise up for you three righteous men in the valley of Dura, Hananiah, Mishael and Azariah."
8. In that hour the Holy One, blessed be He, summoned Michael the angel and said,
9. "Give them (i.e. the witnesses) to her."
10. When she saw them, her eyes shone, ('NHRN 'YYNH')
11. *And she cast* (the witnesses) under the feet of the judges (and said,)
12. *"The man to who owns these, by him am I pregnant.*
13. "Even if I am burned (YQD') I will not reveal him,
14. "because the witnesses which are between me and him
15. "will put[49] in his heart *to recognize* them, *for whose ring, cloak and staff are these?"*
16. (HT,vs.26; P,vs.26) When *Judah recognized* the three pledges
17. he rose on his feet *and said,*
18. "I pray you, my brothers and men of the house of my father, receive from me this matter.
B. 19. "By the measure by which a man measures in the world, by it they measure him in heaven,
B. 20. "whether it is a good measure or a bad measure.
B. 21. "Happy is every man who has good deeds.
A. 22. "it is better not (sic, probably corrupt of LY, "for me") that I am ashamed in this world,
A. 23. "and not be ashamed in the world to come.
A. 24. "It is better for me to burn in the fire which fades

---

[49]Verb is singular although the subject is plural.

A. 25. "and not burn in the fire which consumes fire.
C. 26. "Because I took the cloak of Joseph my brother,
C. 27. "and I dipped it in the blood of the kid
C. 28. "and I oppressed (TLMYT) my father and said to him,
C. 29. "'Recognize now, is this the coat of your son or not?'
B1. 30. "Measure corresponds to measure.
B1. 31. "And judgment (SDR DYN) corresponds to judgment.
   32. "She, Tamar, my daughter-in-law is *justified, by me* she is pregnant.
   33. "Far be it from her, from Tamar my daughter-in-law that she should be pregnant with sons of whoredom.
   34. "(This happened) *because I did not give her to my son Selah.*"
   35. A Bat Qol went forth from the heavens and said,
   36. "Both of you are justified, from before me was the matter."
   37. *And he did not again know her.*

The few structural differences between P and TN are minor and are found in Tamar's prayer and Judah's speech. In Tamar's speech, TN6 is not paralleled by P, neither is the phrase "Illumine my eyes" (TN8). TN10, where the three men go down into the fire and praise God's name, is also missing.

The main difference in Judah's speech is that the order has been altered. Section A is no longer at the beginning but has been placed between sections B and C. In addition, the second part of the *gezera sewa*, the part where Judah is asked to recognize the witnesses, is missing in P. In its place another "Measure" section (B1) has been added. The second phenomenon is a result of the first. The placing of Section A between sections B and C causes section B to modify section A rather than section A. So in order to keep the original emphasis, a second B section, P30-31, is placed after it. One of these lines, P30, is the same as PJ21; the other has the same form. The first B section, P19-21, is like that of TN27-29.

The last significant change is due to the inclusion of the whole of vs. 26 in the expansion. This results in the presence of P34 within Judah's speech and of P37 at the end of the expansion.

Lisbon, 1491

1. (HT,vs.25; Lisbon,vs.25) Tamar, *she was being brought out* (MTPQ') to be burned in the fire.
2. And she sought the three witnesses
3. and she did not find them.
4. For[50] Samuel the angel had come and hidden them from before her.
5. And she lifted her eyes to heaven and said,
6. "I pray to you, God of the living, answer me in this hour, for I am innocent (NYQ').
7. "And I will give to you three righteous (men). They are Hananiah, Mishael and Azariah, in the valley of Dura.

---

[50]KD, lit. "when."

　　　8. "For they will go down into the fire on my account ('L DYLY)."
　　　9. In that hour the Lord signaled to Gabriel,
　　10. and he went down and gave them to her.
　　11. *And she offered* them (i.e. the witnesses) before the feet of the judges and said,
　　12. *"Recognize now, whose ring, cloak and staff are these?"*
　　13. (HT,vs.26; Lisbon,vs.26) *And Judah recognized them and said,*
　　14. "(She is) *justified, from me* is she pregnant
　　15. "and she is not pregnant with sons of whoredom.
B.　16. "In the measure which a man measures, by it they measure him.
C.　17. "When I took the coat of Joseph my brother
C.　18. "and I dipped it in blood,
C.　19. "and I brought it to my father and said,
C.　20. "'Recognize now, is this the coat of your son or not?'
C.　21. "Thus my brothers and all the men of the house of my father say to me,
C.　22. *"'Recognize now, whose ring, cloak and staff are these?'*
A.　(23. "It is better to burn in this world)
A.　(24. "than to burn in the world to come." [Ixar and Bodleian only])
A.　25. "It is better to burn in the fire which fades
A.　26. "than to burn in the fire which consumes."
　　27. Then a Bat Qol went out from the heavens and said,
　　28. "Both of you are justified, from me is this matter."
　　29. *And he did not know her again.*

There are five different occurrences of this expansion in the language of TO. A number of words are based on roots which are not in the Palestinian texts but are in TO. Two of these expansions are found in printed editions of TO.[51] Of the five examples, only three have the expansion in full. The Cambridge fragment is corrupt and breaks off after a few lines (its last line is Lisbon line 9). Ginsburger's tosefta is complete in the manuscript but it finishes at the expansion of verse 25 (Lisbon line 12). Likewise, one of the complete mss., Ixar, has been reduced from a fuller text, but to a lesser degree. So, of the five mss., there are only two complete ones; Lisbon, printed above, and the unpublished fragment in the Bodleian Library.

Despite this fact, it is evident when material is shared across two or more texts at different points that the five mss. are closely related. Ginsburger lacks a large item present in the other texts, Lisbon line 11 (L11). Lines 23-24 are not present in the Lisbon text, although are in both the Ixar printed edition and the Bodleian ms. fragment, as indicated in the translation. There are a number of other differences, among the five texts; a few different roots or places where one text differs in form, but most of the variance is due to the addition or lack of words in lines which are otherwise parallel.

---

[51] *Biblia Hebraica,* Lisbon: 1491; *Biblia Hebraica,* Ixar: 1490.

The similarities between Lisbon and the Palestinian texts, particularly P and TN, are striking. The first three lines are basically the same, but L4, which is present in all the other texts of this group, is not in any of the Palestinian ones. In it, Samuel hides the missing witnesses from Tamar. Tamar's prayer is shorter than in TN – roughly the same length as P – but it has, in different wording, the same idea as TN and PJ that the three righteous men will go down into the fire (TN10, PJ8, L8).

L6 appears to be largely a combination of elements found in P5-6. The opening few words of L6, "I pray to you, God...," are from P5. "...of the living" is unique to Lisbon. But the rest of L6 is from P6, the last phrase "...for I am innocent" being a corruption of P. In P6, the final two words are "hour of my distress," S'H D'NYNQY. But in L6, the three words at the end of the line are "...hour, for I am innocent," S'T' D'N' NQY'. It is evident that the last two words of L6 can be explained as orthographical misreadings – intentional or accidental – of P. The first yod of P has been changed to an aleph, the word has been divided in two, and an aleph has been added at the end of the second word.

Verse 26 is an integral part of Lisbon, as is obvious from the fact that L13 and the first part of L14 quote it. L14 and L15 are based on HT line 6, and are paralleled by P32-33 and TN36-37.

L16 is section B. Like PJ21, it is only one line, unlike PJ, it follows TN27 in its wording. Section C, concerning Joseph's coat, is the closest to its scriptural background. The first four lines, L17-20, follow fairly closely TN and P. The next two lines, L21-22, follow TN34-25. But rather than the inexact quote found in TN, the scripture here is cited so that the parallel words, Hebrew HKR N', are evident.

Unlike the Lisbon text, both the Ixar text and the Bodleian text have four lines in section A. But unlike the palestinian texts, the main verb in all four is "to burn," rather than two lines with "to burn" and two lines with "to be ashamed."[52] The form of the lines in the Ixar text and the Bodleian fragment is like that of Lisbon, which is different from that of the Palestinian.

To complete the expansion, there is the section with the Bat Qol and the last line of vs. 26, "And he did not know her again."

There are two parts of the HT which do not find expression in these texts. HT line 7 is missing, and as in the Palestinian texts, Tamar gives the pledges to the judges rather than to Judah.

These parallels and divergences indicate that Lisbon is based on a text somewhere between the form of PJ and that of TN and P. The following review of the literary elements of the expansion should make clear the nature of this

---

[52]Perhaps the four lines with "to burn" reflect a possible reading of ms. E, which reflects both the aramaic meaning of the root and also a hebraicised meaning.

text, as well as providing a synopsis of the remarks made about each literary unit in the discussion of the various targums.

Tamar's prayer is found in all the targums. The introductory line, in which she raises her eyes to the heavens, is found in all targums (E4, PJ4, TN4, P4, L5). All the mss. have Tamar's offer of the three righteous men (E7, PJ8, TN9, P7, L7). Lisbon (L8) follows PJ8 and TN 10 in that they mention that these men will go down into the fire. Only PJ8 and TN10 state that the three will glorify God's name. All the texts begin the prayer with "I pray...," BB'W, (E5, PJ5, TN5, P5, L6), and have a line in which Tamar asks God to "Answer me in this hour" (E6, PJ6, TN7, P6, L6). Lisbon is like P and E in that it does not elaborate the prayer any further, whereas both PJ and TN contain other items.

God responds to Tamar by sending an angel down to reveal the witnesses to her (E8-10, PJ8-10, TN11-13, P8011, L9-10). The targums differ about whether or not the third line is part of this section or the following one. In PJ and TN, it fits here, but in E and P it belongs to the following section. Lisbon does not have this line. Lisbon and PJ are different from the other three targums, because in them God does not speak to the angel but merely signals. Lisbon is unique in calling the angel Gabriel, the other four call him Michael.

Tamar then takes the witnesses and casts them before the feet of the judges (E11, PJ11, P11, L11). TN14 disagrees with the others by claiming that she gave them into the hands of the judges.

Tamar then speaks to the judges. She begins by saying that she is pregnant by the owner of the pledges. This is a quotation of HT line 3 (E12, PJ12, TN15, P12). Lisbon does not have this line but has rather HT line 4 (L12). In Lisbon, this is the extent of Tamar's speech. In E13-1, Tamar says that she will not reveal the man because the pledges are between the two of them. E15 then quotes HT line 4 and requests recognition of the pledges. PJ13 follows E13 but rather than continuing like E, PF says that God will cause the man to recognize them and save her from judgement (PJ14-15). TN16-17 follow E13-14, but TN18-19 follow PJ14-15. Neither PJ nor TN have HT line 4. P13-15 follow E exactly.

Judah then recognizes the witnesses and begins a speech (E16, PJ16, TN20, P16-17, L13). In both E and PJ, Judah speaks to himself and does not speak out loud until later. In both targums, the second speech begins at the translation of vs. 26 (E21, PJ26). E has the shortest speech since it has only section A (E17-20). Both PJ and TN begin with section A (PJ17-20, TN22-25), but they add to it section B (PJ21, TN27-29) and section C (PJ22-25, TN30-35). PJ and E both have the same order in section A. Judah first worries about being ashamed, then about being burned. For some reason TN reverses this order. This explains TN21 and TN26 which are polite requests for the audience to pay attention. In PJ, section B is only one line (PJ21). TN expands this line (TN27) and then adds a second (TN28) which further explains it. TN29 is added because Judah is now addressing the court rather than talking to self. In PJ22-25, section C is a *gezerah sewa,* based, as I explained earlier, on HKR N'. It is topically balanced: "...according to what I *said*...Thus must I *hear*...." TN takes this and reworks it according to the HT of Gen. 27:31-32.

Turning to P, we find that section B (P19-32) is first, followed by section A (P22-25). Then comes section C (P26-29), which is incomplete since it lacks mention of the second half of the comparison. In its place is a second B section, B1 (P30-31). The B section is based on TN's section B (TN27-29), whereas section B1 is based on PJ's B section, PJ21. P, like TN, has only one speech, which is also introduced by a polite phrase, P18. In Lisbon there is no such politeness. Section B comes first (L6), followed by section C (L17-22) and then by section A (L23-26). Section B is the first line of TN's section B, TN27. The C section is the closest to the HT of all the targums and is the only one to translate the HKR N' of the HT in both parts of the comparison. In Lisbon, the A section consists of only two lines (L25-26) which discuss "burning." The two other texts of this group which are extant here have four lines, but all four discuss "burning," rather than "burning" and "being ashamed" as in the Palestinian targums.

Ms. E continues with line 5 of the HT at E21. E22 translates HT line 6 but it leaves out the MMNY and adds "Tamar." E23-24 bring E to completion by translating the rest of vs. 26. PJ also continues by translating HT line 5 (PJ26). PJ27 expands on E22 by including a phrase which contains MMNY. In TN, the expansion of HT line 6 follows section C. The first line, TN36, is a slight elaboration over PJ27, but TN complements this by adding TN37. P32-33 follow these two lines of TN. In Lisbon, these two lines are also present, somewhat reworked, but they appear at the beginning of Judah's speech (L14-15). It is evident that Lisbon considers the beginning of Judah's speech to correspond to verse 26 since L13 translates HT line 5 (the first line of vs. 26) and L14 expands HT line 6.

At the close of Judah's speech, a Bat Qol comes forth and declares them both justified (PJ28-29, TN38-39, P35-36, L27-28). TN, P and Lisbon all have the same wording, while PJ differs slightly.

That is the end of TN. PJ finishes with PJ31-32, translating and slightly elaborating HT lines 7 and 8. Both P37 and L29 complete their respective expansions by translating HT line 8.

This detailed analysis of the targumic expansion of Gen. 38:25-26 has revealed much about the manner in which it is treated. Different versions show that the structure of the story, as well as the arrangement and choice of words found in earlier texts, was often followed. But in addition, sections were reworked, being increased in size and expanded in topical scope, or cut back and reduced to flow more smoothly. Sometimes a section was redesigned, maintaining the same point but using different phraseology. It has even been seen that whole literary units occasionally are added or removed. This indicates that the expansive material in the targums was not treated as fixed, unalterable text, but that it was reworked to suit the purpose of a redactor.

When the dynamics of the expansions are contrasted with those of the translation, the differences are evident. The Targumist translates with great care, making sure that his translation conforms to the HT in both meaning and form. The different treatments are particularly evident when the translations of Gen. 38:17-24 is compared to the different versions of the expansion. In the translation, it was seen that all the targums closely represent the HT, but that those of TN, D and E tended to be similar. This was not true in the expansion, where those three targums were significantly different from each other.

The differences between the two types of literary activity, translation and redaction, indicates that in the mind of the Targumist there was a distinction between them. This distinction shows that on the one hand, the Targumist translated the HT with accuracy and precision. But on the other hand, it allowed him the freedom to rework the expansions as he saw fit and even to add new material.

Expansions and the Synoptic Versions of the Palestinian Targum

The problem of identifying the interrelationships among the different versions of the PT is complicated by the problem of the relationship between each version and the HT. So often an apparent relationship between two different targums can also be explained as a relationship between each targum and its Scriptural basis. This confusion hampers and even prevents the analysis of inter-targum relationships. The distinction we have made between translation and expansion, however, provides a way out of this impass. By analyzing the relationships among only the expanded material, we bypass altogether the issue of targum/Scripture relationships. We can study the shared material that exists only in the targums and has no direct link to the Scriptural text.

This approach has a second advantage over many previous attempts to determine the relationships among the different targums of the PT; it is free from the restraints and uncertainties inherent in the philogical study of word choice, dialect and other issues of language. These uncertainties arise from what has been explained as the tendency of copyists both to regularize the spelling and word choice of the texts and to "update" them, that is, to make a text's aramaic conform to the form of aramaic known to the copyist. As if this process did not cause enough problems, scholars further suppose that the various copyists were not consistent in their changes. They seem to start at Genesis by changing lots of words and usages and then, after a number of chapters or a book or two, their enthusiasm begins to flag. By the time these copyists reach Deuteronomy, they usually change few words, if any. The activities of these copyists makes it difficult, if not impossible, for scholars to identify the relationships among the different targums. For the copyists have obliterated the original language of the text. It cannot be restored except by conjecture. Thus, the study of language usage in the different targums of the PT is incapable of accurately delineating the relationships amongs them.

By contrast, when we focus on the expansions in the targums and attempt to identify common stories, traditions and formal characteristics, we can delineate the relationships among them without being sidetracked by the problems of targum/Scripture relationships or by the issues of language, dialect or word choice. This approach enables us to accomplish two goals. First, by discovering which expansions are common to all the targums, we can identify a core of material shared by all and that therefore constitutes the source for all of them. This source means that the texts of the PT – in particular, the four complete texts of the PT, Targum Neofiti, Targum Pseudo-Jonathan, and mss. P and V of the Fragmentary Targums – are synoptic. They share material in common that is not merely borrowed from a prior source, but reworked and augmented to reveal the point the targumist wishes to make. As in the synoptic gospels, each expansion has the same tradition or story constructed according to a similar form. However, the exact wording of the expansion, and even the amount of material within the form, varies from targum to targum. Thus by common material we emphasize stories, traditions, and exegetical points, not shared language. An expansion's formal elements are more important than its word choice.

Second, not every expansion in TN occur in all other versions of the PT. Some appear in one or two other targums, while a few appear only in TN. These expansions point to sources that complement the core of material common to all four targums. They identify the links between different texts and reveal the complex weave of interrelationships that bind together the different versions of the PT. By identifying and isolating the material that points to each set of relationships – TN to PJ, P and V to TN, etc. – we take the first step towards the delineating the complex network of sources that underlie the documents of the PT.

In this study, we can identify the core of shared materials that make the four complete versions of the PT – Targum Neofiti, Targum Pseudo-Jonathan, and mss. P and V of the Fragmentary Targums – into synoptic texts. To accomplish this task, we shall use TN as our base and locate its expansions. Then we shall discover which of the other targums possess the same expansions. By constructing a catalogue that lists TN's augmented material and the parallels to them in other texts, we can delineate the core of expansions that reveals the major source common to all targums of the PT. This catalogue will moreover enable us to specify TN's relationships to other targums through expansions that do not constitute part of the source shared by all texts. Although we can complete our primary task of delineating the materials that make the PT synoptic, we cannot investigate all the interrelationships among the texts of the PT within the confines of this paper. We can identify, however, all the relationships that TN has with the other targums. The investigation of the relationships in which the TN does not form a part will have to be postponed to another study.

Rather than list the expansions in the body of the article, I have place the catalogue of expansions in TN into the appendix. It contains two hundred and ninety-two items. Two points immediately become clear. First, there is a significant amount of material that comprise a core of expansions shared among the four versions. One hundred forty-five of the expansions, just less than 50% of the total, are found in all four targums.[53] These pericopae represent the source that make the four versions of the PT into synoptic targums. Second, an intricate network of relationships between TN and other targums exists outside of the core common to all. Most of these expansions find parallels in at least one[54] and more frequently two of the other targums.[55] In fact, 87% of TN's expansions (259 of 292) are paralleled by one of the other versions of the PT.[56] The following two tables help clarify these points.

Table 1

Breakdown by Book and by the Number of Targums Which Parallel TN

	TN+3	TN+2	TN+1	TN	Total
Gen.	65	22	12	5	104
Ex.	23	9	7	6	45
Lev.	6	2	4	2	14
Num.	22	14	11	11	64
Deut.	29	16	17	17	65
Total	145	63	51	33	292

Table 2

Breakdown of List by Size and by the Number of Targums Parallel to TN

	TN+3	TN+2	TN+1	TN	Total
A	39	10	5	1	55
B	37	13	3	1	54
C	69	40	43	31	183
Total	145	63	51	33	292

---

[53]See the appendix, numbers 1 to 145.

[54]See the appendix, numbers 209 to 259.

[55]See the appendix, numbers 146 to 208.

[56]Numbers 1 through 259 have at least one parallel, numbers 260 to 292 have none.

Table 1 shows a breakdown of the the expansions according to the book in which they appear and the number of other targums that parallel the expansion in TN. The nature of the core materials becomes clear from the first column of Table 1. The count shows that the synoptic material is not spread evenly across the five books of the Pentateuch. The largest number of expansions appears in Genesis, some 45% (65 of 145) of the total. Exodus, Numbers and Deuteronomy each have between 15% and 20% of the core material while Leviticus contains only 4%. Thus it is clear that bulk of the common material appears in Genesis. Table 2 records the totals according to size. This is done by means of a ratio between the number of words in the HT and the number of words in TN.[57] The ratio permits the separation of the expansions into three categories; A, those in which the TN expansion is more than five times the size of the HT; B, those in which it is between three and five time the size of the HT; C, those in which the ration is less than three. When we look at the first column of Table 2, we see that the group of shared expansions is weighted towards the smaller ratios; some 47% (69 of 145) of them are in the smallest category, C. The rest are divided evenly into the larger categories of A and B. When we compare the core material to the expansions that are not shared by all four targums, however, we find a significant point. For both categories A and B, the preponderance of expansions are in the core. For A – those expansions with the largest ratios – 71% occur in all four targums, while the percentage for B is 69%. The smallest expansions, by contrast, are spread more evenly among all four options. Thus the larger expansions in general belong to the core of shared material.

When we ask about the material not shared by all four versions of the PT, we find a different situation. The spread of expansions across the different Pentateuchal books varies according to the number of targums in which the expansion appears. For those expansions that occur in three texts (TN+2), most of them appear in Genesis; Numbers and Deuteronomy have about a third less, while Leviticus has very few (see Table 1). These expansions so far are distributed like those belonging to the core source. But Exodus differs significantly, containing much fewer parallel expansions than Numbers and Deuteronomy. When we examine the expansions shared by only two targums (TN+1), the picture again differs. More expansions occur in Deuteronomy than in any other book, whereas it is now Genesis and Numbers that have fewer expansions. Both Exodus and Leviticus again have only a few paralleled expansions. In the expansions where TN has no parallels at all, Deuteronomy and Numbers each have the same amount as they did for one parallel targum. But Genesis has dropped down to the low level of Exodus, with Leviticus again at the bottom. Outside the core of materials shared by all four targums, therefore, only Deuteronomy consistently has a high number of expansions.

---

[57]See the discussion of ratio in the opening paragraphs of Appendix I.

Numbers runs a close second, with Leviticus always at the bottom. But both Genesis and Exodus vary enormously. So although the core of expansions shared by the synoptic targums is heavily weighted toward the beginning of the Pentateuch. The expansions outside the core are not. In fact they appear with greater regularity at the end of the Pentateuch.

The size of the expansions not in the central core follows the same tendency as those that are. Specifically, more appear in the smallest ratios than in the larger two. For expansions that have two parallels, a full two thirds appear in category C. For those expansions of TN that appear in only one other targum, 84% belong to category C (43 of 51), while those expansions unique to TN belong to Category C 94% of the time (31 of 33). Thus overall, the smaller expansions are more numerous.

The one hundred and forty-seven of the expansions that do not belong to the main source shared among all four targums of the PT can be separated into separate sources. For the purposes of this study, the expansions shared by a particular group of targum texts point to an underlying source. We start by identifying the expansions shared by three versions of the PT. Table 3 reveals the number of expansions for each grouping of three texts. (Rather than list the expanded verses here in the text, I have relegated them to the footnotes.) TN, P and V share the most expansions, thirty-one.[58] TN, PJ and V have the next largest group, twenty-one.[59] While TN, PJ and P have the least number in common, eleven.[60] The expansions shared by only two targums appear in Table 4. TN and PJ have the largest number in common, 26,[61] while TN and P have the least, 5.[62] TN and V share 20 expansions.[63] Finally, the 33 expansions that appear only in TN also constitute a source. The nature of these seven sources becomes apparent in the following discussion.

---

[58]The source behind TN/P/V contains Gen. 4:16, 25:34, 30:22, 31:39, 35:9, 44:18, 44:19, 49:2, 49:24, 50:19; Ex. 17:16, 24:6; Num. 12:1, 21:14, 21:15, 21:28, 21:29, 23:10, 23:19, 23:24, 24:7, 24:8, 24:14; Deut. 32:10, 32:24, 32:33, 32:34, 32:35, 32:38, 33:3, 33:9.

[59]The source behind TN/PJ/V contains Gen. 10:2, 10:4, 11:1, 49:4, 49:6, 49:12; Ex. 15:18, 28:17-20, 34:26; Lev. 26:29; Num. 9:8, 20:21, 24:16; Deut. 29:14, 32:15, 32:32, 33:7, 33:10, 33:20, 33:22, 33:28.

[60]The source behind TN/PJ/P contains Gen. 4:13, 4:26, 27:41, 28:17, 31:22, 42:13; Ex. 20:2, 20:13-17, 23:19, 24:11; Lev. 20:7.

[61]The source behind TN/PJ contains Gen. 2:23, 4:23, 4:24, 13:13, 30:30, 38:15, 42:32; Ex. 20:3, 23:3, 23:5, 39:10-13, 39:43; Lev. 13:45, 18:9, 26:13, 26:19; Num. 14:19, 15:24, 27:5, 28:14, 29:35; Deut. 3:24, 5:9, 5:17-21, 14:21, 26:5.

[62]The source behind TN/P contains only Gen. 24:60, 50:21; Ex. 17:12, 20:5; Num.10:10.

Table 3

The Pairing of Targums Which Follow TN, by Size

TN+2	P, V	PJ, V	PJ, P	Total
A	5	3	2	10
B	10	2	1	13
C	<u>16</u>	<u>16</u>	<u>8</u>	<u>40</u>
Total	31	21	11	63

Table 4

The Expansions for Which Only One Targum Parallels TN, by Size

TN+1	PJ	P	V	Total
A	4	0	1	5
B	2	0	1	3
C	<u>20</u>	<u>5</u>	<u>18</u>	<u>43</u>
Total	26	5	20	51

If we examine a listing of TN's expansions in order from Genesis 1 to Deuteronomy 3 – a list such as the index in the Appendix – we discover that, within the guidelines described above, the expansions in general appear to be randomly scattered through the books of the Pentateuch. There are four sections, however, that breaks this random pattern and contain a total of ninety expansions, some 31% of the total. These sections – merely seven chapters in all – are Genesis 49, Numbers 21 and 22-24, and Deuteronomy 32-33. In them lie 34% (50 of 145) of the core of material shared by all four targums. Similarly, they contain 44% of the expansions that appear in three PT texts and 23% of the passages held in common by only two targums. These four sections thus constitute areas on which the targumists concentrated when they were adding expansive material.

This distinction between the expansions in the four sections and those scattered elsewhere throughout the targums reveals a significant fact about the character of the sources external to the shared core of material. Three sources – those that occur in TN/P, TN/PJ, and TN/P/PJ – contain no expansions that appear in any of the four sections. The expanded material they contain is scattered throughout the PT, except in those seven chapters. Since one-fourth of all expansions appear there, statistically speaking we would expect that one-fourth of these sources to have expansions in these particular sections. Similarly, there is a lack of material in these areas in the TN-only source. It contains only one pericope that appears in the four sections.[64] By contrast, the remaining three sources – TN/V/P, TN/V/PJ, and TN/V – all have approximately the same number of expansions occurring in the four special sections as they do scattered through the Pentateuch.[65] How can we explain the difference between the sources that include expansions in the special sections and those that do not?

The key comes from the relationship between TN and V. These two targums both contain every expansion that occurs in the four special sections. Not only do both texts have all the expansions in the sources TN/V, TN/V/P and TN/V/PJ, but they also possess the material common to all four targums, that is, TN/V/P/PJ. Furthermore, in the special sections, neither P nor PJ ever agree with TN against V. This points to an important conclusion; underlying all four versions of the PT is a source – represented by TN/V – that contains every expansion appearing in the special sections. TN, PJ, P and V all draw materials from this TN/V source. We know that P is aware of this source because it appears in TN/V/P and TN/V/P/PJ. We know that PJ knows the TN/V source because it appears in TN/V/PJ and TN/V/P/PJ. This leads us to an important conclusion; the source represented by TN/V is part of the core of materials known to all four targums of the PT, even though every expansion does not appear in all four texts. This means that the core source – the one that makes PT into a set of synoptic targums – contains not merely one hundred and forty-five expansions, but one hundred and eighty-seven. For TN/V, TN/V/P, and TN/V/PJ contain forty-two passages that occur in the four special sections.[66] Increasing the core source to this size means that the core constitutes 63% (two-thirds) of the expansions appearing in TN.

This raises a further question; if PJ and P knew these forty-two expansions, why did they not use them? Each targum has a reason specific to itself. First, for PJ, whenever TN and V share an expansion in the special sections that does not appear in PJ, PJ tends to have a different expansion for that verse. In twenty-two of the thirty-one expansions (71%) that appear in the special areas of TN and V and which PJ does not parallel, PJ has an expansion peculiar to itself. This means that PJ may have once had the expansions but later replaced them

---

[64]This is Num. 24:5, which constitutes an odd passage in a number of ways. Usually, when P or V do not parallel an expansion that occurs in TN, they do not refer to the verse at all. In nearly every case, neither of them contains any material that disagrees with TN. But here, they *share* an expansion different from that in TN.

[65]TN/V/P has 17 expansions in the four special sections and 14 scattered through the rest of the document. TN/V/PJ has 11 expansions in the four special sections and 10 in rest of the text. TN/V has 11 expansions in the sections and 9 throughout the remainder of the Pentateuch.

[66]In addition to the previously identified core of 145 expansions, there are forty-two further passages that I will argue belong to the core. From TN/V come Gen. 49:5; Num. 21:1; Deut. 32:27, 30, 36, 39, 43; 33:11, 12, 19, 24. From TN/V/P come Gen. 49:2, 24; Num. 21:14, 15, 28, 29; 23:10, 19, 24; 24:7, 8, 14; Deut. 32:10, 24, 33, 34, 35, 38; 33:3, 9. From TN/V/PJ come Gen. 49:4, 6,12; Num. 24:16; Deut. 32:15, 32; 33:7, 10, 20, 22, 28.

with other material. This scenario is not unlikely. Since the date for the final redaction of PJ is much later than those of the other versions of the PT and since PJ contains a large number of additions, expansions and borrowings from other sources, it is quite possible a version of PJ prior to the one we now actually contained the expansions in question, which were later replaced by different material. Second, whenever P does not parallel TN and V in the special sections, it is not extant. That is to say, it has no alternate reading or expansion to the one appearing in TN, it simply fails to exist. Thus it is not improbable that the targum from which P was taken contained these expansions, but the redactor failed to select them. This more likely when we remember that the vast majority of these expansions are small and would be overlooked by someone searching for larger expansive material. Both PJ and P, therefore, possess reasons specific to them that can explain why they lack all the expansions of the TN/V source. Although this explanation is perforce hypothetical, it does explain the data before us. Even if it does not hold true, we have shown that there is an important source of expansions shared by TN and V that appear in the seven chapters of Genesis 49, Numbers 21 and 22-24, and Deuteronomy 32-33.

In sum, this paper has shown that source criticism of the expansions in the PT is a profitable method for investigating the relationships among the four versions of the PT. By isolating the material that simply translates Scripture from that which expands upon its ideas, and by ignoring the former, we have been able to study the links between TN, PJ, P and V without interference from the problem of Scripture translation. This enabled us to identify a shared core of expansions that makes these four targums into synoptic targums. It furthermore permitted us to see the sources that were common to some, but not all, texts of the PT.

Abbreviations

A	ms. A, Kahle, MdW
B	ms. B, Kahle, MdW
Br.	FTms. in Klein
BTB	*Biblical Theology Bulletin*
BZAW	*Beihefte Zeitschrift für Alttestamentische Wissenschaft*
C	ms. C, Kahle, MdW
CBQ	*Catholic Biblical Quarterly*
D	ms. D, Kahle, MdW
E	ms. E, Kahle, MdW
F	ms. F, Kahle, MdW
FT	Fragmentary Targums
G	ms. G, Kahle, MdW
HT	Hebrew Text
HTR	*Harvard Theological Review*
HUCA	*Hebrew Union College Annual*
J	ms. J in Klein
JBL	*Journal of Biblical Literature*
JJS	*Journal of Jewish Studies*
JQR	*Jewish Quarterly Review*
JTS	*Journal of Theological Studies*
Klein	Michael L. Klein, *The Fragment-Targums of the Pentateuch*, 2 vols, (Rome: BIP, 1980)
L	ms. L in Klein
MdW	*Masoreten des Westens*, P. Kahle, Stuttgart: 1970
ms.	manuscript
mss.	manuscripts
N	ms. N in Klein
NTS	*New Testament Studies*
P	ms. P in Klein
PJ	Targum Pseudo-Jonathan
PT	Palestinian Targum
TN	Targum Neofiti
TNgl	marginal and interlineal glosses to TN

TO	Targum Onkelos
V	ms. V in Klein
VT	*Vetus Testamentum*
VTS	Supplements to *Vetus Testamentum*
ZAW	*Zeitschrift für Alttestamentische Wissenschaft*

Appendix I
Parallels to the Expansions in Targum Neofiti

The following pages catalogue the expanded verses in TN. Every expansion in TN[67] has been identified and categorized by its size and the number of times another text of the PT contains a version of the same expansion. In order to provide a systematic picture of the number of parallels to each expansion, I have chosen to compare TN only to the targums of the PT that are complete. Thus, the expansions in TN will be compared to those in three other targums: PJ, ms. P, and ms. V. Fragments from other targums are mentioned where extant, but are not included in the computing of statistics about parallels.[68]

The number of parallels per expansion has been used as the main organizing principle. This makes the synoptic character of the expansive material most evident. The secondary principle of organization is based on a ratio between the number of words in the HT and in TN which represents the number of times larger the expansion is over the HT. This permits the separation of the expansions into three categories; A, those which are more than five times the size of the HT; B, those between three and five; C, those less than three. Expansions in sections A and B tend to be cohesive units complete in themselves, whereas those in C are woven with the translation text and are dependent on it.

The ratio has been chosen as a means of evaluating the size of the expansion in TN because it can indicate the relationship between the HT and TN. It is not a perfect measurement because a verse in the HT whose word count is disproportionately high or low tends to upset it. However it is a more useful mechanism than other options. Of these, the first is simply reporting the number of words in the expansion. This is obviously unsatisfactory because it does not indicate the number of words in the HT. The second possibility is to subtract the number of words in the expansion from the number in the HT. This has two faults. First, it provides no indication of the number of words in the HT. Second, it restricts the locus of an expansion to a single verse, and does not provide a means of comparison for an expansion which covers a larger area. The third option, subtracting the number of words in the HT from the number of words in TN, solves the first problem but does not address the second two. This leaves the ratio as the method which is most appropriate.[69]

---

[67]The distinction between translation and expansion is a loose one, particularly since the criterion is size. I have compiled all expansions whose Hebrew/Aramaic ratio is at least 1.5.

[68]Similar studies on the targums to Genesis has been done by A. Shinan, *The Aggadah in the Aramaic Targums to the Pentateuch* (Jerusalem: Makor, 1979) (in Hebrew). Unfortunately, I have not had the opportunity to incorporate his insights into this paper.

[69]I also attempted to categorize the expansions on the basis of form and of relationship to the Hebrew text, but this approach was simply unworkable.

Let me explain the other information provided about the items in the list. For the convenience of the reader, word counts for the HT and TN are provided in addition to the ratio. For the items in which only three or two targums are parallel, those targums are indicated. Where all four are parallel, there is obviously no need for such information. Parallels found in the Cairo Geniza fragments or in targumic tosafot are also mentioned. An index of all the passages is provided at the end.

TN Paralleled by Three Other Targums
(The Synoptic Core of the PT)

A. Ratio of five or greater

1. Gen. 3:18 HT-8, TN-44, r-5.5

2. Gen. 3:24 HT-18, TN-108, r-6.0

3. Gen. 4:8 HT-14, TN-136, r-9.7; also ms. B, TNgl and two targumic tosafot[70]

4. Gen. 15:1 HT-19, TN-139, r-7.3; also in Klein(1)

5. Gen. 16:5 HT-19, TN-98, r-5.2

6. Gen. 18:1 HT-15, TN-77, r-5.1

7. Gen. 20:16 HT-8, TN-47, r-5.9

8. Gen. 21:33 HT-10, TN-54, r-5.4

9. Gen. 22:10 HT-10, TN-70, r-7.0; cf. TNgl

10. Gen. 22:14 HT-13, TN-87, r-6.7

11. Gen. 28:10 HT-6, TN-136, r-22.8

12. Gen. 29:22 HT-8, TN-47, r-5.9; cf. TNgl, also in ms. E

13. Gen. 34:31 HT-5, TN-74, r-14.9; cf. TNgl

14. Gen. 38:25 HT-20, TN-242, r-12.1; also mss. D&E, five targumic tosafot[71]

15. Gen. 40:12 HT-11, TN-78, r-7.1; also in Diez-Macho(1)

16. Gen. 40:18 HT-10, TN-77, r-7.7; partial fragment in Diez-Macho(1), cf. TNgl

17. Gen. 40:23 HT-9, TN-57, r-6.3

---

[70]Ginsburger, pp. 73-4; Sperber, p. 356 (= Epstein, p. 47).
[71]Cf. I (B).

18. Gen. 49:1 HT-14, TN-80, r-5.7; cf. Dt. 6:4

19. Gen. 49:7 HT-7, TN-45, r-6.4

20. Gen. 49:18 HT-3, TN-36, r-12.0; cf. TNgl, also in two targumic tosafot[72]

21. Gen. 49:21 HT-6, TN-37, r-6.2

22. Gen. 49:22 HT-11, TN-143, r-13.0; cf. TNgl

23. Gen. 49:23 HT-5, TN-40, r-8.0

24. Gen. 50:1 HT-5, TN-104, r-20.8

25. Ex. 10:29 HT-9, TN-58, r-6.4

26. Ex. 12:42 HT-16, TN-192, r-12.0; also J, ms. P is at Ex. 15:18, cf. Epstein, pp. 48-9

27. Ex. 15:12 HT-4, TN-65, r-16.25; also in Baars, p. 49, cf. ms. G

28. Lev. 1:1 HT-9, TN-77, r-8.6; cf. TNgl

29. Lev. 22:27 HT-19, TN-170, r-8.9; cf. TNgl, also in ms. F

30. Lev. 24:12 HT-7, TN-118, r-16.8; cf. TNgl, also Nm. 9:8, 15:34, 27:5

31. Num. 10:36 HT-7, TN-87, r-12.4

32. Num. 12:12 HT-10, TN-60, r-6.0; cf. TNgl

33. Num. 12:16 HT-7, TN-75, r-10.7

34. Num. 21:16 HT-13, TN-82, r-6.3

35. Deut. 1:1 HT-22, TN-139, r-6.3; also in TO and Br.

36. Deut. 6:4 HT-6, TN-88, r-14.7; cf. Gen. 49:1

37. Deut. 32:1 HT-7, TN-155, r-22.1

38. Deut. 32:3 HT-7, TN-92, r-13.1

39. Deut. 33:2 HT-16, TN-81, r-5.0

B. Ratio of three or four

40. Gen. 3:9 HT-8, TN-29, r-3.6

41. Gen. 3:15 HT-15, TN-55, r-3.7

42. Gen. 3:22 HT-22, TN-73, r-3.3

43. Gen. 6:3 HT-15, TN-49, r-3.3

---

[72]Ginsburger, pp. 73-4; Sperber, p. 356 (= Epstein, p. 47).

44. Gen. 13:7 HT-15, TN-49, r-3.3

45. Gen. 15:12 HT-13, TN-39, r-3.0; cf. TNgl

46. Gen. 15:17 HT-15, TN-53, r-3.5

47. Gen. 18:17 HT-8, TN-28, r-3.5

48. Gen. 18:21 HT-10, TN-30, r-3.0

49. Gen. 26:35 HT-5, TN-17, r-3.4

50. Gen. 27:40 HT-13, TN-40, r-3.1

51. Gen. 28:12 HT-14, TN-44, r-3.1

52. Gen. 32:3 HT-12, TN-43, r-3.6

53. Gen. 49:3 HT-10, TN-37, r-3.7

54. Gen. 49:17 HT-14, TN-50, r-3.6

55. Gen. 49:19 HT-6, TN-24, r-4.0

56. Gen. 49:27 HT-9, TN-33, r-3.7

57. Ex. 1:21 HT-9, TN-31, r-3.4

58. Ex. 14:13-14 HT-32, TN-118, r-3.7; ms. P is at Ex. 15:3

59. Ex. 14:25 HT-16, TN-58, r-3.6

60. Ex. 15:9 HT-12, TN-44, r-3.7; also in Baars pp. 340-1

61. Ex. 23:2 HT-13, TN-39, r-3.0

62. Num. 5:22 HT-5, TN-19, r-3.8

63. Num. 11:26 HT-20, TN-87, r-4.3

64. Num. 21:18-20 HT-25, TN-78, r-3.1

65. Num. 21:34 HT-26, TN-79, r-3.0

66. Num. 22:30 HT-21, TN-80, r-3.8

67. Num. 24:23 HT-8, TN-26, r-3.25

68. Num. 24:24 HT-9, TN-27, r-3.0

69. Num. 31:50 HT-19, TN-72, r-3.8

70. Deut. 27:15 HT-18, TN-82, r-4.6

71. Deut. 32:4 HT-14, TN-55, r-3.9

72. Deut. 32:5 HT-8, TN-24, r-3.0

73. Deut. 32:19 HT-6, TN-21, r-3.5

74. Deut. 33:15 HT-6, TN-18, r-3.0

75. Deut. 33:17 HT-14, TN-50, r-3.6

76. Deut. 33:29 HT-12, TN-40, r-3.3

C. Ratio of one or two

77. Gen. 1:2 HT-14, TN-32, r-2.3

78. Gen. 3:19 HT-17, TN-32, r-1.9

79. Gen. 4:7 HT-15, TN-40, r-2.7; also in ms. B and a targumic tosafot[73]

80. Gen. 11:4 HT-17, TN-31, r-1.8

81. Gen. 15:2 HT-16, TN-31, r-1.9; also in Klein(1)

82. Gen. 16:13 HT-15, TN-25, r-1.7

83. Gen. 19:18 HT-5, TN-14, r-2.8

84. Gen. 24:62 HT-10, TN-19, r-1.9

85. Gen. 25:22 HT-13, TN-23, r-1.8

86. Gen. 27:27 HT-17, TN-34, r-2.0

87. Gen. 29:18 HT-5, TN-14, r-2.8; also in ms. E

88. Gen. 32:27 HT-11, TN-25, r-2.3; also in ms. C

89. Gen. 36:39 HT-19, TN-33, r-1.7

90. Gen. 41:43 HT-10, TN-23, r-2.3; also in Diez-Macho(1)

91. Gen. 42:36 HT-16, TN-30, r-1.9; also in Diez-Macho(1); cf. Epstein
pp. 45-46

92. Gen. 45:28 HT-11, TN-22, r-2.0

93. Gen. 49:8 HT-11, TN-22, r-2.0

94. Gen. 49:9 HT-12, TN-33, r-2.75

95. Gen. 49:10 HT-14, TN-25, r-1.8

96. Gen. 49:11 HT-12, TN-35, r-2.9

97. Gen. 49:15 HT-14, TN-22, r-2.6

98. Gen. 49:20 HT-7, TN-16, r-2.3

---

[73]Ginsburger, p. 71, not same as other expansions.

99. Gen. 49:25 HT-16, TN-34, r-2.1

100. Gen. 49:26 HT-16, TN-44, r-2.75

101. Ex. 1:19 HT-17, TN-26, r-1.5

102. Ex. 3:14 HT-15, TN-26, r-1.7

103. Ex. 4:25 HT-15, TN-28, r-1.9

104. Ex. 4:26 HT-7, TN-18, r-2.6

105. Ex. 10:28 HT-16, TN-37, r-2.3

106. Ex. 12:33 HT-12, TN-23, r-1.9

107. Ex. 14:15 HT-12, TN-25, r-2.1

108. Ex. 14:20 HT-20, TN-27, r-1.4

109. Ex. 15:1 HT-20, TN-40, r-2.0; also in J

110. Ex. 15:17 HT-12, TN-21, r-1.75; also in Baars p. 341

111. Ex. 20:26 HT-10, TN-20, r-2.0; cf. Klein(3)

112. Ex. 21:14 HT-11, TN-24, r-2.2; cf. Klein(3)

113. Ex. 32:18 HT-12, TN-23, r-1.9

114. Ex. 32:25 HT-12, TN-30, r-2.5

115. Ex. 33:23 HT-9, TN-18, r-2.0

116. Lev. 10:19 HT-22, TN-53, r-2.4

117. Lev. 19:16 HT-10, TN-26, r-2.6

118. Lev. 23:32 HT-15, TN-24, r-1.6; also in ms. F

119. Num. 23:9 HT-13, TN-33, r-2.5

120. Num. 23:23 HT-14, TN-40, r-2.8

121. Num. 24:3 HT-11, TN-20, r-1.8

122. Num. 24:4 HT-11, TN-32, r-2.9

123. Num. 24:15 HT-11, TN-20, r-1.8

124. Num. 24:20 HT-12, TN-30, r-2.5

125. Num. 25:4 HT-19, TN-36, r-1.9

126. Num. 26:11 HT-4, TN-9, r-2.25

127. Num. 28:2 HT-16, TN-36, r-2.25

128. Num. 34:6 HT-12, TN-20, r-1.7

129. Deut. 1:2 HT-10, TN-28, r-2.8; cf. Br.

130. Deut. 3:29 HT-5, TN-14, r-2.8; cf. Br.

131. Deut. 7:10 HT-12, TN-30, r-2.5

132. Deut. 25:13 HT-8, TN-18, r-2.5

133. Deut. 25:14 HT-8, TN-18, r-2.25

134. Deut. 25:18 HT-14, TN-36, r-2.6

135. Deut. 27:8 HT-10, TN-16, r-1.6; also in ms. D

136. Deut. 29:17 HT-30, TN-25, r-1.6

137. Deut. 32:2 HT-12, TN-25, r-2.1

138. Deut. 32:14 HT-19, TN-32, r-1.7

139. Deut. 32:31 HT-6, TN-13, r-3.2

140. Deut. 33:4 HT-7, TN-15, r-2.1

141. Deut. 33:6 HT-7, TN-18, r-2.6

142. Deut. 33:16 HT-12, TN-32, r-2.8

143. Deut. 33:18 HT-7, TN-18, r-2.6

144. Deut. 33:21 HT-17, TN-48, r-2.8

145. Deut. 33:25 HT-5, TN-14, r-2.8

TN Paralleled by Two Other Targums

A. Ratio of five or greater

146. Gen. 35:9 HT-10, TN-103, r-10.3; P,V, also in ms. C and TNgl

147. Gen. 44:18 HT-19, TN-164, r-8.6; P,V, also four targumic tosafot[74] and ms. D

148. Gen. 44:19 HT-10, TN-81, r-8.1; P,V

149. Gen. 49:2 HT-8, TN-82, r-10.25; P,V

150. Gen. 49:12 HT-6, TN-38, r-6.3; PJ,V

151. Ex. 15:18 HT-4, TN-21, r-5.25; PJ,V, cf. Baars, p. 341

---

[74]Diez-Macho (2), pp. 323-4 (= Epstein, p. 46); Ginsburger, p. 73. Sperber, p. 355-6. prints as a composite text tosafot found in *Biblia Hebraica*, Lisbon: 1491, and in *Biblia Hebraica*, Ixar: 1490.

152. Ex. 20:2 HT-9, TN-82, r-9.1; PJ,P, cf. Ex. 20:3; also in ms. F, cf. Diez-Macho(2) and Landauer

153. Ex. 20:13-17 HT-26, TN-168, r-6.5; PJ,P cf. Dt. 5:17-21, also in ms. F

154. Num. 9:8 HT-9, TN-105, r-11.7; PJ,V cf. Lev. 24:12

155. Num. 21:15 HT-14, TN-76, r-5.4; P,V

B. Ratio of three or four

156. Gen. 4:16 HT-9, TN-35, r-3.9; P,V, also in ms. B

157. Gen. 30:22 HT-19, TN-89, r-4.7; P,V

158. Gen. 31:22 HT-7, TN-29, r-4.1; PJ,P, also in ms. E

159. Gen. 31:39 HT-9, TN-32, r-3.6; P,V, also in ms. C

160. Gen. 49:4 HT-12, TN-47, r-3.9; PJ,V

161. Gen. 50:19 HT-6, TN-21, r-3.5; P,V

162. Ex. 17:16 HT-11, TN-48, r-4.3; P,V, also in J

163. Ex. 24:6 HT-11, TN-40, r-3.6; P,V

164. Num. 12:1 HT-14, TN-42, r-3.0; P,V

165. Num. 23:10 HT-14, TN-61, r-4.1; P,V

166. Deut. 32:10 HT-11, TN-48, r-4.4; P,V

167. Deut. 33:3 HT-11, TN-47, r-4.3; P,V

168. Deut. 33:20 HT-11, TN-33, r-3.0; PJ,V

C. Ratio of one or two

169. Gen. 4:13 HT-7, TN-14, r-2.0; PJ,P, also in ms. B

170. Gen. 4:26 HT-14, TN-22, r-1.6; PJ,P

171. Gen. 10:2 HT-9, TN-18, r-2.0; PJ,V

172. Gen. 10:4 HT-6, TN-12, r-2.0; PJ,V

173. Gen. 11:1 HT-7, TN-18, r-2.6; PJ,V

174. Gen. 25:34 HT-14, TN-22, r-1.6; P,V

175. Gen. 27:41 HT-20, TN-51, r-2.6; PJ,P

176. Gen. 28:17 HT-15, TN-26, r-1.7; PJ,P

177. Gen. 42:13 HT-18, TN-30, r-1.7; PJ,P

178. Gen. 49:6 HT-14, TN-23, r-1.5; PJ,V

179. Gen. 49:24 HT-13, TN-20, r-1.5; P,V

180. Ex. 23:19 HT-12, TN-31, r-2.6; PJ,P, same as Ex. 34:26

181. Ex. 24:11 HT-12, TN-21, r-1.75; PJ,P

182. Ex. 28:17-20 HT-32, TN-74, r-2.3; PJ,V

183. Ex. 34:26 HT-12, TN-29, r-2.4; PJ,V, same as Ex. 23:19
184. Lev. 20:17 HT-28, TN-40, r-1.4; PJ,P
185. Lev. 26:29 HT-6, TN-16, r-2.7; PJ,V
186. Num. 20:21 HT-10, TN-21, r-2.1; PJ,V
187. Num. 21:14 HT-12, TN-29, r-2.4; P,V
188. Num. 21:28 HT-13, TN-26, r-2.0; P,V
189. Num. 21:29 HT-14, TN-20, r-1.4; P,V
190. Num. 23:19 HT-14, TN-33, r-2.4; P,V
191. Num. 23:24 HT-14, TN-35, r-2.5; P,V
192. Num. 24:7 HT-11, TN-30, r-2.7; P,V
193. Num. 24:8 HT-13, TN-24, r-1.8; P,V
194. Num. 24:14 HT-13, TN-29, r-2.2; P,V
195. Num. 24:16 HT-13, TN-37, r-2.8; PJ,V
196. Deut. 29:14 HT-17, TN-30, r-1.8; PJ,V
197. Deut. 32:15 HT-12, TN-27, r-2.25; PJ,V
198. Deut. 32:24 HT-14, TN-21, r-1.5; P,V
199. Deut. 32:32 HT-12, TN-20, r-1.7; PJ,V
200. Deut. 32:33 HT-6, TN-16, r-2.7; P,V
201. Deut. 32:34 HT-6, TN-14, r-2.3; P,V
202. Deut. 32:35 HT-13, TN-27, r-2.1; P,V
203. Deut. 32:38 HT-12, TN-19, r-1.6; P,V
204. Deut. 33:7 HT-16, TN-35, r-2.2; PJ,V
205. Deut. 33:9 HT-18, TN-31, r-1.7; P,V
206. Deut. 33:10 HT-11, TN-25, r-2.3; PJ,V
207. Deut. 33:22 HT-8, TN-19, r-2.0; PJ,V
208. Deut. 33:28 HT-14, TN-22, r-1.6; PJ,V

TN Paralleled by One Other Targum

A. Ratio of five or greater

209. Ex. 20:3 HT-7, TN-74, r-10.6; PJ, cf. Ex. 20:2, cf. Diez-Macho(2) and Landauer
210. Num. 15:34 HT-9, TN-104, r-11.6; PJ, cf. V, cf. Lev. 24:12
211. Num. 27:5 HT-6, TN-98, r-16.3; PJ, cf. V, cf. Lev. 24:12
212. Num. 34:15 HT-11, TN-119, r-10.8; V
213. Deut. 5:17-21 HT-27, TN-216, r-8.0; PJ

B. Ratio of three or four

214.   Gen. 4:24 HT-7, TN-27, r-3.8; PJ

215.   Gen. 47:21 HT-10, TN-45, r-4.5; V

216.   Ex. 23:3 HT-4, TN-16, r-4.0; PJ

C. Ratio of one or two

217.   Gen. 2:23 HT-15, TN-31, r-2.1; PJ

218.   Gen. 4:23 HT-17, TN-27, r-1.6; PJ, also a targumic tosafot[75]

219.   Gen. 13:13 HT-6, TN-15, r-2.5; PJ

220.   Gen. 18:12 HT-11, TN-17, r-1.5; V

221.   Gen. 24:60 HT-15, TN-30, r-2.0; P

222.   Gen. 30:30 HT-18, TN-23, r-1.3; PJ, also in ms. E

223.   Gen. 38:15 HT-7, TN-19, r-2.7; PJ

224.   Gen. 42:32 HT-13, TN-24, r-1.8; PJ

225.   Gen. 49:5 HT-6, TN-17, r-2.8; V

226.   Gen. 50:21 HT-13, TN-37, r-2.8; P

227.   Ex. 17:12 HT-23, TN-47, r-2.0; P

228.   Ex. 20:5 HT-21, TN-38, r-1.8; P, cf. Dt. 5:9, cf. Landauer

229.   Ex. 23:5 HT-13, TN-23, r-1.8; PJ

230.   Ex. 39:10-13 HT-30, TN-72, r-2.4; PJ

231.   Ex. 39:43 HT-16, TN-26, r-1.6; PJ

232.   Lev. 13:45 HT-16, TN-27, r-1.7; PJ

233.   Lev. 18:9 HT-15, TN-23, r-1.5; PJ

234.   Lev. 26:13 HT-17, TN-30, r-1.8; PJ

235.   Lev. 26:19 HT-11, TN-30, r-2.7; PJ

236.   Num. 7:13-17 HT-58, TN-120, r-2.1; V

237.   Num. 14:19 HT-13, TN-18, r-1.4; PJ

238.   Num. 17:27 HT-11, TN-18, r-1.6; V

239.   Num. 20:10 HT-18, TN-24, r-1.3; P

240.   Num. 21:1 HT-16, TN-43, r-2.7; V

241.   Num. 28:14 HT-18, TN-41, r-2.3; PJ

242.   Num. 29:35 HT-10, TN-18, r-1.8; PJ

243.   Num. 33:9 HT-13, TN-27, r-2.1; V

244.   Deut. 3:24 HT-21, TN-38, r-1.8; PJ, cf. Br.

---

[75]Ginsburger, p. 72. This expansion does not follow that in Tn and PJ.

245. Deut. 5:9 HT-21, TN-34, r-1.6; PJ, cf. Gen. 49:1, cf. Br.
246. Deut. 14:21 HT-23, TN-48, r-2.1; PJ
247. Deut. 15:11 HT-19, TN-31, r-1.6; V
248. Deut. 22:4 HT-14, TN-22, r-1.6; V
249. Deut. 26:5 HT-20, TN-30, r-1.5; PJ
250. Deut. 30:13 HT-16, TN-27, r-1.7; V
251. Deut. 32:27 HT-16, TN-37, r-2.3; V
252. Deut. 32:30 HT-14, TN-31, r-2.2; V
253. Deut. 32:36 HT-15, TN-31, r-2.1; V
254. Deut. 32:39 HT-18, TN-32, r-1.8; V
255. Deut. 32:43 HT-13, TN-31, r-2.4; V
256. Deut. 33:11 HT-12, TN-20, r-1.7; V
257. Deut. 33:12 HT-14, TN-26, r-1.9; V
258. Deut. 33:19 HT-14, TN-20, r-1.4; V
259. Deut. 33:24 HT-11, TN-25, r-2.3; V

TN Not Paralleled

A. Ratio of five or greater
260. Num. 24:5 HT-6, TN-44, r-7.3, cf. P and V

B. Ratio of three or four
261. Ex. 18:11 HT-12, TN-37, r-3.1

C. Ratio of one or two
262. Gen. 16:8 HT-15, TN-24, r-1.6
263. Gen. 22:1 HT-13, TN-22, r-1.7
264. Gen. 30:2 HT-13, TN-24, r-1.8
265. Gen. 30:8 HT-12, TN-19, r-1.6; also in ms. E
266. Gen. 30:11 HT-7, TN-13, r-1.8
267. Ex. 1:10 HT-19, TN-33, r-1.7
268. Ex. 9:16 HT-13, TN-30, r-1.5
269. Ex. 22:22 HT-12, TN-18, r-1.5
270. Ex. 22:30 HT-12, TN-24, r-2.0
271. Ex. 23:21 HT-14, TN-24, r-1.7
272. Lev. 20:4 HT-16, TN-23, r-1.4
273. Lev. 23:16 HT-11, TN-23, r-2.1; also in ms. F
274. Num. 7:18-23 HT-68, TN-134, r-2.1

275. Num. 7:24-29 HT-67, TN-133, r-2.0
276. Num. 7:30-35 HT-67, TN-133, r-2.0
277. Num. 7:36-41 HT-66, TN-134, r-2.0
278. Num. 7:42-47 HT-66, TN-133, r-2.0
279. Num. 7:48-53 HT-66, TN-133, r-2.0
280. Num. 7:54-59 HT-68, TN-135, r-2.0
281. Num. 7:60-65 HT-66, TN-132, r-2.0
282. Num. 7:66-71 HT-66, TN-140, r-2.1
283. Num. 7:72-77 HT-68, TN-135, r-2.0
284. Num. 7:78-83 HT-68, TN-135, r-2.0
285. Num. 10:31 HT-14, TN-24, r-1.7
286. Num. 29:10 HT-6, TN-13, r-2.2
287. Num. 29:14 HT-17, TN-29, r-1.7
288. Num. 29:15 HT-8, TN-13, r-1.6
289. Deut. 2:6 HT-11, TN-29, r-2.6; cf. Br.
290. Deut. 15:4 HT-18, TN-26, r-1.4
291. Deut. 24:6 HT-8, TN-19, r-2.4
292. Deut. 28:23 HT-10, TN-23, r-2.3

Gen.	1	:2	77		10	:2	171
	2	:23	217			:4	172
	3	:9	40		11	:1	173
		:15	41			:4	80
		:18	1		13	:7	44
		:19	78			:13	219
		:22	42		15	:1	4
		:24	2			:2	81
	4	:7	79			:12	45
		:8	3			:17	46
		:13	169		16	:5	5
		:16	156			:8	262
		:23	218			:13	82
		:24	214		18	:1	6
		:26	170			:12	220
	6	:3	43			:17	47

	:21	48			:18	16
19	:18	83			:23	17
20	:16	7		41	:43	90
21	:33	8		42	:13	177
22	:1	263			:32	224
	:10	9			:36	91
	:14	10		44	:18	147
24	:60	221			:19	148
	:62	84		45	:28	92
25	:22	85		47	:21	215
	:34	174		49	:1	18
26	:35	49			:2	149
27	:27	86			:3	53
	:40	50			:4	160
	:41	175			:5	225
28	:10	11			:6	178
	:12	51			:7	19
	:17	176			:8	93
29	:18	87			:9	94
	:22	12			:10	95
30	:2	264			:11	96
	:8	265			:12	150
	:11	266			:15	97
	:22	157			:17	54
	:30	222			:18	20
31	:22	158			:19	55
31	:39	159			:20	98
32	:3	52		49	:21	21
	:27	88			:22	22
34	:31	13			:23	23
35	:9	146			:24	179
36	:39	89			:25	99
38	:15	223			:26	100
	:25	14			:27	56
40	:12	15		50	:1	24

		:19	161				:5	229
		:21	226				:19	180
Ex.	1	:10	267				:21	271
		:19	101			24	:6	163
		:21	57				:11	181
	3	:14	102			28	:17-20	182
	4	:25	103			32	:18	113
		:26	104				:25	114
	9	:16	268			33	:23	115
	10	:28	105			34	:26	183
		:29	25			39	:10-13	230
	12	:33	106			39	:43	231
		:42	26	Lev.	1	:1		28
	14	:13-14	58		10	:19		116
		:15	107		13	:45		232
		:20	108		18	:9		233
		:25	59		19	:16		117
	15	:1	109		20	:4		272
		:9	60			:17		184
		:12	27		22	:27		29
		:17	110		23	:16		273
		:18	151			:32		118
	17	:12	227		24	:12		30
		:16	162		26	:13		234
	18	:11	261			:19		235
	20	:2	152			:29		185
		:3	209	Num.	5	:22		62
		:5	228		7	:13-17		236
		:13-17	153			:18-23		274
		:26	111			:24-29		275
	21	:14	112			:30-35		276
	22	:22	269			:36-41		277
		:30	270			:42-47		278
	23	:2	61			:48-53		279
		:3	216			:54-59		280

	:60-65	281			:14	194
	:66-71	282			:15	123
	:72-77	283			:16	195
	:78-83	284			:20	124
9	:8	154			:23	67
10	:31	285			:24	68
	:36	31		25	:4	125
11	:26	63		26	:11	126
12	:1	164		27	:5	211
	:12	32		28	:2	127
	:16	33			:14	241
14	:19	237		29	:10	286
15	:34	210			:14	287
17	:27	238			:15	288
20	:10	239			:35	242
20	:21	186		31	:50	69
21	:1	240		33	:9	243
	:14	187		34	:6	128
21	:15	155			:15	212
	:16	34	Deut.	1	:1	35
	:18-20	64			:2	129
	:28	188		2	:6	289
	:29	189		3	:24	244
	:34	65			:29	130
22	:30	66		5	:9	245
23	:9	119			:17-21	213
	:10	165		6	:4	36
	:19	190		7	:10	131
	:23	120		14	:21	246
	:24	191		15	:4	290
24	:3	121			:11	247
	:4	122		22	:4	248
	:5	260		24	:6	291
	:7	192		25	:13	132
	:8	193		25	:14	133

	:18	134		:10	106
26	:5	249		:11	256
27	:8	135		:12	257
	:15	70		:15	74
28	:23	292		:16	142
29	:14	196		:17	75
	:17	136		:18	143
30	:13	250		:19	258
32	:1	37		:20	168
	:2	137		:21	144
	:3	38		:22	207
	:4	71		:24	259
	:5	72		:25	145
	:10	166		:28	208
	:14	138		:29	76
	:15	197			
	:19	73			
	:24	198			
	:27	251			
	:30	252			
	:31	139			
	:32	199			
	:33	200			
	:34	201			
	:35	202			
	:36	253			
	:38	203			
	:39	254			
	:43	255			
33	:2	39			
	:3	167			
	:4	140			
	:6	141			
	:7	204			
	:9	205			

Chapter Four

The Relationship Between Topic, Rhetoric and Logic: Analysis of a Syllogistic Passage in the Yerushalmi

Richard E. Cohen
Brown University

I. Logical Discourse

Every document that makes a systematic statement exhibits certain qualities which distinguish it from other such documents. First, each composition formulates its arguments according to a particular set of logical patterns. Second, it expresses these arguments through a particular repertoire of rhetorical forms. And third, it uses these logical patterns and rhetorical forms to address a particular range of topics. The Palestinian Talmud (ca. A.D. 400) or "Yerushalmi" is characterized by its distinct choice of logic, rhetoric and topic. By inductively analyzing the Yerushalmi in each of these three dimensions, we shall be able to determine the characteristics which distinguish this document from the other books of the Rabbinic corpus.

The Yerushalmi's distinct mode of argumentation, as we shall see, is characterized by the interdependence of rhetoric and logic. We cannot understand the one without the other. On one hand, an analysis of the logical patterns allows us to understand the point that individual stories, statements and citations are intended to make. On the other hand, it is only through the analysis of these rhetorical forms that we are able to detect the implicit logical patterns. Logic and rhetoric are two aspects of the text's mode of argumentation – one implicit, the other explicit. The logical patterns are the assumed structures of argumentation, which the audience must share in order to accept the text's conclusions. The rhetorical forms are the vessels or vehicles of expression, which communicate the arguments. In other words, the text assumes that the audience accepts the logic and understands the rhetoric. When we ask *what* the text says, we are led in many directions according to the diffuse topical content. But when we ask *how* the text argues and expresses its points, we discover the uniform logical and rhetorical patterns which characterize the Yerushalmi as a whole.

The Yerushalmi is a systematic exposition which expresses religious truth through the presentation of logical arguments. Logical discourse is a distinct mode of expression which derives conclusions from authoritative premises through formal patterns of argumentation. In contrast, other modes of expression, such as art, poetry, story-telling, music, dance, and physical mannerisms, obviously communicate through different means.[1] The Yerushalmi is a remarkably uniform document which consistently adheres to a systematic exposition of ideas. It usually formulates its arguments according to syllogistic patterns, but it occasionally appeals to other types of logic, such as exegesis. In other words, syllogistic and exegetical discourse are two types of logical argumentation. These two species within the genus of logical discourse are distinguished according to the particular authoritative premises and the particular formal patterns of argumentation.

GENUS: LOGICAL DISCOURSE

premise(s)   —>   formal pattern of argumentation   —>   conclusion

Species I.   Syllogistic Argumentation

proposition(s)   —>   abstract causal relationship   —>   new proposition

Species II.   Exegetical Argumentation

textual citation   —>   philological and literary-critical analysis   —>   new proposition

Syllogisms argue according abstract causal relationships: "If propositions A and B are true, then, proposition C must theoretically also be true." Propositions A and B function as premises. These premises are arranged according to a fixed pattern, which necessarily yields a certain conclusion (proposition C). The sample passage of the Yerushalmi consists entirely of syllogistic arguments. In this article, I shall analyze the various abstract causal relationships appearing in the passage and classify the rhetorical forms according to these syllogistic patterns. The exegetical passages of the Yerushalmi require a different classification scheme, because exegetical passages reflect a different set of logical patterns. Exegesis derives conclusions by analyzing the words and the literary traits of citations of authoritative sources, such as Scriptural[2] and

---

[1]On the use of narrative, particularly stories, as a mode of discourse, see Jacob Neusner, *Judaism and Story: The Evidence of The Fathers According to Rabbi Nathan* (in press).

[2]See for example, Saul Lieberman, *Hellenism in Jewish Palestine, Studies in the Literary Transmission, Beliefs and Manners of Palestine in the I Century B.C.E. - IV Century C.E.* (New York: Jewish Theological Seminary of America, 1962), chapter 5, "Rabbinic Interpretation of Scripture" and chapter 6 "The Hermeneutic Rules of the *Aggadah*;" and Jacob Neusner, *What is Midrash?* (Philadelphia: Fortress Press, 1987). Neusner distinguishes between the different types of exegesis used by various Midrashic texts. See also the five-hundred-item bibliography of Aggadic narrative by Joseph Davis, elsewhere in this volume.

Mishnaic[3] pericopae. Therefore, if I were studying an exegetical passage, I would classify the particular patterns of philology and literary-criticism and classify the rhetorical forms used to express these arguments.[4]

II.   Three Maps: Topic, Rhetoric, and Logic

This article is in four parts. First, I shall present a translation of a sample passage of the Yerushalmi. Then I shall superimpose three "maps"[5] – topical, rhetorical, and logical – on this text.[6] When cartographers originally developed a map of a certain territory, they began on the small scale and then combined and simplified the detail maps in various stages in order to produce large-scale maps. However, they presented the end product in the reverse order, beginning with the large-scale map and then moving to the details. Likewise, I argue that the analysis of logical patterns of argumentation guides our understanding of the

---

[3]Relatively little attention has been given to the *exegesis* of Mishnah in Rabbinic Literature, in general, of the Talmud of the Land of Israel, in particular. Lieberman makes the following one-sentence remark in the middle of a long footnote in his chapter on "Heathen Idolatrous Rites in Rabbinic Literature:"

> we know that the Rabbis sometimes interpreted the Mishnah by the same methods as they interpreted Scripture (See *TP* [The Talmud of the Land of Israel] *Rosh Hashanah* I. 10, 57c. Comp. also I. Heinemann, *The Methods of the Aggadah* [Hebrew], p. 198, n. 28).(Lieberman, *Hellenism in Jewish Palestine*, p. 137, n. 87)

Another example of exegesis of Mishnah in the Yerushalmi is *TP Rosh Hashanah* I. 5:

> [Mishnah:] Whether the new moon was exposed [*b'alil*] or whether it was not exposed, etc.
> [Commentary:] What is the meaning of *b'alil*? Exposed, as you find it said, *as purified silver exposed to the earth, refined seven times* (Psalms 12:7).

[4]Such a classification scheme of exegetical passages would provide an interesting contrast to the results of this article. The mode of argumentation used by a text provides important information about the authors' theology and epistemology. On one hand, exegesis presupposes the self-evident authority of the *content* of a source, indicating a belief that the material contains revealed truth. On the other hand, syllogistic discourse presupposes that a source is structured according to valid *logic*, indicating a belief that the material contains rationally derived truth. Therefore, it would be probative to compare the kind of material which receives exegetical analysis with the kind of material which serves as the premise of a syllogism.

[5]Jonathan Z. Smith (*Map Is Not Territory: Studies in the History of Religions*. Leiden: Brill, 1978, *passim*, esp. ch 13) introduced the map metaphor to the historical study of religion. This metaphor is apt for at least two reasons: First, a map is just a map; it is not the same as territory. Maps are evaluated according to usefulness and accuracy. No map can claim to be the absolutely true representation of an area or a text. Every map represents a particular perspective, bias, and purpose. Likewise, our categories of analysis (topical, rhetorical, and logical) are not the only or the ultimate way of viewing a systematic exposition. They are merely maps which are evaluated according to their usefulness as a tool for research and their accuracy in fitting the texts on which they are superimposed. Second, because maps are superimposed onto territory, they make no claim to explain the origins of that territory. Likewise, our maps do not presuppose or claim any authorial intention. If the maps fit, they fit, whether or not the authors of our document were aware of these logical patterns and rhetorical forms.

[6]Of course, the translation itself is an interpretation of the Hebrew and Aramaic text, and therefore it is also a "map."

rhetorical forms, which in turn, guides our understanding of the topics emphasized by the text. However, the presentation of results moves in the opposite direction. First, I present a topical map, in which I identify the main issue of each cogent discussion. I then present a rhetorical map, because our ability to discern these cogent discussions results from our understanding of the literary structure of the text. And finally, I present the logical patterns, because our ability to classify the literary forms derives from the analysis of the logical arguments which the rhetoric expresses.

By *topic,* I mean what the text says. I am interested in the main points made by the text. I therefore focus on the cogent units of discourse which express complete arguments. If we were to focus on the philology and exegesis of individual words and sentences – the atoms and molecules of a text – we would fail to see how complete paragraphs are carefully formulated to make a particular point. The discrete particles provide bits of information about certain details, but little about the overall topical program of the document. Indeed, the main point of each paragraph is greater than the sum of its parts. Each paragraph has an implicit "topic sentence," as it were, which establishes the focus of the paragraph as a whole. The topical program of entire passages, and of the document as a whole, is defined by the main issues addressed by the individual paragraphs.

By *rhetoric,* I mean how the text expresses its points. By using regular and recognizable, literary forms, a text communicates messages to its audience over and above the meaning contained in discrete particles of language. Because sentences follow regular grammatical patterns, which the audience presumably recognizes and understands, they convey more meaning than is contained in the individual words. Likewise, groups of sentences are constructed according to formal patterns of rhetoric. These patterns of arrangement communicate more meaning than a random collection of sentences. For example, let us consider a common rhetorical form, the story. A narration may consist of only two or three sentences, but the rhetorical patterns tell the reader more than the sentences themselves. As we shall see, the following the four short sentences (16 words in the original Aramaic) in **I.D.1.** convey a complete story:

I

D. 1. *Samuel went up to visit Rav. He saw* [Rav] *eating with a napkin* [covering his hands]. *He said to him, "how so?* [I.e., are you doing this to avoid washing?]" *Rav replied,* "[No], I am fastidious [therefore I **wash as well as cover** my **hands with a napkin.**]."

The first sentence establishes the setting. The second sentence creates tension or dissonance when Rav acts in an unexpected way. And the last sentence brings resolution when he explains his action. Obviously, this construction would convey less meaning if the sentences were randomly arranged. Because the reader recognizes the pattern of this construction, these few sentences represent a coherent story.

By *logic*, I mean how the text argues its points. Every systematic exposition constructs arguments which support or prove conclusions. The arguments must begin somewhere, and they are therefore based on premises, propositions assumed to be self-evident to the audience. The premises function as the authoritative ground. Structures of argumentation are built on these premises, in order to support conclusions. The structures are logical patterns, also assumed to be self-evident to the audience. If the premises (ground) and the logic of argumentation (structure) are sound, the conclusion will be solidly supported, and the text will have convincingly made its point. The premises are already considered self-evidently authoritative. The conclusions, on the other hand, are legitimated by being connected to the premises. The structures of the argumentation demonstrates that the conclusions are logically connected to authoritative premises.

Let me describe the document as a whole in order to put our sample passage in context. The Yerushalmi is, in large part, a commentary on another document, the Mishnah, composed two centuries earlier (ca. A.D. 200). The Talmud is structured around successive verses of the Mishnah, which I call the base pericopae. Each Mishnaic pericope is followed by a passage of the Talmud. The cogent units within the passage relate to the Mishnaic citation in a limited variety of ways.[7] Some units analyze all or part of the Mishnaic pericope, while others discuss a related topic. A third group bears no obvious connection to the base pericope. In other words, the Yerushalmi contains material which is either (1) directly related, (2) indirectly related, or (3) unrelated to the base Mishnaic pericope.

---

[7] In the introduction to his translation, *The Talumd of the Land of Israel: A Preliminary Taranslation and Explanation*, Vol 35, Introduction and Taxonomy (Chicago: The University of Chicago Press, 1983), pp. 9ff., Jacob Neusner classifies the cogent units of discourse according to the six ways that they relate to the base Mishnaic pericope.

1. *Mishnah Exegesis.* The text comments directly on all or part of the base Mishnaic pericope, discussing particular words and phrases.

2. *Tosefta: citation and exegesis.* The text quotes (or paraphrases) and analyzes the relevant passage of the Tosefta, a third-century commentary on the Mishnah. Individual words and phrases of the Toseftan material are often discussed.

3. *Legal speculation and reflection primary to the Mishnah.* The text discusses a legal principle indirectly related to the topic of the base Mishnaic pericope.

4. *Harmonization of distinct laws of the Mishnah.* A legal principle behind the base Mishnaic pericope is compared to the principle behind another Mishnaic pericope.

5. *Legal speculation and reflection independent of the passage of the Mishnah at hand.* The text discusses a legal principle unrelated to the base Mishnaic pericope.

6. *Anthology, relevant to the Mishnah only in theme.* The text presents non-legal material, usually stories about sages or Scriptural references, thematically related to the base Mishnaic pericope.

III. The Sample Passage

The sixteenth-century printed editions of the Yerushalmi, the only original-language versions in use today,[8] present the text without differentiating between individual pericopae. Our sample passage appears as three pages of unbroken text between Mishnah Berakhot 8:2 and 8:3. In the translation below, I divide the text into units of discourse which address a single point. We may think of these cogent units as paragraphs.[9]   A new paragraph begins when the text addresses a new point. As we shall see, these shifts in argument are reflected in the rhetorical forms and logical patterns, as well as in the topical content. Such shifts are the only way we have of determining the boundaries of paragraphs, because the cogent units do not begin with a topic sentence or an introductory phrase. Furthermore, cogent units typically discuss only one aspect of a larger issue which is usually not explicitly introduced. The reader must infer the topical context. In my translation, I identify the specific point made by each cogent unit, and the general issue to which it applies. I introduce each paragraph by posing a question (in brackets), which the paragraph answers. In this way, I test whether I have properly identified the cogent units, because, by definition, a cogent unit of discourse answers a single question.

The following translation is in outline form in order to distinguish the smaller and larger units. I shall follow the same notation system in the topical, rhetorical and logical maps. Paragraphs are assigned capital letters. The sentences within a paragraph are outlined with numbers and small letters. Groups of paragraphs which deal with a single general issue are identified with Roman numerals. For example, the first general issue (**I.**) concerns required ritual washings. The first paragraph (**I.A.**) answers the question, "Are washings required – before mixing a cup of wine to be blessed?" The second paragraph (**I.B.**) answers the question, "Are washings required – even if it is inconvenient?" Words in Aramaic, the spoken language of the time, are italicized. Hebrew words are given in plain text. In order to clarify the point of each paragraph, I often put the main arguments in bold type. The translation is presented with brief commentaries explaining the meaning of each section. I shall explain the more difficult units in greater detail later in the article, when I discuss the rhetorical forms and logical patterns.

---

[8]There is no critical edition of the text. Jewish seminaries and university Judaica departments still use fascimilies of sixteenth-century printed editions. The only version which divides the text into cogent units of discourse is the American translation by Jacob Neusner *(The Talmud of the Land of Israel: A Preliminary Translation and Explanation* [Chicago: University of Chicago Press, 1982-89]; volumes 20-35 are now in print).

[9]We must remember that the paragraph metaphor is anachronistic, because the authors were unaware of the modern convention of indenting to distinguish complete units of thought. We must also remember that the paragraph is a *literary* device, whereas the Talmud of the Land of Israel was created in a mixed media environment, in which "authors" used oral material, articulated verbally and transmitted through memorization, in addition to written material.

IV.   Translation

[Base Mishnaic Pericope (M. Ber. 8:2):]

House of Shammai say: they wash the hands, and then mix the cup.
House of Hillel say: they mix the cup, and then wash the hands.

In the base Mishnaic pericope, a dispute is reported between the followers of
Shammai and Hillel about whether a man[10] must wash his hands before he
prepares a cup for the blessing over the wine. In context of chapter eight of
Mishnaic tractate Berakhot, this dispute clearly refers to the ritual of a Sabbath
or Festival meal. The sanctification process of the Mishnaic religious system
requires a high degree of ritual purity, hence the question of washing hands.

I
A. [Are washings required – before mixing the cup of wine to be
    blessed?]
    1. [Reasoning of the houses (cf. T. Ber. 5:26):]
        a. *What is the reasoning of the House of Shammai?* [The cup cannot
            be mixed without washing the hands] lest hands make unclean the
            liquid [on the outside of the cup] and, in turn, the cup [and its
            contents].
        b. *What is the reasoning of the House of Hillel?* [The cup can be
            mixed without washing the hands because] the outside of a cup is
            always unclean [so washing would not help to protect the cup].
            Another matter – hands should only be washed immediately before
            blessing [without interrupting to mix the cup].
    2. *R. Biban in the name of R. Yohanan* [said]: *"The opinion of the House
        of Shammai is in accord with R. Yosé and that of the House of Hillel
        with R. Meir* [i.e., the House of Shammai and the House of Hillel in M.
        Ber. 8:2, agree with the views of R. Yosé and R. Meir, respectively,
        found in M. Kel. 25:7-8]
    3. *"as we have learned there* [in M. Kel. 25:7-8]:
        '[In all vessels, the outside, the inside, and the handle are distinguished
        (with respect to the transfer of uncleanness).] R. Meir says: "For unclean
        and clean hands." [I.e., unclean hands only make unclean the parts of a
        cup which they actually touch, not the entire cup.] R. Yosé says: "For
        unclean hands only." [I.e., unclean hands which touch any part of a cup
        make the entire cup unclean.]'"

The first paragraph of our sample passage comments directly on the base
Mishnaic pericope, exploring the reasoning behind each side of the dispute. The
House of Shammai advocate washing before mixing the cup in order to prevent
the cup from being made unclean. On the other hand, the House of Hillel
believe that there is no reason to protect the cup, because they consider the
outside of the cup to be permenantly unclean. Furthermore, the Hillelites

---

[10]My translation and commentary follow the gender usage of the original text.

advocate a different order to the ritual: because washing is part of the sanctification process, one must wash immediately before saying the blessing. Biban compares the base Mishnaic pericope with another Mishnaic verse. The reason that the Shammaites are concerned with washing before touching the cup is that they agree with Yosé that, if uncleanness is transferred to the outside of the cup, the entire cup, including the contents, will be made unclean. The Hillelites agree with Meir that uncleanness on the outside of the cup is not automatically transferred to other parts of the cup.

I

B. [Are washings required – even if it is inconvenient?]
    1.   a.   R. Yosé in the name of R. Shabbetai and R. Hiyya in the name of R. Simeon b. Laquish said: "For dough-offering and for washing of the hands, a man goes four miles [if necessary to find water]." [I.e., **washings are required, even if it is inconvenient.**]
          b.   R. Abbahu in the name of R. Yosé b. R. Hanina said: "This is what was said, '[If the water is] before him [i.e., on his way, he must wash], but if it is behind him [i.e., out of his way], they do not trouble him [to wash].' " [I.e., **washings are *not* required, if it is inconvenient.**]
    2.   a.   Regarding men who guard gardens and orchards [for whom water is neither before or behind], what do you do for them, as to the inner sides and outer sides [of a cup]? [I.e., how would R. Abbahu rule in a situation in which a man is stationary without water to wash?]
          b.   Let us infer the solution from this:
              (1)   The woman sits and cuts off her dough-offering while she is naked, because she can cover herself up, but a man cannot [prepare the dough-offering unless he is dressed [Mishnah Hallah 2:3].
              (2)   Now, does not a woman sit in the house, yet you say they do not trouble her [to even cover herself]? [Likewise], here they would not trouble those who guard gardens and orchards to wash their hands.

This paragraph asks whether a person must do ritual washings even if it is inconvenient to do so. Yosé says yes, even if the person has to walk four miles to find sufficient water. Abbahu says no, a person need not go out of his way in order to wash. Does Abbahu's lenient ruling only apply to people who are on their way somewhere? This question is answered by reference to another Mishnaic pericope in which a person is not put to trouble in order to fulfill an obligation. By analogy, therefore, Abbahu's lenient position applies to stationary people as well as to travelers.

I

C. [Are washings required – before and after meals?]
    1.   a.   [Tannaitic Teaching:] *It has been taught:*
              (1)   (a)   **Washing before the meal is optional.**
                    (b)   **But after the meal it is obligatory.**

(2) (a) But with the first [washing], *he washes and interrupts.*
    (b) And with the second [washing], he washes but does not interrupt.

  b. [Commentary on the Tannaitic teaching:]
    (1) What is the meaning of "He washes and interrupts?"
    (2) R. Jacob b. Aha said: "[It means that] he washes and repeats [the washing]."
    (3) R. Samuel b. Isaac asked: "[If by obligation] *he washes and repeats,* [how] *do you say it is optional* [before the meal]?" [I.e., Washing is **required before the meal** as well as after the meal.]

  2. Said R. Jacob b. Idi: "On account of [missing] the first washing, pork was eaten. On account of [missing] the second washing, women left her house – and some say, three souls were killed. [I.e., **washing is required before and after the meal.**]

A ruling is quoted which requires washing after, but not before, eating. Yet Samuel son of Isaac questions this position. He implies that, because one must wash twice before eating (according to the interpretation of Jacob son of Isaac), washing must be required. Jacob son of Idi concurs by relating a story about the negative consequences that supposedly result from the failure to wash before and after a meal.

I

D. [Are washings required – even if hands do not touch the food?]
  1. *Samuel went up to visit Rav. He saw* [Rav] *eating with a napkin* [covering his hands]. *He said to him, "how so?* [I.e., are you doing this to avoid washing?]" *Rav replied,* "[No], I am fastidious [therefore I **wash as well as cover my hands with a napkin.**]."
  2. *When R. Zeira came up here* [to Palestine], *he saw priests eating with a napkin* [covering their hands]. *He said to them, "This is in accord with the* [above] *story about Rav."*

We learn from these stories about Rav and the Palestinian priests, that one should wash his hands even if they are covered and will not touch the food.

I

E. [Are washings required – for all types of food?]
  1. R. Yosé b. Kahana came [and said] in the name of Samuel: "One washes hands for **Priests' rations**, one does **not** wash hands **for unconsecrated food.**"
  2. R. Yosé says: "for Priests' rations, **and** for **unconsecrated food.**"
  3. R. Yosah in the name of R. Hiyya Bar Ashi, and R. Johan and R. Hiyya Bar Ashi in the name of Rav, [said]: "one washes hands **up to the wrist for Priests' rations and up to the knuckles for unconsecrated food.**"

4. *Measha, grandson of R. Joshua b. Levi, said "If one was eating with my grandfather and did not wash his hands up to the wrist, grandfather would not eat with him."* [I.e., wash **up to the wrist for all food.**]
5. R. Huna said, "One washes hands **only for bread."**
6. Taught R. Hoshaia : "[One washes hands] **for anything containing liquid."**
7. R. Zeira said: *"Even for cutting beets he would wash his hands."*

Here we have seven different positions on the types of food which call for washing.

I

F. [Are washings required – more than once a day?]
   1. Rav said: "[If] he washed his hands in the morning, they do not trouble him to wash in the afternoon." [I.e., **once in the morning is sufficient for the day.**]
   2. R. Abina ordered his wine-steward: "[Washing once] **whenever you find sufficient water** is enough for the day."
   How many times must one wash in one day? Rav and Abina agree that once a day is enough, although Rav seems to further stipulate that this one washing be done in the morning. This is a more lenient attitude than we have seen in previous paragraphs (e.g. **I. C.**).

II

A. [Does the same man say the blessings before and after the meal?]
   1. *R. Zeira went up to visit R. Abbahu. He found him saying,* "I shall go to eat."
   2. *He gave him a chunk of bread to cut.* [**Before eating** they discussed **who should bless** it.]
      a. *[R. Zeira] said to him, "make the blessing."*
      b. *[R. Abbahu] replied,* "[You should make the blessing, because] *the host knows the value of his loaf."*
   3. *After eating* [they discussed **who should bless**] –
      a. [R. Abbahu] *said to him, "make the blessing."*
      b. [R. Zeira] replied, *"Rabbi, does the rabbi* [you] *know R. Huna, a great man, who would say,* "He who opens [says the blessing before the meal] *must close [and say the blessing after the meal]."* [I.e., **R. Huna says, the same man says the blessings before and after the meal.**]

So far, this new paragraph is topically unrelated to the previous units. A relatively long story introduces Huna's position that the same person says grace before and after meals. This position differs from a teaching supposedly from the Tannaitic period (i.e., the two centuries before the closure of the Mishnah):

B. 1. *A Tannaitic teaching differs from R. Huna, as it has been taught:*
   2. "The order of washing hands is this: (1) With up to five people, they begin with the greatest. (2) With more than this, they begin with the

least.   (3) In the middle of the meal, they being with the eldest.   (4)
After the meal, they begin with the one who blesses."

3.   a.   Do they not [begin the washing after the meal with the one who
          says the blessing] so that he may prepare himself for the blessing?

     b.   *If you* [R. Huna] *say* he who opens also closes, he would know from
          the beginning of the meal that he would say the grace after the meal
          [and would not need time to prepare].

C.   R. Isaac said, "[**R. Huna's position stands,** because you can] explain it
     as referring to those who come in one by one [after the blessing was said
     before the meal] and do not know who had said the blessing."

We now see, in **B.2.**, the relationship of the entire paragraph to the base
Mishnaic pericope.   This Tannaitic teaching considers the issue of ritual
washings connected to meals.   This teaching conflicts with the statement
attributed to Huna, because it should be unnecessary to begin the post-meal
washings with the person who will say grace, if the purpose of doing so is to
give him time to prepare.   If Huna is correct, the man would know from the
beginning of the meal that he was saying the blessing afterwards, so he would
not need any more time to prepare.   Therefore, Huna's opinion must be in error.
However, Isaac is able to restore Huna's position by saying that it applies only
to the special situation in which the participants in the meal did not know who
said grace before the meal.

V.   Topical Analysis

In the above translation, I have divided the text into cogent units of
discourse, paragraphs which address a single point.   I have identified the main
point of each cogent unit by posing a question which the paragraph answers.
These questions function as the implicit "topic sentence" of each paragraphs.   By
listing these questions, we can develop a map of the topical program of the
passage as a whole.   Let us compare the topical focus of the base Mishnaic
pericope to the topics addressed by this passage of the Yerushalmi.

Topical Map

Base Mishnaic Pericope:

House of Shammai say: they wash the hands, and then mix the cup.
House of Hillel say: they mix the cup, and then wash the hands.

Commentary:

Topical Focus	Relationship to Base Mishnaic Pericope
I. Are washings required –	
A. before mixing the cup of wine to be blessed?	Direct
B. even if it is inconvenient?	Indirect
C. before and after meals?	Indirect
D. even if hands do not touch the food?	Indirect
E. for all types of food?	Indirect
F. more than once a day?	Indirect
II. Does the same man say blessings before and after the meal?	Tangential

The paragraphs in this passage exhibit three types of relationship to the topic of the base Mishnaic pericope. The first paragraph (**I.A.**) is directly related to the topic of the whole pericope (the order of washing the hands and mixing the cup before the Sabbath meal). The next five paragraphs (**I.B.-I.F.**) consider various aspects of a subtopic of the base Mishnaic pericope (washing the hands before any meal during the week). The topic of the last paragraph (**II.A.**) is only tangentially related to this pericope, directing our attention toward a different set of issues (the man who says grace). The passage begins by closely analyzing the issues of the base Mishnaic pericope and then moves far afield. This movement from direct relationship, to indirect relationship, and finally to tangential relationship compares to the arrangement of passages in the Tosefta, a third-century commentary on the Mishnah often quoted by the Yerushalmi:

> the Tosefta's arrangers ... will tend (1) to keep as a group passages that cite and then comment on the actual words of the Mishnah's base-passage; then (2) to present passages that amplify in the Tosefta's own words opinions fully spelled out only in response to the Mishnah's statements, and, finally, (3) to give at the end, and as a group, wholly independent and autonomous sayings and constructions of such sayings.[11]

Likewise, the Yerushalmi's commentary is not limited to the topics of the base Mishnaic pericope. The commentary does not exhaust the potential questions which could be asked of this pericope. Although the Yerushalmi is structured as a commentary to the Mishnah, this Talmud has its own distinct topical program. As we have seen, the sample passage considers a select group of issues, addressing some topics related, and some topics unrelated, to the base Mishnaic pericope. The Mishanic pericope addresses the relatively narrow issue of when

---

[11]Jacob Neusner, *The Oral Torah: The Sacred Books of Judaism* (San Francisco: Harper and Row, 1986), 39-40. See also Jacob Neusner, *The Tosefta: Its Structure and Its Sources* (Atlanta: Scholars Press, 1986), 202ff.

one should wash during the Friday night meal. In contrast, the main concern of the Yerushalmi is the more general issue of when washings are required before eating.

My focus on complete paragraphs differs from the usual emphasis by Talmudic scholars on words, phrases, and sentences. If we focus exclusively on these particles, we fail to see the shape and purpose of the larger constructions. We must look at entire cogent units of discourse – that is, complete paragraphs – in order to see the main points of the passage. Furthermore, the Yerushalmi compiles many citations of sources composed at other times and places, each reflecting the concerns of the particular historical context. Because many of the individual sentences are take verbatim from other sources, the philological and exegetical analysis of discrete words and sentences tells us little about how this document differs from the other documents in which these words and sentences also appear. We must consider how borrowed and original materials are combined in the construction of complete arguments, in order to learn about the distinct topical program of the document at hand. Any analysis of the topical content of the Yerushalmi must therefore focus on complete paragraphs.

VI.   Rhetorical Analysis

Now that the text has been divided into paragraphs, each of which address a particular issue, let us analyze the rhetorical forms used make each point. The Yerushalmi employs a limited number of rhetorical patterns to express its arguments. These rhetorical forms are comparable to the blueprints used to build houses in a neighborhood. If more that one house follows a single blueprint, the basic structure of these houses will be identical. Likewise, different paragraphs in our document often follow a common rhetorical pattern, even though the topics and constituent materials vary. I study the rhetoric of each cogent unit found in the passage at hand, in order to hypothesize the general pattern which it reflects. In other words, I look at the structure of each paragraph and attempt to recreate the "blueprint" used to construct it.

Paragraphs, like houses, are made up of a number of distinct components. First of all, we can talk about the main part of a house, as distinct from the garage or other structures annexed to it. In a like manner, we can identify the main structure of a paragraph as distinct from any appendices. Secondly, the main structure of a house can be divided into individual sections (e.g., bedroom, kitchen, stairway, basement, attic) each of which has been constructed according to a blueprint of its own. Similarly, a cogent unit of discourse can be divided into distinct components, each of which follows a rhetorical pattern. In fact, we can identify three types of rhetorical unit in a paragraph. I call the main structure of a paragraph the "independent unit," for reasons which will become clear below. In contrast, we also find two types of dependent subunit. As I shall explain, these are (1) "appended subunits" which are derivative additions to an independent unit, and (2) "constituent subunits" which are integral parts of a larger construction (either an independent unit or an appended subunit).

The independent unit is a complete, self-contained discussion which conveys the main argument of the paragraph. Every paragraph in our sample begins with a fully developed discussion. We need not refer to any other component in the paragraph in order to comprehend the way the argument is constructed. When I say that an independent unit is a complete, self-contained discussion, I mean that it is a fully developed logical argument. I do not mean that the message of the independent unit will always be self-evident to the modern reader. The text assumes a great deal of information. Allusions are often made to customs, ideas and quotations. There are no footnotes to assist the uninitiated. Therefore, the modern reader often must refer to other Rabbinic documents, Greek literature, archeological evidence, art history and other extraneous material to understand what the text is talking about (the informational content or *realia*). Furthermore, the text does not explicitly state the topic of an independent unit. In order to determine the main point of any discussion, we often must look at the other paragraphs in the passage. Even though the independent units are not self-sufficient in terms of information and topic, I shall demonstrate that they represent self-contained and fully developed logical arguments. I focus on the ways that the independent units are formulated, because these units convey the main arguments of the text. In contrast to the independent units, we distinguish two types of dependent material, the appended subunit and the constituent subunit.

Occasionally, we find a single appended subunit affixed to an independent unit in order to amplify or support this main structure. The independent unit conveys the main point of the paragraph. The appended subunit merely comments on all or part of this discussion. Therefore, the appended subunit does not represent a self-contained argument; it derives its meaning from its relationship to the independent unit. Appended subunits are formulated according to certain rhetorical patterns, in the same way that the construction of a garage follows a blueprint. These appendices do not alter the main structure of a paragraph.[12] In other words, independent units will not deviate from a regular rhetorical pattern, regardless of what type of appended subunit, if any, is added. A builder may construct a number of houses according to the same blueprint, yet

---

[12] I can prove that appended subunits do not affect the primary structure of a paragraph by demonstrating that two independent units in our sample passage follow the same rhetorical pattern, even though one has an appended subunit. The independent units of paragraphs **I.B.** and **I.F.**, share a common rhetorical pattern, which I describe below as a dispute. Paragraph **I.F.** presents a dispute between Rav and Abina without any appended material. Paragraph **I.B.**, on the other hand, attaches an appended subunit to a dispute between Yosé and Abbahu. This appendix amplifies Abbahu's position. We see that the main structure of both paragraphs follows the dispute "blueprint," even though the latter case contains an appended subunit. We can therefore conclude that the rhetorical pattern of the independent unit is unaffected by the addition of an appended subunit.

attach a different type of garage to each. Or conversely, a builder may specialize in garages and build the same type of garage onto different types of houses. I hypothesize that independent units and appended subunits are each constructed according to a limited repertoire of thetorical forms, and that any type of appended subunit can be attached to any type of independent unit.[13]

A rhetorical form is a constituent subunit when it occurs as part of a larger logical construction. Two types of constituent subunit appears in our sample passage. On one hand, we find citations of Mishnah, Tosefta or other teachings attributed to the "Tannaitic period" (the first two centuries of the Common Era). On the other hand, we also find sayings and actions often explicitly attributed to authoritative sages of the "Amoraic period" (after ca. A.D. 200). A constituent subunit is a distinct component constructed according to a regular rhetorical pattern, in the same way that an attic, bedroom or stairway follows what architects call a "detail drawing." But this component, by itself, does not function as a complete discussion. The significance of a constituent subunit depends upon the context of the larger construction. A pericope may be capable of standing on its own – and indeed may appear elsewhere as an independent discussion – but I call it a constituent subunit when it is part of the formulation of a larger argument. The larger argument may give the constituent subunit a different meaning than it would have on its own terms, out of context.[14] Therefore, we must focus on the entire construction in order to understand the function of these individual "building blocks." If we study constituent subunits in isolation, we would learn about the rhetoric of these subunits – perhaps created centuries earlier – but we would miss the particular way that this document uses such material in the construction of its main arguments. As I have said, we must look at how complete arguments are formulated, in order to see the distinct perspective of this particular document.

The following map identifies the various types of rhetorical form in the sample passage. The first column distinguishes the independent rhetorical units from the dependent subunits. By identifying the independent units, we are able

---

[13]If our sample were larger, we could test this hypothesis by investigating whether a special relationship exists between certain types of appended subunit and certain types of independent unit.

When I refer to the "framers" I do not mean to imply that one group necessarily created the entire document. It is conceivable that the independent units were formulated at a one time, and a later group of redactors added the appended subunits.

[14]The quotation of a Tannaitic teaching in paragraph I.C. is a good example of how material takes on a different meaning when it is part of the formulation of a new argument. If the Tannaitic teaching is understood on its own terms, out of context, it has one meaning – washings before meals are optional. However, in the paragraph at hand, this quotation is an integral part of a larger construction which makes the opposite point – washings before meals are required. The reason that we need to distinguish between independent units and their constituent elements is that we are interested in analyzing the rhetorical patterns the authors use to make complete arguments.

to isolate the primary rhetorical patterns which convey the main points of the document. The second column indicates the rhetorical form of each unit. The outline follows the same notation system as the translation and topical map above.

Rhetorical Map

I. A. **Independent Unit** — **Analysis of the Logical Derivation of the Base Mishnaic Pericope**

    1. Constituent Subunit — Quotation of Tosefta
    2. Constituent Subunit — Commentary
    3. Constituent Subunit — Quotation of a Mishnaic Pericope

  B. 1. **Independent Unit** — **Dispute**
      a. Constituent Subunit — Opinion
      b. Constituent Subunit — Opinion
    2. Appended Subunit — Application of a Principle to a Specific Situation

      a. Constituent Subunit — Commentary on Second Opinion
      b. (1) Constituent Subunit — Quotation of a Mishnaic Pericope
        (2) Constituent Subunit — Commentary on this Mishnaic Pericope

  C. 1. **Independent Unit** — **Logical Analysis of a Single Source**

      a. Constituent Subunit — Quotation of a Tannaitic Teaching
      b. Constituent Subunit — Commentary on the Tannaitic Teaching

    2. Appended Subunit — Negative Precedent

  D. 1. **Independent Unit** — **Precedent**
    2. Appended Subunit — Precedent

  E. **Independent Unit** — **Series of Disputes**
    1. Constituent Subunit — Opinion
    2. Constituent Subunit — Opinion
    3. Constituent Subunit — Opinion
    4. Constituent Subunit — Precedent
    5. Constituent Subunit — Opinion
    6. Constituent Subunit — Opinion
    7. Constituent Subunit — Opinion

  F. **Independent Unit** — **Dispute**
    1. Constituent Subunit — Opinion
    2. Constituent Subunit — Narrated Opinion

II. A. **Independent Unit** — **Harmonization of Conflicting Sources**

    1. Constituent Subunit — Narrated Opinion
    2. Constituent Subunit — Conflicting Tannaitic Teaching
    3. Constituent Subunit — Commentary on the Narrated Opinion

We see that every paragraph contains a single independent unit which always appears at the beginning of the paragraph. All of the independent units contain constituent subunits (except **I.D.**, because it is a unitary syllogism, as we shall see). The constituent subunits are indented in the outline to indicate their subservient status. Appended subunits, on the other hand, are derivative but not subservient. Therefore, the map situates the appended units parallel to the independent units. Three of the seven paragraphs in our sample contain such appendices.

In the second column, I indicate the various rhetorical forms. I shall concentrate on the forms which express the arguments of the independent units: (1) analysis of the logical derivation of the base Mishnaic pericope, (2) dispute, (3) logical analysis of a single source, (4) precedent, and (5) harmonization of conflicting sources. We recall that rhetorical forms are constructed in order to express logical arguments. In other words, logical patterns of argumentation are implicitly contained in the rhetorical forms. Therefore, we must analyze the logical patterns, before we can describe how the rhetorical forms express these arguments. In the next part of this article, I shall distinguish the three types of syllogistic logic appearing in the sample passage. Then I shall classify the rhetorical forms according to these three categories. And finally, I shall demonstrate how each rhetorical form is specially constructed, or is cited from another source, in order to express a syllogistic argument.

VII.   Logical Analysis

The Yerushalmi is a systematic exposition that argues according to certain logical patterns which I call "syllogisms." I define the word syllogism to characterize a mode of argumentation, not a specific logical formula.[15] For our purposes, the word "syllogism" – from the Greek *logizesthai* ("to reason") and *syn* ("together") – means to derive new propositions (conclusions) from other propositions (premises) through regular patterns of abstract causal reasoning. Aristotle defined syllogistic logic as "a discourse in which, certain things being

---

[15]Previous comparisons between syllogistic and Talmudic reasoning have been much narrower in definition. For example, Louis Jacobs begins his *Studies in Talmudic Logic and Methodology* (London: Vallentine, Mitchell, and Co., 1961) with the following statement:

Adolf Schwarz, in his well-known work, *Der Hermeneutische Syllogismus in der Talmudischen Litteratur* [Karlsruhe, 1901], suggests in the title, and develops in the work itself, the idea that the Talmudic mode of *qal wa-homer* is identical with the Aristotelean Syllogism. It will be shown here that not only is there no connection between the two forms of reasoning, but that an analogy to the Syllogism *is* found in the Talmudic literature as something quite different form the *qal wa-homer*.

Jacobs goes on to define the syllogism according to the logical formulae of the Greek philosophers: "all men are mortal; Socrates is a man; therefore Socrates is mortal." He then argues that *qal wa-homer* (also called argument *de minore ad majus*, which I define as, "if a weak case for a certain point is true, all the more so should a strong case for that point be true") is not a syllogism, but that another logical formula found in Rabbinic literature, "the *'ha-kol'* formula" is "identical with the Syllogism" (pp. 3-8)

stated, something other than what is stated follows of necessity from their being so."[16] In plain English, this means that a syllogism is an argument which is so constructed that it necessarily yields a certain conclusion. In our sample passage, the independent rhetorical units reflect three different types of syllogistic pattern, which I call (1) the unitary syllogism, (2) the constructive syllogism, and (3) the supportive syllogism.

All three types of argument contain constituent subunits which function as logical propositions. Propositions are assertions of a single point which can be declared either true or false. These constituent subunits are the indivisible building blocks of syllogistic discourse. One type of proposition is the premise. A premise is a proposition which is assumed to be self-evidently true. By definition, a premise does not require any proof, justification or apology. Another type of proposition is the conclusion. Conclusions, unlike premises, require proof, hence the need for the syllogistic argument. In our sample passage, three types of material function as premises.[17]

- citations from authoritative texts
- quotes of statements by authoritative sages
- reports of actions by authoritative sages

In a syllogism, the premise is the "grounding" or foundation on which the logical argument is built. The formal patterns of logic are the structures which

---

[16]Antony Flew, ed., *A Dictionary of Philosophy* (London: Macmillan, 1979), p. 322. In Greek philosophy, syllogisms contain propositions which are indicative sentences, with a subject and a predicated adjective or nominative. A typical syllogism is in three parts, with two propositions functioning as premises and a third serving as the resulting conclusion.

1.	**Premise**	—	Sweepy is a clown.
2.	**Premise**	—	All clowns are funny.
3.	**Conclusion**	—	(Therefore) Sweepy is funny.

By definition, the two premises of a syllogism must have a common term – in our example, "clown". Logicians label the word "M" (for "middle term" or "medium"). Through a process analogous to subtraction, we can derive the relationship between the other two terms – "funny" and "Sweepy" – by removing the middle term.

1.	S —	MS	— "Sweepy"
2.	M —	PP	— "funny"
3.	S —	P	

[17]Greek philosophers also argue through propositional discourse. However, whereas the Greek philosophers appeal to reason and observation as the sources of truth for their propositions, the framers of our document appeal to information passed on to them from authoritative sources and sages. The two groups would not accept each other's premises. This Talmud's framers would not be convinced that something is true just because any rational person can reason or observe that it is so. Conversely, the Greek philosophers would not be convinced that something is true just because a past authority once said so. The role of the historian is to describe the sources of authority not to evaluate the respective truth-claims. In other words, I am interested in the modes of argumentation not in the veracity of truth-claims – be they derived from abstract reason, empiricism, or tradition.

support the conclusions. In other words, the conclusions rest upon the patterns of logic, which, in turn, rest upon the premises.

The analysis of syllogistic patterns allows us to more clearly specify the difference between independent rhetorical units and appended subunits. We recall that an independent unit is defined as a fully developed discussion which conveys the main point of a paragraph. When I say that a discussion is fully developed, I mean that it is a complete logical argument. In other words, a syllogistic argument can function as an independent unit. The distinguishing charactersitic of an independent unit is that it contains all the premises from which its conclusion is derived.[18] The logic of an independent unit is self-sufficient, because it does not rest on any external propositions. Appended subunits also express syllogistic arguments. However, an appended subunit, by definition, refers to all or part of an independent unit. Therefore, it is not logically self-sufficient, because one or more of the premises of an appended unit is external to its construction.

The simplest logical pattern in our sample is the unitary syllogism. In such a construction, a single proposition is, at one and the same time, a premise and a conclusion. For a proposition to be a premise, the text must (1) assume it to be true and (2) assume that the audience considers it to be self-evident. A conclusion, on the other hand, is the point which the text attempts to prove or justify. If an authoritative source (premise) is cited in order to make a point (conclusion), I call it a unitary syllogism. A unitary syllogism is a self-contained argument which is not part of a larger logical construction. Therefore, a unitary syllogism functions as an independent rhetorical unit. In contrast, a proposition which requires further elaboration or logical discussion in order to derive a conclusion, is a constituent subunit. In other words, a proposition is a constituent subunit when it functions as *either* the premise *or* the conclusion of a syllogism. On the other hand, a proposition which functions as *both* a premise *and* a conclusion is a unitary syllogism, and therefore comprises an independent rhetorical unit (or an appened subunit).

In other patterns of syllogistic discourse, the conclusions, whether explicit or implied, are *separate* from the premises. For example, in a constructive syllogism, new propositions (conclusions) derive from other propositions (premises). The premise is the source of authority. Therefore, in order for a conclusion to be authoritative, it must derive from a premise. That is, a conclusion must be the logical outcome of a premise. Through presumably self-evident logical patterns, the authority of premises passes to conclusions. In

---

[18]When I call a portion of text an "independent" unit, I mean that it is logically self-sufficient. However, even a *logically* independent unit may *topically* depend upon external knowledge in order to convey meaning: as we shall see, the content often alludes to information not contained within the confines of the rhetorical construction.

syllogistic argumentation, the patterns of logic are based upon abstract causal relationships (i.e., "If propositions A and B are true, then, proposition C must also be true"). To rephrase our definition, a supportive syllogism derives *new conclusions* from authoritative sources through a formal pattern of argumentation implicitly based upon principles of logically necessity .

The third type of syllogism appearing in our sample passage is the supportive syllogism. In this logical pattern, the text begins with the conclusion and moves backward, explaining how this proposition is logically derived from a certain premise. In other words, a supportive syllogism announces the conclusion at the outset and then cites *new premises* to reinforce the authority of this conclusion. In the constructive syllogism, new propositions are implicitly or explicitly presented as the logical conclusion of an argument. In the supportive syllogism, on the other hand, the text does not establish a new proposition. The text merely reaffirms a proposition already known to the audience.

VIII.   Classification of Rhetorical Forms According to Syllogistic Patterns

I shall now present a preliminary classification scheme for the independent rhetorical units of the Yerushalmi which express syllogistic arguments. Our sample passage contains three different types of argument: (1) unitary syllogism, (2) constructive syllogism and (3) supportive syllogism. For each of these categories, I shall describe the logical structure and then present the rhetorical forms which express the type of argument. I expect these rhetorical forms to represent general patterns which will appear elsewhere in the Yerushalmi. After outlining the general rhetorical and logical characteristics of each rhetorical form, I shall present the one or more paragraphs from our sample passage which contain an independent unit exemplifying this form. With each paragraph cited, I will analyze the independent rhetorical units and occasional constituent and appended subunits in order to explain the relationship to our classification scheme.

Logical Pattern I.   Unitary Syllogism

We recall that in a unitary syllogism, a single proposition functions as both the premise and the conclusion of a logical argument. In our sample passage, we find only one example of a single proposition functioning as an independent rhetorical unit – the precedent.[19]

Rhetorical Form A. Precedent. Rhetorically, the precedent is a series of declarative sentences which has the following features identifying it as a story:

---

[19] I expect that, elsewhere in the Talmud of the Land of Israel, other types of material (e.g., narrated opinions and Tannaitic teachings) function as unitary syllogisms.

1. **Establishment of the setting**

   (I.e., Rabbi X goes to visit Rabbi Y.)

2. **Creation of tension or dissonance**

   (I.e., Rabbi Y acts in a strange, unexpected or seemingly unacceptable manner.)

3. **Resolution**

   (I.e., Rabbi Y explains his action.)

Rabbi Y's statement justifying his action functions as the establishment of a ruling. Sages are assumed to act in an exemplary manner. Therefore, stories about them set a precedent for normative behavior. In other words, if the authors wished to argue that a certain action was proper, they could simply cite a story of a sage acting accordingly. The story begins without an introduction identifying the narrator or the issue under consideration (e.g., "Rabbi X used to tell a story about..."). The narration is in Aramaic, although the characters may speak Hebrew. Precedents refer to sages who lived "here" in Palestine or "there" in Babylonia during the post-Mishnaic or "Amoraic" period. Logically, a precedent can function as an independent unit, because it contains all of the necessary features of a syllogism, in single proposition: it is at one and the same time a premise and a conclusion. The premise is that a certain authoritative sage is reported to have acted in a certain way. The conlusion is that such action is normative.

Example:

I

D. [Are washings required — even if hands do not touch the food?]

   1. *Samuel went up to visit Rav. He saw* [Rav] *eating with a napkin* [covering his hands]. *He said to him, "how so?* [I.e., are you doing this to avoid washing?]*" Rav replied,* "[No], I am fastidious [therefore I **wash as well as cover my hands with a napkin.**]."

   2. *When R. Zeira came up here* [to Palestine], *he saw priests eating with a napkin* [covering their hands]. *He said to them, "This is in accord with the* [above] *story about Rav."*

The first story, about Rav, is an independent unit, because it contains all of the premises on which its conclusion is based. In contrast, the story about the Palestinian priests is an appended subunit, because it is not logically self-sufficient. In the latter story, two authoritative sources or premises are harmonized – the report of the action of the priests and the report of the action of Rav. This harmonization is a strong argument for the conclusion that such action represents normative behavior. However, since one of these premises (Rav's action) is external to this story, I call this precedent an appended subunit and not an independent rhetorical unit. This appended subunit reinforces the point made in the first story, but it is not an integral or necessary part of that independent unit.

Even though the rhetoric and logic of the first precedent function independently, the message depends upon external material. In other words, the topic alludes to information not contained in the rhetorical unit. In fact, the primary point for the citation of the story is not explicitly stated. Hand-washing is not even mentioned. We only realize the significance of the napkin when we put these stories in context of the surrounding paragraphs: the use of a napkin signifies that the food is protected from contact with the hands. By presenting these stories about covering hands with a napkin, the text makes the point that hands should be washed, even if they do not touch the food.

Logical Pattern II. Constructive Syllogism

A constructive syllogism establishes a new proposition through a formal pattern of logic. In other words, an argument derives a new conclusion from certain authoritative sources. Citations of authoritative sources function as the premises of syllogistic discourse. The logic pattern of the syllogism necessarily leads from the premise to a certain conclusion. Therefore, because the conclusion can be inferred from the logic of argumentation, the conclusion is not always explicitly stated as a separate proposition. We find three types of constructive syllogism in our sample passage. The first type derives a conclusion from the logical analysis of a single authoritative source. The second type derives a conclusion from the harmonization of two sources. And the third type derives a conclusion from two or more sources without resolving contradictions between these sources.

All three patterns presuppose the principle of logical consistency. The first type of constructive syllogism analyzes the internal, logical coherence of a single proposition. Because the proposition is found to be self-contradictory, the contradiction must be explained or corrected. Through this pattern of argumentation, a new, modified proposition is presented or implied. The new proposition is the conclusion of the syllogism. As we shall see, the "logical analysis of a single source" at I.C. is an example of such a syllogism. Second, propositions must be logically consistent with all other known authoritative sources. If a proposition from one source is found to conflict with a proposition from another source, one of these propositions will be reinterpreted in order to resolve the contradiction. In other words, a new, reinterpreted proposition is derived from the harmonization of two propositions. The "harmonization of conflicting sources" at II. A. exemplifies this type of syllogism. Third, the principle of logical consistency applies even in the "dispute" form, in which contradictory positions are presented and remain unresolved (e.g. I.B.2.). The "conclusion" of a dispute syllogism is the point of agreement and the range of acceptable disagreement.

Rhetorical Form B.   Logical Analysis of a Single Source. This form identifies a logical contradiction in the citation of a single source and resolves this contradiction in order to derive a new conclusion. The rhetorical pattern contains four components:

1. An authoritative source containing two parts (part A and part B) is cited.
2. The meaning of part A of this citation is questioned.
3. An Amora clarifies the meaning of part A of the citation.
4. A second Amora declares that such an interpretation of part A conflicts with part B.

In other words, parts A and B of an authoritative source are shown to be logically inconsistent. By implication, the inconsistency is resolved by changing part A to A$_1$, thereby changing the cited source. Logically, the authoritative source functions as the initial premise of a syllogistic argument. A fixed pattern of argumentation derives a conclusion (A$_1$) from this premise (A), by identifying and resolving a logical contradiction within the source. Indeed, the premise and the conclusion, A and A$_1$, may be logically opposite. This conclusion is the implicit fifth component of the pattern.

5. [Implicit:] Part A is modified so as not to conflict with part B. The modified version of part A (part A$_1$) functions as the conclusion of this argument.

This conclusion need not be explicitly stated, because it is the logically necessary outcome of the syllogistic argument.

Example:

I

C. [Are washings required – before and after meals?]
   1. a. [Tannaitic Teaching:] *It has been taught:*
          (1) (a) **Washing before the meal is optional.**
              (b) **But after the meal it is obligatory.**
          (2) (a) But with the first [washing], *he washes and interrupts.*
              (b) And with the second [washing], he washes but does not interrupt.
      b. [Commentary on the Tannaitic Teaching:]
          (1) What is the meaning of "He washes and interrupts?"
          (2) R. Jacob b. Aha said: "[It means that] he washes and repeats [the washing]."
          (3) R. Samuel b. Isaac asked: "[If by obligation] *he washes and repeats,* [how] *do you say it is optional* [before the meal]?" [I.e., Washing is **required before the meal** as well as after the meal.]
   2. a. Said R. Jacob b. Idi: "On account of [missing] the first washing, pork was eaten. On account of [missing] the second washing, women left her house – and some say, three souls were killed. [I.e., **washing is required before and after the meal.**]

In the independent unit (**I.C.1.**) of this paragraph, a source is quoted and then corrected in favor of a more stringent ruling. In the present example, a Tannaitic teaching functions as the authoritative source. The three-letter introductory formula in Aramaic ("It has been taught") identifies this constituent subunit as a Tannaitic teaching. This citation contains a series of declarative sentences in Mishnaic-style Hebrew. The quoted position requires ritual washings after the meal but not before the meal. Furthermore, when a person washes before the meal, he must wash and interrupt. Through exegesis on the meaning of the word "interrupts," the commentary determines that he is required to wash twice before the meal. Therefore, this interpretation of line **I.C.1.(2)(a)** – one must wash twice before the meal – conflicts with line **I.C.1.a.(1)(a)** – washing before the meal is optional. The Talmud has identified a contradiction in the Tannaitic teaching. It implicitly resolves the problem by modifying the quoted material and sides with the more stringent position [**I.C.1.b.(3)**], that washing is required before the meal.[20]   The syllogism therefore produces a new proposition (washing is required before meals), even though this conclusion conflicts the original premise of the authoritative source (washing is optional before meals).

The story told by Jacob b. Idi is an appended subunit, because it refers to the independent unit. On its own terms, the story is a rather cryptic statement. But when we compare it to a more complete version of the same story in the Babylonian Talmud, we learn of a supposed situation in which forbidden meat was eaten and a women was divorced (or three men killed) on account of hands not being washed. I call this form a negative precedent because it illustrates the unfortunate consequences resulting from the failure to act in the prescribed manner. By reversing the logic of the statement, we can determine the position of Jacob b. Idi: if missing washings before and after the meal leads to negative results, then these washings must be required. This view supports the position of the preceding independent unit.

Rhetorical Form C. Harmonization of Conflicting Sources. This form is a three part argument which resolves a contradiction between two conflicting sources.

1. One proposition is presented.

2. A second proposition is presented and shown to logically conflict with the first proposition.

3. A sage interprets one of the propositions so as to resolve the logical

---

[20]We know that the text advocates the more stringent position for two reasons. First, the topic of the paragraph is the question of whether washing is required before and after meals, not the manner of washing. Therefore the commentators have an interest in disproving I.C.1.a.(1)(a), that washing before the meal is optional, but they have no interest in disproving I.C.1.a.(2)(a) that one washes and interrupts. Second, the appended subunit attributed to Jacob b. Idi, reinforces the position that washings are required before, as well as after, meals.

contradiction.

In the example from our sample passage, the propositions are (1) a narrated opinion and (2) a Tannaitic teaching. I hypothesize that this general rhetorical pattern could be constructed using other combinations of constituent subunits, such as a Tannaitic teaching and a conflicting precedent. Logically, these authoritative sources function as the premises of a syllogism. The syllogism produces a new conclusion through a set pattern of logic which harmonizes two contradictory propositions. The logical pattern narrows the application of one premise to a specific situation, so that the other premise can can function as the general rule without contradiction.

Example:

II. [Does the same man say the blessings before and after the meal?]

A. 1. *R. Zeira went up to visit R. Abbahu. He found him saying,* "I shall go to eat."

   2. *He gave him a chunk of bread to cut.* [**Before eating** they discussed **who should bless** it.]
      a. *[R. Zeira] said to him, "make the blessing."*
      b. *[R. Abbahu] replied,* "[You should make the blessing, because] *the host knows the value of his loaf.*"

   3. *After eating* [they discussed **who should bless**] –
      a. [R. Abbahu] *said to him, "make the blessing."*
      b. [R. Zeira] replied, *"Rabbi, does the rabbi* [you] *know R. Huna, a great man, who would say, "He who opens* [says the blessing before the meal] *must close [and say the blessing after the meal]."* [I.e., **R. Huna says, the same man says the blessings before and after the meal.**]

B. 1. *A Tannaitic teaching differs from R. Huna, as it has been taught:*

   2. "The order of washing hands is this: (1) With up to five people, they begin with the greatest. (2) With more than this, they begin with the least. (3) In the middle of the meal, they being with the eldest. (4) **After the meal, they begin with the one who blesses.**"

   3. a. Do they not [begin the washing after the meal with the one who says the blessing] so that he may prepare himself for the blessing?
      b. *If you* [R. Huna] *say* he who opens also closes, he would know from the beginning of the meal that he would say the grace after the meal [and would not need time to prepare].

C. 1. R. Isaac said, "[**R. Huna's position stands,** because you can] explain it as referring to those who come in one by one [after the blessing was said before the meal] and do not know who had said the blessing."

This form harmonizes two propositions. In the present example, the propositions are a narrated opinion and a Tannaitic teaching. Let me describe the rhetorical and logical traits of these constituent subunits. The narrated opinion (II.A.) presents a statement of a sage as part a story. Whereas the positive precedent expresses a sage's position by describing his behavior, the narrated opinion quotes a sage directly in the context of a story. In other words, a narrated opinion is a simple proposition in which the premise of argumentation is the quote of a statement by an authoritative sage. Rhetorically, the narrated opinion is a list of declarative sentences with at least one direct quotation. The stories can be relatively long with numerous statements by different sages. The narration is in Aramaic, but individual statements may be in Hebrew. The story as a whole is unattributed.

As to logic, only one of these statements functions as the proposition; the other statements are part of the narration that introduces this proposition.[21] We recall that a proposition is the assertion of a point. Here, the point is that the same man says the blessings before and after the meal. This statement functions as a premise for the syllogistic argument of the independent unit as a whole. In the second proposition (II.B.1.-2.), an introductory formula in Aramaic ("A Tannaitic teaching differs..., as it has been taught...") identifies this subunit as [1] a Tannaitic teaching which [2] conflicts with the first proposition. After this introduction, the Tannaitic teaching appears in Mishnaic-style Hebrew. The Tannaitic teaching is then interpreted and shown to conflict with Huna. Isaac expresses the conclusion of this syllogism when he resolves the contradiction (in II.C.) by limiting the application of Huna's position, so that it no longer conflicts with the general applicability of the Tannaitic teaching. The Yerushalmi has thereby succeeded in harmonizing two conflicting opinions.

Rhetorical Form D.   Dispute. The most common form in our sample passage is the dispute, the juxtaposition of opposing positions without any explicit resolution. As we shall see our sample passage contains two different forms, the implicit and the explicit dispute. Rhetorically, a dispute is a list of two or three constituent subunits each of which expresses the position of a different sage.

1. A report of by Rabbi X demonstrates that he holds a certain position.

2. A report of a statement or an action by Rabbi Y demonstrates that he holds a certain position (which conflicts with the position of Rabbi X).

3. [Optional] A report of a statement or an action by Rabbi Z demonstrates that he holds a certain position (which conflicts with the positions of Rabbis X and Y).

---

[21] Any statement within a narrated opionion could function as a logical proposition. Conceivably, this narrated opinion could be cited elsewhere, with a different statement within the construction functioning as the proposition.

The disputes in our sample passage contain only the positions of the disputants, without any prefatory remarks introducing the precise point of disagreement. Conflicting positions are presented without any commentary explicitly declaring the relationship between the statements, such as "Rabbi X disagrees with Rabbi Y on issue A for the following reason...." Therefore the reader must reflect on the relationship between the various positions in order to reconstruct the disputed issue. The disputants share common assumptions and only disagree on relatively minor issues.[22] In terms of logic, each statement functions as a proposition validated by the attribution to an authoritative sage. In other words, propositions serve as the premises of a logical argument. *The implicit conclusion of a dispute syllogism is the point of agreement and the range of acceptable opinion.* For example, in **I. E. 5-7.**, Huna, Hoshaia and Zeira dispute whether one washes his hands for bread alone, for anything containing liquid, or for everything including beets. They disagree on the types of food requiring washing, but they all agree that hands should be ritually washed before eating. We find examples of disputes containing either two or three contrary positions. I call these bilateral and trilateral disputes, respectively. We can also distinguish between explicit and implicit disputes according to the ways the individual positions of the disputants are phrased.

Rhetorical Form D (1). Explicit Disputes. In an explicit dispute, the disputants' positions are expressed as opinions, almost identically phrased, except for the difference of a word or two. For example, the following would be an explicit dispute:

> Rabbi X said: One washes for A.
>
> Rabbi Y said: One washes for B.

The explicit dispute gives opinions in a highly abridged formula without regard for the original context of these statements. In the above model, Rabbis X and Y agree that one needs to wash. They disagree on whether one is required to washes for A or for B. By reflecting on the difference between A and B we can reconstruct the principle behind their dispute. The positions of the disputants are phrased in rhetorical and logical contradistinction to each other. Because of the formulaic nature of explicit disputes, the slight difference in wording highlights the common assumptions as well as the precise issue on which the dispute is based. In other words, the rhetoric of an explicit dispute enables us to infer the

---

[22]Louis Newman, in *The Sanctity of the Seventh Year: A Study of the Mishnah Tractate Shebiit* (Chico, CA: Scholars Press, 1983), p. 32., analyzes the dispute form in the Mishnah: "the juxtaposition of two alternative responses to a single issue points toward the principle upon which the disputants agree, the common ground from which their disagreement arises.... the contrasting rulings themselves express alternative ways of resolving the problem...." See also Martin S. Jaffee, *Mishanah's Theology of Tithing: A Study of Tractate Maaserot* (Chico, CA: Scholars Press, 1981), pp. 16-7.

the logical conclusion (the point of agreement and the range of acceptable opinion) with relative ease.

Rhetorical Form D (2). Implicit Disputes. The positions of an implicit dispute are not phrased in logical or rhetorical contradistinction to each other. In contrast to the explicit dispute which contains only highly formulaic *opinions*, the implicit dispute is constructed out of three different forms of proposition:

1. Opinion. A statement is attributed to a sage.

2. Narrated Opinion. The statement of a sage is presented as part of a story.

3. Precedent. A story describing a sage's behavior, reflects his position on the disputed issue.

An implicit dispute can be constructed out of any combination of these constituent subunits. This form has an advantage and a disadvantage compared to the explicit dispute. The advantage is that, because the positions are not as severely abridged into formulae, they purport to give more information about the original context of the sage's statement or action. The disadvantage is that, because the positions are not formulated in contradistinction to each other, the common assumptions and the precise issue of the dispute are less obvious. In other words, the logical conclusion of an implicit dispute is more difficult to infer.

First example:

I

E. [Are washings required – for all types of food?]

    1. R. Yosé b. Kahana came [and said] in the name of Samuel: "One washes hands for Priests' rations, one does *not* wash hands for unconsecrated food."

    2. R. Yosé says: "for Priests' rations, *and* for unconsecrated food."

    3. R. Yosah in the name of R. Hiyya Bar Ashi, and R. Johan and R. Hiyya Bar Ashi in the name of Rav, [said]: "one washes hands up to the wrist for Priests' rations and up to the knuckles for unconsecrated food."

    4. *Measha, grandson of R. Joshua b. Levi, said "If one was eating with my grandfather and did not wash his hands up to the wrist, grandfather would not eat with him."* [I.e., wash up to the wrist for all food.]

    5. R. Huna said, "One washes hands only for bread."

    6. Taught R. Hoshaia : "[One washes hands] for anything containing liquid."

    7. R. Zeira said: *"Even for cutting beets he would wash his hands."*

This paragraph is a series of three disputes, each dealing with different aspects of a single topic. We could consider each dispute to be a separate paragraph. This pattern of arranging three disputes on a related topic is reminiscent of the

Mishnah which commonly groups in groups three or five pericopae in order to facilitate memorization.

1. Opinion $\Big\}$ **Explicit Bilateral Dispute**
2. Opinion   (Topic: Does one wash for consecrated food?)

3. Opinion $\Big\}$ **Implicit Bilateral Dispute**
(Topic: How thoroughly does one wash for
4. Precedent   unconsecrated food?)

5. Opinion

6. Opinion $\Big\}$ **Explicit Trilateral Dispute**
(Topic: Does one wash for all kinds of food?)
7. Opinion

Second example:

I

F. [Are washings required – more than once a day?]
    1. Rav said: "[If] he washed his hands in the morning, they do not trouble him to wash in the afternoon." [I.e., **once in the morning is sufficient for the day.**]
    2. R. Abina ordered his wine-steward: "[Washing once] **whenever you find sufficient water** is enough for the day."

This is an implicit dispute with Rav's position expressed as an opinion and Abina's position expressed as a narrated opinion. The views are quite similar, with each sage assuming that a single washing is sufficient for the entire day. Apparently, the disputed issue is whether this one washing must be done in the morning, before eating, as Rav advocates.

Third example:

I

B. [Are washings required – even if it is inconvenient?]
    1. a. R. Yosé in the name of R. Shabbetai and R. Hiyya in the name of R. Simeon b. Laquish said: "For dough-offering and for washing of the hands, a man goes four miles [if necessary to find water]." [I.e., **washings are required, even if it is inconvenient.**]
        b. R. Abbahu in the name of R. Yosé b. R. Hanina said: "This is what was said, '[If the water is] before him [i.e., on his way, he must wash], but if it is behind him [i.e., out of his way], they do not trouble him [to wash].'" [I.e., **washings are *not* required, if it is inconvenient.**]

2. a. Regarding men who guard gardens and orchards [for whom water is neither before or behind], what do you do for them, as to the inner sides and outer sides [of a cup]? [I.e., how would R. Abbahu rule in a situation in which a man is stationary without water to wash?]

    b. Let us infer the solution from this:

      (1) The woman sits and cuts off her dough-offering while she is naked, because she can cover herself up, but a man cannot [prepare the dough-offering] unless he is dressed [Mishnah Hallah 2:3].

      (2) Now, does not a woman sit in the house, yet you say they do not trouble her [to even cover herself]? [Likewise], here they would not trouble those who guard gardens and orchards to wash their hands.

The independent unit of the paragraph is an implicit bilateral dispute between Yosé and Abbahu. The positions of the disputants are both expressed as opinions, yet it is an implicit dispute, because the opinions are not phrased in contradistinction to each other. I have given their positions as abridged formulae in brackets to clarify the issue under dispute.

An appended subunit (**I.B.2.**) amplifies the position of one of the disputants by applying it to a special situation. Rhetorically, this appendix contains two parts, a question and an answer.

Question: Unattributed question about part of the previous independent unit

Answer: (1) Citation of another Mishnaic pericope

      (2) Unattributed commentary on this pericope, explaining how it answers the question

In the independent unit, Abbahu, one of the disputants, says that a man is required to wash only if he happens upon water while he is on his way somewhere. In other words, a person need not go to the trouble of backtracking his steps in order to do his ritual washing before meals. The first part of the appended subunit (**I.B.2.a.**) asks, what about a person who is not on his way somewhere, but is stationary, guarding a garden or an orchard? Another Mishnaic pericopeprovides the answer.[23] The text cites a pericope of Mishnah tractate Hallah, and then explains the relevance of this citation: if a woman need not trouble herself to dress while preparing the dough-offering, then surely a guard of an orchard or a garden need not go out of his way to wash his hands.

Logically, the second constituent subunit of the independent unit provides a premise for the argument of this appended subunit.

---

[23]Conceivably, this type of question could be answered through other rhetorical forms, such as the report of a statement or an action of an authoritative sage. Elsewhere in this Talmud, I would expect to find other combinations of rhetorical forms functioning as questions and answers.

First Premise: Opinion of Abbahu [**I.B.1.b.**]

Challenge: Commentary questions the applicability of this opinion to a special situation [**I.B.2.a.**]

Second Premise: Citation of another Mishnaic Pericope [**I.B.2.b.(1)**]

Conclusion: Application of Abbahu's opinion to a special situation [**I.B.2.b.(2)**]

We recall that an appended unit is a rhetorical unit which does not contain all of the premises necessary to its argument. Because the first premise is part of the independent rhetorical unit, I call the form at hand an appended subunit. This appendix does not effect the dispute between Yosé and Abbahu (the independent unit), but merely elaborates the position of the second disputant. The appendix raises the philosophic question about the difficulty of applying general principles to specific real-life situations. This Talmud answers the question by citing a Mishnaic pericope, rather than using abstract philosophic prose. The text assumes that the Mishnah is a coherent logical system. Principles learned from any part of the Mishnah can be applied to problems arising elsewhere in the Mishnah and to problems arising within discussions among the sages of the Talmudic period. In order to state a principle, the text cites a pericope where the principle is operative. Using this logical pattern, the Yerushalmi expresses complex philosophic matters in concrete terms and in compact language.

Logical Pattern III.   Supportive Syllogism

In all syllogisms, a formal pattern of logic derives a conclusion from certain premises. A *supportive* syllogism begins with the conclusion and moves backwards, explaining how this proposition is logically derived from other premises. In other words, a supportive syllogism cites "new" premises in order to demonstrate the authority of the conclusion. In contrast, we recall that a *constructive* syllogism moves forward from authoritative premises in order to derives "new" conclusions.

Rhetorical Form E.   Analysis of the Logical Derivation of the Base Mishnaic Pericope.

This rhetorical form uses two pieces of quoted material in order to demonstrate two levels of reasoning logically prior to the base Mishnaic pericope. This form contains three components:

1.   A citation of relevant Toseftan material,

2.   An attributed statement comparing the base Mishnaic pericope with another Mishnaic pericope, and

3.   A quotation of the other Mishnaic pericope.

Let us look at the rhetorical features more closely. The Toseftan material is presented without introduction. This quotation is in Mishnaic-style Hebrew and directly analyzes the logic of the base Mishnaic pericope. The second component begins with an attribution to an Amora in Aramaic. This sage explains, also in Aramaic, which elements of the base Mishnaic pericope relate to which elements of the second Mishnaic pericope. The third component begins with a formulaic introduction to the quotation of the latter pericope, *"as we have learned there."* The text then presents the second Mishnaic pericope (or enough of the text to serve as a footnote referring the reader to the approprate pericope of the Mishnah.)

Logically this form uses two successive syllogisms to establish authoritative premises which support the conclusion. The base Mishnaic pericope functions as the conclusion of a syllogistic argument. This conclusion derives from a certain premise. This premise, in turn, is a conclusion which derives from a logically prior premise. In other words, the base Mishnaic pericope is the third stage of a three-stage argument.

Argument:	Stage One	Stage Two	Stage Three
Rhetoric constituent subunits:	second Mishnaic pericope	Tosefta citation	base Mishnaic Pericope
Logic first syllogism:		premise $\rightarrow$	conclusion
		$\parallel$	
second syllogism:	premise $\rightarrow$	conclusion	

The first syllogism moves us back one step in the argument, from the third to the second stage, by paraphrasing the relevant material from the Tosefta. The Toseftan material straightforwardly explains the reasoning of the base Mishnaic pericope. The innovation of the Talmud is to take us behind the reasoning of the Tosefta, from the second to the first stage of the argument, with a second syllogistic argument. As we have seen already seen, the authors of the Talmud assume that the Mishnah is a logically consistent document. Therefore, they explain the reasoning of the first stage of the argument by referring to another Mishnaic pericope where such reasoning is operative. Through such comparisons, they are able to express complex legal principles in compact form, without using abstract language. Because the base Mishnaic pericope in our present example is a bilateral dispute, the reasoning of each side must be explained at every stage of the argument. But theoretically this general form can explain a Mishnaic pericope which does not contain a dispute. In such cases, only one reason would be given at each stage of the argument.

Example:

I

A. [Are washings required – before mixing the cup of wine to be blessed?]

   1. [Reasoning of the houses (cf. T. Ber. 5:26):]

a. *What is the reasoning of the House of Shammai?* [The cup cannot be mixed without washing the hands] lest hands make unclean the liquid [on the outside of the cup] and, in turn, the cup [and its contents].

b. *What is the reasoning of the House of Hillel?* [The cup can be mixed without washing the hands because] the outside of a cup is always unclean [so washing would not help to protect the cup]. Another matter – hands should only be washed immediately before blessing [without interrupting to mix the cup].

2. *R. Biban in the name of R. Yohanan* [said]: *"The opinion of the House of Shammai is in accord with R. Yosé and that of the House of Hillel with R. Meir* [i.e., the House of Shammai and the House of Hillel in M. Ber. 8:2, agree with the views of R. Yosé and R. Meir, respectively, found in M. Kel. 25:7-8]

3. *"as we have learned there* [in M. Kel. 25:7-8]:
   '[In all vessels, the outside, the inside, and the handle are distinguished (with respect to the transfer of uncleanness).] R. Meir says: "For unclean and clean hands." [I.e., unclean hands only make unclean the parts of a cup which they actually touch, not the entire cup.] R. Yosé says: "For unclean hands only." [I.e., unclean hands which touch any part of a cup make the entire cup unclean.]'"

The base Mishnaic pericope reports a disagreement of the Houses as to whether hands must be washed before one mixes a cup of wine to be blessed. Why do they differ? The first component (**I.A.1.**) takes us one back to an earlier in the argument. The reasoning of each side of the dispute in the base Mishnaic pericope is given, in a paraphrase of the relevant material from the Tosefta (T. Ber. 5:26). The House of Shammai advocates washing before mixing to ensure that unclean hands do not make the contents of the cup unclean. The House of Hillel advocates washing only after mixing because washing is useless in protecting the outside of a cup from uncleanness, and because hands should be washed immediately prior to the blessing. The point of disagreement is difficult to discern because the reasons of the Houses are not expressed in logical or rhetorical contradistinction to each other. We can clarify the issue under dispute by putting the answers in parallel form.

The House of Shammai holds that, if unclean hands touch the outside of a cup, the contents of the cup become unclean.

The House of Hillel holds that, even if unclean hands touch the outside of a cup, the contents of the cup remain clean.

In other words, the reason the Houses dispute in the base Mishnaic pericope over whether washing is required before mixing the cup is that they disagree on whether unclean hands which touch the outside of a cup make the contents unclean. Without the questions, the relationship between the sentences would be unclear. Identical questions are posed, and then answered, on the reasoning of each side of the dispute. The formulaic nature of these questions, expressed in Aramaic, gives unity to the Toseftan material and identifies it as a dispute.

Logically, the second component (**I.B.1.**) explains the first component in the same way that the first component explains the base Mishnaic pericope. We have already seen how the first component explains the dispute in the base Mishnaic pericope by presenting a logically prior argument. Likewise, the analysis attributed to Yohanan explains this first component by taking us to an even earlier stage in the argument. On the surface, Yohanan simply compares two Mishnaic pericopae showing the similarities in reasoning. However, the purpose of this comparison is much more complex: the reference to the second Mishnaic pericope explains the presuppostions of the base Mishnaic pericope. The reason why the Shammaites are concerned with unclean hands touching the outside of the cup is that they (along with Yosé) presuppose that the parts of a cup are not distinct with respect to the transfer of uncleanness. If unclean hands touch the outside of the cup, they believe the inside of the cup and the contents become unclean. The Hillelites, on the other hand, are not concerned with unclean hands touching the outside of the cup, because they (along with Meir) presuppose that each part of the cup is distinct with respect to the transfer of uncleanness. If unclean hands touch the outside of the cup, they believe the inside of the cup and the contents do not become unclean. The Talmud has outlined two stages of argument behind the base Mishnaic pericope:

Stage One (second Mishnaic pericope): Whether or not the parts of a cup are distinct with respect to the transfer of uncleanness.

Stage Two (Toseftan material): Whether or not unclean hands touching the outside of a cup do make the inside of a cup and its contents unclean.

Stage Three (base Mishnaic pericope): Whether or not hands must be washed before mixing a cup of wine to be blessed.

The disagreement at each stage is rooted in a logically prior dispute. The Toseftan material may appear independently in another context, but here it is a constituent subunit. This subunit is a necessary component of the larger logical construction, serving as a bridge between the argument in the base Mishnaic pericope (stage three, above) and the argument of the second Mishnaic pericope (stage one).

The individual paragraphs of our sample passage have been carefully constructed according to syllogistic patterns. The independent units consist of supportive, constructive and unitary syllogisms. The appended subunits are also constructed accrding to syllogistic patterns. In fact, we find no extraneous material; as the following logical map demonstrates, every word in the passage functions as part of a syllogistic argument.

Logical Map

Topical Relation to the Base Mishnaic Pericope	Independent Unit Logical Pattern	Rhetorical Form	Appended Subunit Logical Pattern
I. A. Direct	Supportive	Logical Derivation of the Base Mishnaic Pericope	—
B. Indirect	Constructive	Dispute	Application of a Principle to a Specific Situation (I.B.2.)
C. Indirect	Constructive	Logical Analysis of a Single Source	Negative Precedent (I.C.2.)
D. Indirect	Unitary	Precedent	Precedent (I.D.2.)
E. Indirect	Constructive	Series of Disputes	—
F. Indirect	Constructive	Dispute	—
II. A. Tangential	Constructive	Harmonization of Conflicting Sources	—

The paragraphs appear in a specific order. The passage begins with a supportive syllogism followed by a number of unitary and constructive syllogisms. The supportive syllogism appears first, immediately following the citation of the base Mishnaic pericope, because this pericope functions as the implicit conclusion of the construction. The syllogism identifies authoritative sources which reinforce the authority of this pericope. In the sample passage, we do not find any other logical patterns in which the base Mishnaic pericope functions as a proposition – either as a premise or a conclusion.[24] All subsequent paragraphs contain unitary and constructive syllogisms which have no logical connection to the base Mishnaic pericope. They neither derive conclusions from this pericope nor identify premises to support it. These syllogisms derive new conclusions from other authoritative sources besides the base Mishnaic pericope. They therefore appear at the end of the passage, removed from the citation of the base Mishnaic pericope.

The arrangement of paragraphs according to the type of syllogism corresponds to our earlier finding that paragraphs are arranged by topic. The supportive syllogism takes the base Mishnaic pericope as its conclusion. Therefore, by definition, a paragraph with a supportive syllogism will address a topic directly related to this pericope. In contrast, the unitary and constructive syllogisms take us far afield from the topical focus of the base Mishnaic pericope. Because these syllogisms bear no logical connection to this pericope,

---

[24]In the appended subunit **I.B.2.**, a Mishnahic pericope from another tractate, functions as the premise of argumentation.

they can be used to address different issues. We have already determined that paragraphs which are only indirectly or tangentially related to the topic of the base Mishnaic pericope occur at the end of the passage.

Not only are paragraphs arranged according to topical focus and type of syllogism, but also by complexity of construction. We can see why **I.A.** appears first: it is a supportive syllogism which is directly related to the topical focus of the base Mishnaic pericope. We can also see explained why **II.A.** occurs last: it is a constructive syllogism with only a tangential relationship to this pericope. But we have yet to explain the order of the intermediate units, **I.B. – I.F.** We note that the first three paragraphs in this group, **I.B. – I.D.**, contain appendices, whereas the subsequent paragraphs do not. The addition of an appended subunit makes a paragraph more complex. It becomes a two-tiered discussion, with a primary and a derivative argument. I see no other reason why these three paragraphs should occur together. There is no topical, rhetorical or logical characteristic which distinguishes them, except for the inclusion of an appendix. I hypothesize that the editors preferred to place the more complex constructions at the beginning of a group of paragraphs that have a similar topical relationship to the base Mishniac pericope and a similar syllogistic pattern. Our analysis is limited to a single passage, and we cannot use this small sample to generalize about the patterns of arrangement which characterize the document as a whole. But even in this one passage, it is clear that the editors were not haphazardly gathering material. The paragraphs have been arranged according to an identifiable pattern.

IX. Conclusion

The Yerushalmi is a logically uniform document which makes its points through two types of syllogistic argumentation. On one hand, supportive syllogisms reinforce the authority of an existing ruling by identifying new grounds for this position. On the other hand, constructive and unitary syllogisms derive new rulings from authoritative sources. If the Yerushalmi is a uniform document, the logical patterns appearing in our sample passage should recur throughout the document. In this syllogistic mode of discourse, the authors assume that certain logical patterns of thought allow them and their audience to interpolate and extrapolate religious truth from authoritative sources. Therefore, human reason appears as a source of knowledge along with divine revelation and the wisdom of the ages.

This Talmud also has a uniform rhetorical style. The document is an immense compilation of three types of material – stories, statements and citations. The choice of material is significant: the use of citations indicates that certain texts were considered authoritative, and the use of statements and stories demonstrates that the words and deeds of certain sages were also considered authoritative. These literary units are the building blocks of this Talmud's syllogistic discourse. The stories, statements and citations appear to be haphazardly collected, until we realize that they have been carefully selected and arranged in certain patterns in order to make a point. They function as the propositions of syllogistic arguments. As we have seen, the Yerushalmi contains three types of logical patterns – the supportive, constructive and unitary syllogism. Each type of logical pattern is expressed through a variety of rhetorical forms. In our sample passage, for example, we identified three rhetorical forms which express constructive syllogisms – the dispute, the logical analysis of a single source and the harmonization of conflicting sources. The repertoire of rhetorical forms is limited. The same forms are used again and again, each time to make a different point. In other words, the topical content varies, but the rhetorical forms remain constant.

The Yerushalmi is not characterized by a distinct topical focus. In contrast to the the limited repertoire of logical patterns and rhetorical forms, the Yerushalmi addresses a virtually unlimited number of topics. The document contains thousands of paragraphs, each of which is a cogent discussion on a different issue. Because it is a commentary on successive Mishnaic pericope and not an exposition on a particular topic, the text does not move from one subject to another according to a topical program, nor does it systematically treat various subtopics of a general topic. Therefore, we cannot abstract the topical focus of a passage, a tractate, or the document as a whole. Topical analysis leads us in many directions according to the diverse interests of the authors in the Mishnaic pericope under consideration. Topically, each discussion is idiosyncratic. An analysis of the topics addressed in one tractate does not allow us to predict the topics that will occur in any of the other thirty-eight tractates. Therefore, in order to determine the characteristics which give unity and definition to the document as a whole, I focus on the recurrent logical patterns and rhetorical forms instead of the diffuse topical content.

While the topics vary, the relationship between rhetoric and logic remains constant throughout the document. The rhetoric is the surface texture. The logic is the deeper structure which holds the document together. Let us look at a specific example. In I.E.3-4., Rav and Joshua b. Levi dispute over which types of food require thorough ritual washing:

I

E. 3.   R. Yosah in the name of R. Hiyya Bar Ashi, and R. Johan and R. Hiyya Bar Ashi in the name of Rav, [said]: "one washes hands **up to the wrist for Priests' rations and up to the knuckles for unconsecrated food.**"

4.   *Measha, grandson of R. Joshua b. Levi, said "If one was eating with my grandfather and did not wash his hands up to the wrist, grandfather would not eat with him."* [I.e., wash **up to the wrist for all food.**]

We recall that a syllogism – meaning, "to reason together" – combines propositions in order to make a new argument. The argument as a whole conveys more information than the sum of the parts viewed separately. The implicit conclusion of a dispute syllogism is the point of agreement and the range of acceptable opinion. Therefore, in the above dispute, the conclusion is that one must wash up to the wrist for Priest's rations, but that it is debatable whether one must do the same for unconsecrated food as well.

The Yerushalmi is more concerned with the underlying relationship between the two positions than in the way the individual positions are expressed. Rav's position is expressed in the form of a statement and Joshua b. Levi's position is expressed in the form of a story. The type of literary form is unimportant to the argument. Both forms, the statement and the story, function identically as the premises of the dispute syllogism. Logically, it makes no difference whether a proposition is expressed in the form of a story, a statement, or a citation.[25] The syllogism is structured so that the premises automatically lead to a conclusion. Because the conclusion is the logically necessary outcome of the syllogism, it is not rhetorically necessary to explicitly state the conclusion. The syllogistic patterns allow for a very compact rhetorical style: if the conclusion of an argument can be inferred, it need not be expressed. Therefore, the implicit logical patterns give meaning to rhetorical forms, turning discrete sentences into cogent arguments.

This article has analyzed the topic, rhetoric and logic of a short passage of the Yerushalmi. As I have demonstrated, this passage repeatedly uses a particular type of logical pattern, which I call the "syllogism." All of the rhetorical forms appearing in the sample passage express syllogistic arguments. I have distinguished between three categories of syllogism and then described the rhetorical forms which express each type of logical pattern. I expect the syllogistic mode of argumentation and the subsequent rhetorical forms of expression to recur elsewhere in this Talmud. Therefore, the now-completed

---

[25]Scholars have completely overlooked the point that stories function as propositions in syllogistic discourse, because they differentiate Halakhic [legal] material from Aggadic [non-legal] material. Studies in Talmudic reasoning focus on the Halakhah and neglect the supposedly Aggadic stories, folklore and legends. For example, Jacobs, in *The Talmudic Argument*, studies only *Halakhic* (legal) material and ignores stories because they are *Aggadic* (non-legal):

> Finally, it must be noted that all the passages considered in this book belong to the Halakhah, the legal element in the Talmud, which is after all the largest component in the gigantic work. Considerations of space dictated that the Aggadic element – the religion, history, folklore, medicine, science, legends and stories of the saints – be omitted. In the Aggadic passages there is, naturally, more poetry, less prose; more appeal to emotions, less to the intellect; more attention to literary composition, less to acute analysis. Nevertheless, no hard and fast distinction between the Halakhic and Aggadic passages can be drwn. It can be shown that the type of argumentation exhibited in the Halakhah is not entirely absent from the Aggadah and, as we have seen, a striving for literary effect is present throughout the Halakhah (p. 211).

"Halakhah" and "Aggadah" may be useful categories for Jewish law and theology, but they confound the analysis of the rhetorical and logical dimensions of a syllogistic passage. As we have seen, stories, statements and citations all function as propositions in the Yerushalmi's syllogistic mode of argumentation.

analysis yields a preliminary classification scheme of the rhetorical forms which express syllogistic patterns of logic in the document as a whole.[26] This classification scheme can be tested and improved by applying it to other syllogistic passages in the Yerushalmi. In time to come, I anticipate, the project will go forward along the lines of classification proposed here.

---

[26]Louis Jacobs writes: "It has to be said that there is no actual classification of the different types of argument in the Talmud itself and the names for them are our invention" *(The Talmudic Argument: A Study in Talmudic Reasoning and Methodology* [Cambridge: Cambridge University Press, 1984], p. 17). When Jacobs refers to the Talmud, he means the Babylonian Talmud (ca. A.D. 600). The state of research on the Yerushalmi is more primitive. To my knowledge, there has been no systematic study of the mode of argumentation employed by this document.

Chapter Five

System or Tradition?
The Bavli and Its Sources

Jacob Neusner

Brown University

I. Tradition or System?

A variety of writings containing statements attributed to sages, or rabbis who lived over the course of nearly seven hundred years (ca. 200 B.C. to A.D. 500), came to closure between the editing of the Mishnah, in ca. A.D. 200, and the formation of the Bavli, the Talmud of Babylonia, in ca. A.D. 600. These writings in the history of Judaism have formed not only a literary corpus, exhibiting traits in common, but – in the judgment of that same Judaism – also a tradition and a theological and legal canon. The writings at hand are represented as an incremental tradition formed out of prior sources, which are seen to be making a cogent and authoritative statement in common and to form a continuous set of writings. That increment, formed in an allegedly sedimentary process out of prior sources, moreover, is understood to derive from a continuous process of tradition, with sayings handed on from an earlier generation to a later on until a complete and final statement came to full expression in the Bavli. Hence the Bavli is supposed to stand in relationship to prior writings as a summary statement stands to the sources that are summarized. It is supposed to respond to a received program and to restate a vast corpus of already-circulating and traditional materials.

In stating matters in literary terms, I mean to point to a broader theoretical issue. It is, for the case at hand, whether a tradition can live with, and within, a system. By "system" in the case of a Judaism, I mean a coherent and cogent statement of a world view, way of life, addressed to a well-defined "Israel." A systemic statement will be not a composite – a kind of necklace of discrete gems, strung together in whatever overall order makes sense, but a tapestry, in which discrete threads lose their separate existence and join to form a single well-crafted composition, proportioned and purposive, beginning to end.

The case at hand involves the Bavli, which as we shall see, is made up not of a conglomerate of diverse sources transformed into a single source, but comprises an essentially independent construction, one that stands upon its own ground and takes its own position. The Bavli's statement is framed in a balance and proportion of its own, and so issues its own distinctive statement. The Judaic system of the dual Torah certainly recognizes a corpus of authoritative writings. But that corpus as we now have it does not merely state or represent a composite tradition formed out of prior and unreworked sources. As we shall see, the Bavli does not fall into the classification formed by books that take over from the precedecessors' materials to be handed on to equally reverential imitator-continuators. The Bavli therefore does not take its place as part of a traditional literature, each of the documents of which stand in close relationship with its neighbors, fore and aft, each borrowing from its predecessor, handing on to its successor, a nourishing tradition. The Bavli's authorship makes its own statement in its own way, occasionally utilizing received materials, but not bound to follow their program. The Bavli follows its own logic, pursues its own program, and makes of whatever it receives out of earlier documents whatever its own authorship has chosen to make: a system, not a mere stage in a sedimentary and incremental tradition. How to show that that is the fact?

II.   The Bavli as Tradition or System

Asking, in a concrete and particular instance, whether a system of applied reason and sustained, rigorous rational inquiry can coexist with a process of tradition, I argue that it cannot. So far as a process of tradition takes over the formation of a cogent and sustained statement, considerations extraneous to rational inquiry, decided, not demonstrated facts – these take over and divert the inexorable processes of applied reason from their natural and logically necessary course. And the opposite is also the case. Where a cogent statement forms the object of discourse, syllogistic argument and the syntax of sustained thought dominate, obliterating the marks of a sedimentary order of formation in favor of the single and final, systematic one. So far as an authorship proposes to present an account of a system, it will pay slight attention to preserving the indicators of the origins of the detritus of historical tradition, of which, as a matter of fact, the systemic statement itself may well be composed.

The metaphor selected by Judaism for the Bavli's components is *massekhet*, which means, tractate, a metaphor drawn from textile weaving. The threads of the textile or tapestry serve the artist's vision; the artist does not weave so that the threads show up one by one. The weavers of a tractate of the Bavli, as we shall see, make ample use of available yarn. But they weave their own tapestry of thought. And it is their vision and not the character of the threads in hand that dictate the proportions and message of the tapestry. In that same way, so far as processes of thought of a sustained and rigorous character yield writing that makes a single, cogent statement, tradition and system cannot form a compatible unit. Where reason governs, it reigns supreme and alone, revising the received materials and, through its own powerful and rigorous logic, restating into a compelling statement the entirety of the prior heritage of information and thought.

At stake in the literary analysis therefore is a hypothesis concerning culture and intellect. Specifically, I contrast thought received as truth transmitted through a process of tradition against thought derived from active rationality by asking a simple question: does what is the most rigorously rational and compelling statement of applied reason known to me, the Talmud of Babylonia or Bavli, constitute a tradition and derive from a process of traditional formulation and transmission of an intellectual heritage, facts and thought alike? Or does that document make a statement of its own, cogent and defined within the requirements of an inner logic, proportion, and structure, imposing that essentially autonomous vision upon whatever materials its authorship has received from the past? We shall know the answer through a sequence of simple tests, which concern the framing of the program of inquiry and the character of the sustained discourse of the Bavli. Specifically, if I can show that in literary terms the Bavli is not traditional, formed out of the increment of received materials, the form of the reception of which governs, but – in the sense now implied – systemic, that is, again in literary terms orderly, systematic, laid out in a proportion and order dictated by the inner logic of a topic or generative problem and – and therefore – authoritative by reason of its own rigorous judgment of issues of rationality and compelling logic, then I can offer a reasonable hypothesis resting on facts of literature. I can contribute a considerable example to the debate on whether tradition may coexist with the practical and applied reason of utter, uncompromising logical rationality and compelling, autonomous order.

Since, quite clearly, I use tradition in a literary sense, as referring to a process by which writings of one kind and not another take shape, let me then define what I mean by tradition and place into the context of Judaism the issue I have framed, to begin with, in such general terms. For if any noun follows the adjective, "Rabbinic," it is not "Judaism" but "tradition." And by "tradition" people mean two contradictory things.

First, when people speak of "tradition," they refer to the formative history of a piece of writing, specifically, an incremental and linear process that step by step transmits out of the past an essential and unchanging fundament of truth *preserved in writing*, by stages, with what one generation has contributed covered by the increment of the next in a sedimentary process, producing a literature that, because of its traditional history as the outcome of a linear and stage by stage process, exercises authority over future generations and therefore is nurtured for the future. In that sense, tradition is supposed to describe a *process* or a chain of transmission of received materials, refined and corrected but handed on not only unimpaired, but essentially intact. The opening sentence of tractate Avot, "Moses received Torah from Sinai and handed it on to Joshua," bears the implication of such a literary process, though, self-evidently, the remainder of that chapter hardly illustrates the type of process alleged at the outset.

The second meaning of tradition bears not upon process but upon content and structure. People sometimes use the word tradition to mean a fixed and unchanging essence deriving from an indeterminate past, a truth bearing its own stigmata of authority, e.g., from God at Sinai.

These two meanings of the same word coexist. But they are incompatible. For the first of the two places a document within an on-going, determinate historical process, the latter speaks of a single statement at the end of an indeterminate and undefined process, which can encompass revelation of a one-time sort. In this book I use only the first of the two meanings. When, therefore, I ask whether or not the Bavli is a traditional document, I want to know whether the present literary character of the Bavli suggsts to us that the document emerges from a sedimentary process of tradition in the sense just now specified: an incremental, linear development, step by step, of law and theology from one generation to the next, coming to expression in documents arrayed in sequence, first to last. The alternative is that the Bavli originates as a cogent and proportioned statement through a process we may compare – continuing our geological metaphor – to the way in which igneous rock takes shape: through a grand eruption, all at once, then coalescence and solidification essentially forthwith. Either the Bavli will emerge in a series of layers, or it will appear to have formed suddenly, in a work of supererogatory and imposed rationality, all at once, perfect in its ultimate logic and structure.

When – it must follow – I maintain that the Bavli is not a traditional document, I issue a judgment as to its character viewed as literature in relationship to prior extant writings. Everyone of course must concur that, in a theological sense, the Bavli is a profoundly traditional document, laying forth in its authorship's terms and language the nature of the Judaic tradition, that is, Judaism, as that authorship wishes to read the tradition and have it read. But this second sense will not recur in what follows. In framing the issue of tradition versus system, I sidestep a current view of the literature of formative Judaism. That view, specified presently, ignores the documentary character of each of the writings, viewing them all as essentially one and uniform, lacking all documentary definition. In a variety of studies I have argued precisely the opposite. Before proceeding, let me allude to these prior works, which come to conclusion in this last statement of the matter as I see it after fifteen years of study.

III.   The State of the Question in Prior Research

I began in 1972 with the Mishnah and the Tosefta, at first seeing them as Mishnah-Tosefta, only later on understanding that they are essentially distinct statements, each with its tasks and purpose. My *History of the Mishnaic Law* (Leiden, 1974-1986) in forty-three volumes, and associated studies worked on that matter, yielding *Judaism: The Evidence of the Mishnah* (Chicago: University of Chicago Press, 1981). Subsequent studies of the Yerushalmi, The Fathers According to Rabbi Nathan, Genesis Rabbah, Leviticus Rabbah, Pesiqta de Rab Kahana, Pesiqta Rabbati, and the Bavli, have shown me that each of these documents is subject to precise definition in its own terms, as to both rhetorical and logical plan and topical program. Three works provide a good picture of the basic argument and method worked out in a variety of monographs and books: *The Integrity of Leviticus Rabbah: The Problem of the Autonomy of a Rabbinic Document* (Chico: Scholars Press for Brown Judaic Studies, 1985), *Comparative Midrash: The Plan and Program of Genesis Rabbah and Leviticus Rabbah* (Atlanta: Scholars Press for Brown Judaic Studies, 1986), and *From Tradition to Imitation. The Plan and Program of Pesiqta deRab Kahana and Pesiqta Rabbati* (Atlanta: Scholars Press for Brown Judaic Studies, 1987). In two other works, I have applied the results to specific allegations concerning the character of that same literature deriving from Orthodox-Jewish literary critics, who see the whole as uniform and interchangeable, lacking all documentary specificity. The systematic reply to these approaches, which restate in literary terms the received theology of Judaism and its hermeneutic, is in these works: *Canon and Connection: Judaism and Intertextuality* (Lanham: University Press of America, 1987), which addresses the propositions on the character of the canonical writings of formative Judaism currently set forth by Shaye J. D. Cohen, Lawrence H., Schiffman, and Susan Handelman; and *Midrash and Literature: The Primacy of Documentary Discourse* (Atlanta: Scholars Press for Brown Judaic Studies, 1987), which addresses the characterization of Midrash-compilations deriving just now from James Kugel. In the concluding chapter of this book I go over some of the results of the former work. In all instances I lay forth sizable samples of the literature, and test the allegations of the Orthodox Jewish literary critics against that evidence. In my view the results prove somewhat one-sided, but, of course, the way forward lies through further dialogue on these interesting questions.

Now to the issue at hand. When I ask whether or not the documents of the Judaism of the dual Torah exhibit shared traits of logic, rhetoric, or topic that justify imputing to them not merely points of intersection or connection but continuities and commonalities, I do not ask an invented question. It is a position maintained by a sizable sector of those who revere the Torah and interpret it today. I shall show that, as a statement of the continuities of a traditional character, deriving from a long and incremental process of handing on materials from generation to generation and – more to the point – document to document – that position contradicts the evidence of the Bavli, which, we must remember, constitutes the single most authoritative canonical writing of Judaism. What I shall show in this book is a simple proposition.

The Judaism of the dual Torah knows not traditions to be recited and reviewed but merely sources,[1] to be honored always but to be used only when pertinent to a quite independent program of thought.

That is to say, to go over the first definition of tradition with which I commenced, the components of the Torah of that Judaism do not contribute equally and jointly to a single comprehensive statement, handed on from generation to generation *and from book to book,* all of them sources forming a tradition that constitutes the Torah. Each has a particular message and make a distinctive statement. Obviously, all fit together into a common statement, the Torah or Judaism. That fundamental theological conviction defines Judaism and cannot – and should not – give way before the mere testimony of literary evidence. But it is the fact that whatever traits join the whole of the rabbinic corpus together into the single Torah of Moses our Rabbi, revealed by God to Moses at Sinai, they are not literary traits of tradition.

In literary terms, the various rabbinic documents commonly (and, from a theological perspective, quite correctly) are commonly represented as not merely autonomous and individual statements, or even connected here and there through shared passages, but in fact as continuous and and interrelated developments, one out of its predecessor, in a long line of canonical writings (to Sinai). The Talmud of Babylonia, or Bavli, takes pride of place – in this picture of "the rabbinic tradition" – as the final and complete statement of that incremental, linear tradition, and so is ubiquitously described as "*the* tradition," par excellence. In this concluding monograph I shall demonstrate that, vis-à-vis its sources, the Bavli represents an essentially autonomous, fresh, and original statement of its own. How so?

Its authorship does not take over, rework, and repeat what it has received out of prior writings but makes its own statement, on its own program, in its own terms, and for its own purposes.

Every test I can devise for describing the relationship between the authorship of the Bavli and the prior and extant writings of the movement of which that authorship forms the climax and conclusion yields a single result. The authorship at hand does not pursue anyone else's program, except only that of the Mishnah. It does not receive and refine writings concluded elsewhere. It takes over a substantial heritage and reworks the whole into its own sustained and internally cogent statement – and that forms not the outcome of a process of sedimentary tradition but the opposite: systematic statement of a cogent and logical order, made up in its authorship's rhetoric, attaining comprehensibility through the syntax of its authorship's logic, reviewing a received topical program in terms of the problematic and interests defined by its authorship's

---

[1]And I should imagine that, when work on the traditions used by the Bavli's authorship makes solid progress, we shall have good reason to say the same of the Bavli's authorship's approach to traditions as much as to sources.

larger purposes and proposed message. The samples of the Bavli we shall review constitute either composites of sustained, essentially syllogistic discourse, in which case they form the whole and comprehensive statement of a system, or increments of exegetical accumulation, in which case they constitute restatements, with minor improvements, of a continuous tradition. In my view, the reader is going to review sustained, directed, purposive syllogistic discourse, not wandering and essentially agglutinative collections of observations on this and that, made we know not when, for a purpose we cannot say, to an audience we can scarcely imagine, so as to deliver a message that, all together and in the aggregate, we cannot begin to recapitulate. But it is for the reader to judge the evidence.

True, the authorship of the Bavli drew upon a sizable corpus of materials indeterminate character and substance, which we assuredly do classify as traditions handed on from their predecessors. Hence the authorship of the Bavli made use of both sources, completed documents, and also traditions, transmitted sayings and stories, ordinarily of modest proportions, not subjected to ultimate redaction. But the authorship of the Bavli did whatever it wished with these materials to carry out its own program and to make its own prevailing statement. These received materials, undeniably formulated and transmitted in a process of tradition, have been so reworked and revised by the penultimate and ultimate authorship that their original character does not define the syntax of argument and the processes of syllogistic discourse, except by way of supplying facts for someone else's case. Whether or not we can still discern traces of received statements, even in wordings that point to an origin other than with or authorship, is beside the point. Proof of my case does not derive from the failure or success of scholars to identify the passages of the Bavli that antedate the penultimate or ultimate work of composition.

To be sure, I regard as ultimately unsuccessful the convoluted effort by such scholars as David Weiss Halivni, in his *Sources and Traditions*,[2] to tell us not only the original form but also the later (by them utterly undocumented) literary history, of these unredacted sayings. Endless speculation on what may have been masks the simple fact that we do not know what was. But that is not much to the point anyhow. The point is what we have, not what we do not have, and we have the Bavli to tell us about the work of the penultimate and ultimate authorship of the Bavli. That suffices. The facts are what they are.

In its final, literary context defined by the documents or sources we can identify, the Bavli emerges as anything but the seal of "tradition" in the familiar sense. For it is not based on distinct and completed sources handed on from time immemorial, subserviently cited and glossed by its own authorship, and it does not focus upon the systematic representation of the materials of prior documents, faithfully copied and rehearsed and represented. We have, of course, to exclude

---

[2]Referred to in Chapter One.

the Mishnah, but this fundamental document is treated by the authorship of the Bavli in a wholly independent spirit, as I shall demonstrate. The upshot is that the Bavli does not derive from a process of tradition in the first sense stated above, although, as a faithful and practicing Jew, I believe that the Bavli truly constitutes "tradition" in that second, theological sense to which I referred: a new statement of its own making and a fresh address to issues of its own choosing. But as I shall now show, the *literary* character of the process that created the Bavli is irrelevant to the demonstration of that *theological* proposition, which derives its proof from the entire history of Judaism from the Bavli onward. Viewed as literature, the Bavli is not a traditional document at all. It is not the result of an incremental and linear process; it does not review and restate what others have already said; its authorship does not regard itself as bound to the program and issues received from prior ages. The Bavli constitutes a systemic and not a traditional statement.

IV. The Literary Context of Judaic Tradition

The premise of this inquiry is simple. The Talmud of Babylonia, or Bavli, draws upon prior materials. The document in no way was not made up out of whole cloth by its penultimate and ultimate authorship, the generations that drew the whole together and placed it into the form in which it has come down from the seventh century to the present day. The Bavli's authorship both received out of the past a corpus of *sources*, and also stood in a line of *traditions* of sayings and stories, that is, fixed wordings of thought the formulation and transmission of which took place not in completed documents but in ad hoc and brief sentences or little narratives. These materials, deriving from an indeterminate past through a now-inaccessible process of literary history, constitute traditions in the sense defined in the preface: an incremental and linear process that step by step transmits out of the past an essential and unchanging fundament of truth and writing.

Traditions: some of these prior materials never reached redaction in a distinct document and come down as sherds and remnants within the Bavli itself. These are the ones that may be called traditions, in the sense of materials formulated and transmitted from one generation to the next, but not given a place in a document of their own.

Sources: others had themselves reached closure prior to the work on the Bavli and are readily identified as autonomous writings. Scripture, to take an obvious example, the Mishnah, tractate Abot (the Fathers), the Tosefta (so we commonly suppose), Sifra, Sifré to Numbers, Sifré to Deuteronomy, Genesis Rabbah, Leviticus Rabbah, the Fathers according to Rabbi Nathan, Pesiqta deRab Kahana, Pesiqta Rabbati, possibly Lamentations Rabbah, not to mention the Siddur and Mahzor (order of daily and holy day prayer, respectively), and various other writings had assuredly concluded their processes of formation before the Bavli's authorship accomplished their work. These we call *sources* – more or less completed writings.

The Bavli supposedly draws upon and reshapes available ideas and reworks them into a definitive statement, hence turns sources into a tradition. To test that claim I have devised a simple experiment.

If the authorship at hand resorts to prior writings and presents us with what is at its foundations a systematic and comprehensive summary and restatement of them, then the Bavli will take up an honorable position at the end of a long process of tradition.

But if we find that the authorship of the Bavli follows an essentially independent and fresh program of its own, then the Bavli will prove to have inaugurated a tradition but not to have received and transmited one. It will follow that, for the Judaism of the dual Torah, holy scripture, authoritative sources whether preserved orally or in writing, as such play no categorical role whatsoever.

The Bavli will then constitute an independent and fresh statement of its own authorship, not a restatement of what its authorship has received from prior generations, and assuredly not a statement of a cumulative and incremental tradition. The Bavli, rather, will come forth as a statement that in time to come, beyond its redaction, would *become* traditional, but for reasons not related to its own literary let alone theological and legal traits. That set of choices explains the interest and importance of determining the relationship between the Bavli and the extant sources of the Judaism of the dual Torah that reached closure prior to the Bavli.

To state the result that, in highly graphic form, the reader is about to survey: the Bavli is mostly the work of its own authorship, acting independently on its singular program of Mishnah-exegesis and amplification, alongside its distinctive program of Scripture-exegesis and amplification, both programs demonstrably unique to that authorship alone so far as extant sources and documents indicate for our sample. In the Bavli-sample at hand we look in vain for large tractates or even sizable units of discourse that refer to, or depend upon, the plan and program of prior documents. When, moreover, we survey how earlier authorships dealt with the same materials – [1] the Mishnah-chapter before us, and [2] an important set of verses of Scripture pertinent to the theme of the tractate – we come up with a single and uniform result. Our sample of Bavli tractate Sukkah will show us this fact:

What earlier authorships wished to investigate in the Mishnah, the points they wished to prove by reference to verses of Scripture important in our tractate – these have little or nothing in common with the points of special concern systematically worked out by the authorship of the Bavli. The Bavli's authorship at ca. 600 approaches Mishnah-exegesis with a program distinct from that of the Yerushalmi's authorship of ca. 400, and the Bavli's authorship reads a critical verse of Scripture within a set of considerations entirely separate from those of interest to the authorships of Leviticus Rabbah and Pesiqta de Rab Kahana of ca. 450 and 500. Any notion that the Bavli's authorship has taken as its principal task the restatement of received ideas on the Mishnah-topics and Scripture-verses at hand derives no support to speak of from the sample we shall examine.

That finding, alas, will contradict familiar and much-cherished convictions concerning the character of the Bavli, and of Judaism, that is to say, the larger canonical corpus of which it forms a principal representative. Reaching the world of commonly held opinions in the the song, *Tradition,* that conviction leads us to expect the principal document of Judaism to say pretty much what had been said before, and, many would add, beginning at Sinai. That corpus is held to form a continuous statement, beginning in an earlier writing, standing behind, generating, and therefore continuing in a later one. Consequently, the corpus is called "traditional," in the sense that one document leads to the next, and all of the documents come to their climax and conclusion in the final one of late antiquity. To the documents of the Torah – oral and written – is imputed not only the status of tradition in the sense just now defined but also a relationship of continuity which we may call imputed canonicity, so that, we are told, we may freely cite a passage from one document alongside a counterpart from another, treating them as part of a single – hence, continuous statement, and, in theological terms, one might say, canonical one, though our issue is not to be confused with canonical research. And that claim for the Bavli and the literature prior to it of *traditionality* bears with it not merely theological, but literary implications about the nature of the documents and the correct way of reading them. Because of those implications as to literature we can test the claim at hand and ask whether it indeed so describes the documents as to find substantiation in literary facts.

It is, therefore, legitimate to ask whether the Torah – that is, the tradition formed out of prior sources of Judaism – constitutes a cumulative tradition. And it is correct to answer that question by assessing the traits of continuity that join document to document – so it is alleged – in a single textual community, one formed out of a long process of formulation and transmission in a continuous relationship of tradition, hence, in an exact sense, a traditional literature.

I therefore want to know whether and how – again, in concrete, literary terms – a document makes its part of such a traditional statement, speaking, for its particular subject, in behalf of the entirety of the antecedent writings of the Judaic system at hand and standing in a relationship of continuity – not merely connection – with other such writings.

How, in other words, does the authorship of a corpus of writings that unfold on after another take up sources and turn them from traditions into a systematic and cogent statement. I ask the question in the case of a given topic. To answer the question, for obvious reasons I turn to the document universally assigned canonical and official status in Judaism from antiquity to the present day, the Talmud of Babylonia. In the centuries beyond the closure of the Bavli in ca. A.D. 600, people would universally turn to the Bavli as the starting point for all inquiry into any given topic, and rightly so. Since the Bavli made the first and enduringly definitive statement, we impute to the Bavli canonical status. If, therefore, we wish to ask about how a variety of sources turned into a tradition, that is to say, about the status as statements of a continuous tradition of documents of the formative age of the Judaism of the dual Torah, we shall inquire into the standing of a Bavli-tractate as testimony on its subject within the larger continuous system of which it is reputed to form a principal part. What we want to know about that testimony therefore is how the Bavli relates to prior documents. The reason is that we want to know whether or not the Bavli constitutes a statement of a set of such antecedent sources, therefore a step in an unfolding tradition, so Judaism constitutes a traditional religion, the result of a long sedimentary process. As is clear, the alternative and complementary issue is whether or not the Bavli makes its own statement and hence inaugurates a "new tradition" altogether (in that theological sense of tradition I introduced in the preface). In this case the Judaism defined by the Bavli is not traditional and the result of a sedimentary process but the very opposite: fresh, inventive, responsive to age succeeding age.

I take up a Bavli tractate specifically because, on any given topic, a tractate of the Bavli presents the final and authoritative statement that would emerge from the formative period of the Judaism of the dual Torah. That statement constituted not only an authoritative, but also an encompassing and complete account. That is what I mean by the making of a traditional statement on a subject: transforming in particular the received materials – whatever lay at hand – into a not merely cogent, but fixed and authoritative statement. What I wish to find out is the canonical status of the Bavli, insofar as the authorship of the Bavli transformed its antecedents, its sources, into traditions: the way things had been, are and must continue to be, in any given aspect of the life and world-view of Israel, the Jewish people, as the Bavli's authorship understood the composition of that Israel. Accordingly, I mean to investigate how a principal authorship in Judaism has taken up whatever sources it had in hand and transformed them into the tradition of Judaism: the canonical statement, on a given subject, that would endure.

V. The Literary Corpus and its Cogency: Criteria of Systemic Composition

How will I know whether we deal with a traditional or systemic statement? Let me set forth the issue of cogency as a principal criterion for *traditionality* as I here frame that issue in literary terms. Do we have a collection of books that happen to make, each its own particular statement? Or do the books form a cogent and whole statement all together? If the former, then "the tradition" – so to speak – *begins* with each book and its authorship. If the latter, then we may speak of sources which do accumulate, in a continuous process of transmission, and which do comprise and constitute an incremental and linear tradition. That is, we may really claim to discover, describe, analyze and interpret "the (ancient, on-going, linear) tradition." That is why I identify as a principal criterion for traditionality the matter of cogency from book to book – attested not through mere collusion of conceptions but concrete intersection of specific formulations, the material and verbally demonstrable interplay of unfolding conceptions formulated in the same language. That criterion marks an important way to test the hypothesis of traditionality imputed to the writings of the rabbinic corpus. In this context, one may even invoke the notion of canon, in the sense of a theologically-recognized body of writings deemed (if only after the fact) to make a single, correct statement. But not canonicity but rather traditionality in the literary sense now fully spelled out, is the issue here.

Since all inquiry – however aimed at a theoretical result – begins with some one document and its material traits, I conduct a simple, empirical experiment. The specific research problem of this book – to come down to earth – is how the Bavli (the Talmud of Babylonia), as exemplified in one tractate, relates to its sources, by which I mean, materials it shares with other and (by definition) earlier-redacted documents. The question that defines the problem is how the Bavli has formed of available writings (redacted in documents now in hand) a single, cogent, and coherent statement presented by the Bavli's authorship as summary and authoritative: a canonical statement on a given subject. In what ways does a Bavli-tractate frame such a (theologically-canonical) statement out of what (as attested in extant writings) its authorship has in hand?

The result of pursuing these questions should yield the answer to yet another: can we discern within the Bavli's treatment of a subject documentary traits of *traditionality*, that is, laying down a summary, final and experienced judgment for all time? And can we see within the Bavli elements of a program to turn sources into a single tradition, on a given topic? When I can answer that program of questions, I can form a hypothesis, resting on literary facts, concerning the literary and doctrinal traditionality of a sample item within the rabbinic corpus of late antiquity. That is to say, I can frame a theory on – to state with emphasis: *how the Judaism of the dual Torah speaking through the Bavli in conclusion constituted of its received materials a whole and proportioned system – way of life, world-view, addressed to a defined Israel – and turned into a systemic statement, that is,* a statement of the tradition *handed down in and formed out of prior sources, a variety of available writings on any given subject.*

The question before us arises from the fact that that Judaic system – the Judaism of the dual Torah, as authoritatively stated by the Bavli – encompassed also extant and prior documents, making of the these diverse writings now more than a mere collection of books, but *a tradition formed out of prior sources,* that is (from the system's perspective) a single, whole, homogeneous, cogent and (therefore) authoritative statement. So a still more wide-ranging theoretical statement is in order. The matter may be expressed in a simple way. I discern three dimensions by which any document of that Judaism may be measured: autonomy, connection, continuity. As to *autonomy*: a book in the tradition formed out of prior sources at hand stands by itself, within its own covers. But, as to *connection*, that same book also relates to other books of the same tradition formed out of prior sources through specific connections, indicated by intrinsic traits of rhetoric, topic, and logic or by shared materials, common to a number of documents. And, as to *continuity*, it also forms part of an undifferentiated tradition formed out of prior sources, that is, the Torah, or (a) Judaism, through the dimension of complete continuity. Hence among those three dimensions, autonomy, connection, continuity, we now address the third. It follows that the Judaism of the dual Torah transformed a variety of writings from a literary *corpus* into a systemic theological-legal *tradition formed out of prior sources*. The problem of this book therefore is to take the first step toward the description of that Judaism. We begin by turning to the authoritative literature and asking where and how that literature exhibits internal traits of traditionality, I mean, coherence to a broad, systemic composition.

So far as traditionality constitutes a literary question concerning rules of how one writes a canonical document, giving the signals to the community that one's writing constitutes a final, authoritative statement, through inductive inquiry into relationships I should be able to answer that question and describe those rules: why this not that. That interest requires me to collect answers to questions deriving from these comparative inquiries, and at the end we shall revert to these same questions:

1. *The topical program* of prior writings on the subject as compared to the topical program of the Bavli on the same subject, with attention to questions such as these: does the Bavli follow the response to the Mishnah characteristic of the authorship of the Tosefta? the Sifra (or Sifré to Numbers or Sifré to Deuteronomy, where relevant) Does the Bavli follow the response to relevant passages of Scripture that have caught the attention of compilers of Midrash-exegeses in Genesis Rabbah, Leviticus Rabbah, Pesiqta deRab Kahana, and other documents generally thought to have come to closure prior to the Bavli?

2. *The Bavli's use or neglect of the available treatments ("sources") in the prior literature*: if the Bavli does make use of available materials, does it impose its own issues upon those materials or does it reproduce those materials as they occur elsewhere? Has the authorship of the Bavli carried forward issues important in prior writings, or has it simply announced and effected its own program of inquiry into the topic at hand?

3. *The traits of the Bavli's statement, that is, derivative and summary at the end, or essentially fresh and imputed retrospectively?* In consequence of the detailed examination of the Bavli's authorship's use of and response to available sources, how may we characterize the statement of the Bavl as a whole in

comparison to prior statements? And, since that statement is canonical by the definition of the entire history of Judaism, we ask about the upshot: the shape and character of a canonical statement on a given subject.

I have used different type faces to indicate what is unique to the Bavli and what is shared by the Bavli with prior writings. Regular type is what is unique; italics, for the Mishnah, and boldface type, for the Tosefta and other documents, are used. The acres of regular type present a landscape distinctive to the territory before us. The Bavli is a special place, with its own flora and fauna, a kind of Australia of Judaism.

VI.   The Bavli in Relationship to the Yerushalmi

Our first exercise requires us to ask whether the Bavli carries forward the exegetical program of the prior Talmud, the Talmud of the Land of Israel, which reached closure, it is commonly thought, two centuries before the completion of work on the Bavli. Since the Talmud of Babylonia constitutes the second of the two Talmuds devoted to Mishnah-exegesis, separated from the first by about two centuries, the Bavli by definition stands connected to two prior documents, the Mishnah and the Yerushalmi. But – also by definition – it stands autonomous of the entirety of the rabbinic canon. Why so? Because it can be, and usually is, studied entirely on its own, delivering its own message in its own terms. And – again by definition – the Bavli forms part of, and stands continuous with, "the one whole Torah of Moses, our rabbi." Accordingly, proponents of the document claim in its behalf a critical place within the canon of Judaism. So the Bavli forms part of a larger continuity of texts, all of them making their contribution to Judaism. Among the three dimensions by which we describe and analyze any document, in this case, the Bavli – autonomy, connection, continuity – however, it is the issue of connection that for the moment seizes and retains our attention – in this case, connection to the Yerushalmi.

To state the issue simply, if the Bavli carries forward the exegetical program of the Yerushalmi, repeating, refining, restating that received plan of Mishnah-commentary, then the Bavli stands in a traditional relationship to its predecessor, the Yerushalmi. A single, unbroken chain of tradition reaches into the Bavli. If, on the other hand, the authorship of the Bavli can be shown to have made its own decisions, worked out its own program, and so made a statement in its own behalf upon an entire, received heritage, the Bavli will emerge not as traditional in intent and execution but as systemic and singular. The document will stand not at the end of a long line of tradition, but at the outset of a fresh program entirely – and that despite the undeniable fact that the Bavli makes ample use of prior documents, particular Scripture and the Mishnah, as well as, in much less measure to be sure, the Tosefta. But use of what is in hand does not signify traditional intent and program, any more than a composer's working within the received canon of harmony or an artist's utilizing a familiar palette attests to traditionalism.

Since, as I said, the Bavli forms the second of the two Talmuds that undertake the systematic exegesis of Mishnah-tractates and the restatement, in encompassing terms, of the Torah's message on their respective topics, the Bavli's relationship to its predecessor provides indicative data. If we wish to assess the Bavli's use of prior sources, therefore, we ask first of all about the relationship of the Bavli to the Yerushalmi. With the issue clear, let me make the criteria concrete.

If we can demonstrate a systematic exercise of refinement, completion, summary, we may assign to the Bavli a position at the end of a sustained and continuous process of thought – tradition in the exact sense. It will stand to reason that, for the case at hand, the power of the Bavli to make what we stipulate to be the canonical statement on its topic derives from its character as a summary and conclusion. The Bavli will fall into the classification of a traditional document, one that encompasses a long past of thought and development of doctrine and law, topic by topic, problem by problem.

If, on the other hand, the authorship of the Bavli has defined an essentially fresh and therefore original program of Mishnah-exegesis, we shall have to see the Bavli as an original statement of an essentially fresh system. We shall then close off the possibility that a corpus of writings yields as its canonical statement a conclusion that encompasses and harmonizes the whole of an antecedent body of writings, joining each of its extant elements into a single cogent statement. The Bavli will then turn out to have made a statement not of tradition, deriving from prior sources, but of a system of its own, based upon a wholly autonomous act of intellect and reflection. In that sense the choice – as well as I can phrase it in two words – is tradition or system.

Let me now specify the operative question and the criteria for answering it:

Does the Bavli carry forward the exegetical program of the Yerushalmi?

Or does the authorship of the Bavli invent its own, altogether singular and distinctive topical-exegetical program for the same chapter of the Mishnah?

A comparison of the two documents will allow us to settle at the outset a number of important questions. These concern the relationships of connection between the Bavli and prior writings. For what we shall now see is that the Bavli is autonomous, singular, distinctive. Its authorship delivers its message in a way that is its own and works out an exegetical program, on precisely the same chapter of the Mishnah, that is particular to itself, not dictated by the prior Talmud's treatment of the same materials. It therefore is in substantial measure distinct from the other Talmud. The Bavli is far more than a secondary development of the Yerushalmi.

We need hardly dwell on the simple fact that both the Yerushalmi and the Bavli organize their materials as comments on Mishnah sentences or paragraphs. A further important but equally obvious fact is that the two compositions differ from all other documents of the rabbinic canon both in their focus – the

Mishnah – and in their mode of discourse. That is to say, Mishnah exegesis and expansion find their place, in the entire corpus of rabbinic writings of late antiquity, solely in the two Talmuds. What is shared between the two Talmuds and the remainder of the canon deals with Scripture exegesis, on the one side, and deeds and sayings of sages, on the other.

To give one simple example, while Leviticus Rabbah contains exegeses of Scripture found also in one or another of the two Talmuds, there is not a single passage of the Mishnah subjected, in Leviticus Rabbah, to modes of analysis commonplace in the two Talmuds, even though on rare occasion a Mishnah sentence or paragraph may find its way into Leviticus Rabbah. So the two Talmuds stand together as well as take up a position apart from the remainder of the canon. These two facts make the definitive points in common sufficiently clear so we may address the more difficult issue of whether and how the two Talmuds differ from one another, meaning, whether, where, and how the authorship of the Bavli has accepted the program of its predecessors and so given us the seal of tradition, and when that authorship has gone its own way and so given us its own systemic statement. That is what is now at stake.

To unpack and explore that issue, we shall entertain a series of propositions and examine evidence marshalled to test those propositions. We begin from the simplest point and move to the more complex and subtle ones. I can imagine no more obvious and self-evident point of entry than this: the two Talmuds not only treat the Mishnah paragraphs in the same order, they also say much the same thing about them. We take up the simplest proposition.

A. The two Talmuds say pretty much the same thing in the same words. The Bavli, coming later, depends upon and merely amplifies or augments the Yerushalmi.

or:

B. The two Talmuds treat the Mishnah paragraph in distinct and distinctive ways. They use different language to make their own points. Where they raise the same issue, it derives from the shared text, the Mishnah, and its logic. Both Talmuds respond to the Mishnah; the Bavli does not depend overall on a conventional program supplied by the Yerushalmi.

The modest sample at hand will decisively settle matters in favor of B. In what follows, I compare and contrast the exegetical program of the Yerushalmi, given in the left-hand column, against that of the Bavli, given in the right. I have given only a selection, but the result, for the chapter at hand, is uniform, and is given in my *Judaism: The Classical Statement. The Evidence of the Bavli* (Chicago: University of Chicago Press, 1986). My précis of each unit of discourse deals only with the issue at hand: what did the exegetes of the Mishnah paragraph wish to ask? Unless there is a clear reproduction of the same discussion in both Talmuds, I do not present the actual texts. The system of division and signification worked out in my translation of Yerushalmi as well as

Bavli Sukkah is followed throughout. It has the merit of consistent principles of division, so we are comparing passages that, in a single, consistent way, are identified as whole and complete. Where passages are congruent I indicate in the Bavli column by cf. and the Yerushalmi unit. Where they intersect, I indicate with an equal sign (=). I present the Mishnah-passages in italics.

Mishnah-Tractate Sukkah
1:1A-F
A. *A sukkah that is taller than twenty cubits is invalid.*
B. *R. Judah declares it valid.*
C. *And one which is not ten handbreadths high,*
D. *one which does not have three walls,*
E. *or one, the light of which is greater than the shade of which,*
F. *is invalid.*

Yerushalmi	Bavli
I. Basis for Judah's dispute with rabbis: analogy to the Temple's dimensions. M. Er. 1:1.	I. Relationship of M. Suk. 1:1 to M. Er. 1:1: what differentiates sukkah from erub law. = Y. I.
II. Why sages regard a sukkah that is too tall as invalid.	II. Scriptural basis for position of sages at M. 1:1A. [cf. Y. I.]
III. Rab: A larger sukkah is valid even if it is very tall.	III. If sukkah roofing touches walls of sukkah, the sukkah may be higher than twenty cubits.
IV. Hoshaiah: If one builds an intervening floor, so diminishing the distance from roof to floor in part of a sukkah, what is the status of the space unaffected by the intervening floor?	IV. Dispute of Judah/sages + precedent supplied by T. Suk. 1:1A-E = Y. III.
V. If one lowered the sukkah roof by hanging garlands, does that lower the roof to less than the acceptable height?	V. Sukkah must hold person's head and greater part of his body. Discourse: M. Suk. 2:7.
VI. How do we know that air space ten handbreadths above the ground constitutes a domain distinct from the ground? M. Shab. 1:1.	VI. Who stands behind view that house not 4 x 4 cubits is not regarded as a house. = Y. II.
	VII. Diminishing the height of a sukkah by raising the floor. [cf. Y. IV.]

VII. Rabbi, Simeon, Judah: Sukkah must be given dimension in length, breadth, and must have four walls. Dispute.

VIII. Hiyya-Yohanan: Sukkah is valid if it has two walls of normal size and a third of negligible dimensions.

IX. A braided wall as a partition.

X. M. Kil. 4:4.

XI. Tips of laths that protrude from sukkah roofing are treated as part of the sukkah.

XII. Citation and discourse on M. 1:1E-F: If light is half and half, it is valid/invalid.

VIII. Diminishing the height of a sukkah by lowering the roof with hangings. = Y. V.

IX. Putting sukkah roofing on posts.

X. M. 1:1C: Scriptural basis for rule that sukkah less than ten handbreadths in height is invalid.

XI. Continues X.

XII. Continues X.

XIII. Sukkah has to have three walls, with the third of negligible [cf. Y. VIII] dimensions. = Y. VII-VIII.

XIV. Where does builder set the little wall?

XV. Continues foregoing.

XVI. M. 1:1E-F: definition of valid roofing = Y. XII.

XVII. Sukkah must be permanent, not temporary, in character. Various authorities who take that view.

XVIII. Continues XVII.

XIX. Two sukkah, one inside the other.

XX. Sukkah built for gentiles, women, cattle, Samaritans is valid, if the roofing is valid.

Before proceeding to the comparison of the two Talmud's treatment of the same passage, let us briefly review how, overall, each one has composed its materials.

Yerushalmi to M. Suk. 1:1A-F. The Yerushalmi provides a substantial discussion for each of the Mishnah's topical clauses in sequence, furthermore bringing together parallel rulings in other tractates to enrich the context for discussion. It would be difficult to point to a more satisfactory inquiry, on the part of either Talmud, into the Mishnah's principles and problems. Unit I takes up the noteworthy parallel between M. 1:1A and M. Er. 1:1A. The main point in both cases is the scriptural basis for the dimensions specified by the law. The effort to differentiate is equally necessary. Hence the difference between one sort of symbolic gateway and another, or between one wall built for a given purpose and another wall built for some other purpose, has to be specified. Unit II undertakes a complementary discourse of differentiation. It is now between a sukkah and a house. The two are comparable, since a person is supposed to dwell in a sukkah during the festival. Unit III, continuous with the foregoing, further takes up the specified measurement and explains it. Unit IV raises a difficult question, dealing with the theory, already adumbrated, that we extend the line of a wall or a roof or a cornice in such a way as to imagine that the line comes down to the ground or protrudes upward. At unit IV we seem to have a sukkah roofing at an angle, extending from the middle of a sukkah outwards, above the limit of twenty cubits. Unit V asks about lowering the sukkah roofing by suspending decorations from it or raising the sukkah floor by putting straw or pebbles on it. Both produce the effect of bringing the sukkah within the required dimensions of its height. Unit VI does not belong at all; it is primary at Y. Shab. 1:1. I assume it was deemed to supplement M. 1:1C. Unit VII takes up the matter of the required walls for the sukkah, M. 1:1D. Once again the scriptural basis for the rule is indicated. Unit VIII carries forward this same topic, now clarifying the theoretical problems in the same matter. At unit IX we deal with an odd kind of partition, a braid partition. This discussion is primary to Y. Er. 1:9 and is inserted here because of IX and X. The inclusion of unit X is inexplicable, except as it may form a continuous discourse with unit IX. It is primary at Y. Er. 1:8. Units XI and XII are placed where they are as discussions of M. 1:1E. But only unit XII takes up the exegesis of the Mishnah's language.

Bavli to M. Suk. 1:1A-F. The protracted Bavli passage serving M. 1:1A-F not only works its way through the Mishnah paragraph but systematically expands the law applicable to that paragraph by seeking out pertinent principles in parallel or contrasting cases of law. When a unit of discourse abandons the theme or principle connected to the Mishnah paragraph, it is to take up a secondary matter introduced by a unit of discourse that has focused on that theme or principle. Unit I begins with an analysis of the word choice at hand. At the same time it introduces an important point, M. Er. 1:1, namely, the comparison between the sukkah and a contraption erected also on a temporary basis and for symbolic purposes. Such a contraption is a symbolic gateway that transforms an alley entry into a gateway for a courtyard and so alters the status of the alley and the courtyards that open on to it, turning them into a single domain. As one domain, they are open for carrying on the Sabbath, at which time people may not carry objects from one domain (e.g., private) to another (e.g., public). That comparison is repeatedly invoked. Units II and III then move from language to scriptural sources for the law. Unit IV then stands in the same relationship to unit III, and so too unit V. Unit VI reverts to an issue of unit V. Thus the entire discussion, II-VI, flows out of the exegetical requirements of the opening lines of the Mishnah paragraph. But the designated unit-divisions seem to mark discussions that could have stood originally by themselves. Unit VII then reverts to the original topic, the requisite height of the sukkah (= Y. IV-V). It deals with a fresh problem, namely, artificially diminishing or increasing the height of the sukkah by alterations to the inside of the hut. One may raise the floor to diminish the height or lower the floor to increase it. Unit VIII pursues the same interest. It further introduces principles distinct from the Mishnah's rules but imposed upon the interpretation of those rules or the amplification of pertinent cases. This important exercise in secondary expansion of a rather simple rule through the introduction of fresh and rather engaging principles – "curved wall," fictional extension of walls upward or downward and the like – then proceeds in its own terms. Unit IX is continuous in its thematic interest with unit VIII. Unit X reverts to the Mishnah paragraph, now M. 1:1C, and asks the question usually raised at the outset about the scriptural authority behind the Mishnah's rule. This leads us into a sizable digression on scriptural exegesis, with special interest in establishing the analogy between utensils in the temple and dimensions pertinent to the sukkah. The underlying conception, that what the Israelite does on cultic occasions in the home responds to what is done in the cult in the temple, is familiar. Units XI and XII pursue the same line of thought. Then unit XIII reverts once more to the Mishnah's rule, M. 1:1D. Now we take up the issue of the walls of the sukkah. These must be three, in the rabbis' view, and four in Simeon's. Each party concedes that one of the requisite walls may be merely symbolic. The biblical source for the required number of walls forms the first object of inquiry. Unit XIV then takes up the symbolic wall. Unit XV reverts to a statement on Tannaite authority given in unit XIII. Subject to close study is a somewhat complicated notion. There are diverse kinds of sukkah buildings. One, we know, is a sukkah erected to carry out the religious duty of the festival. But a person may build a sukkah to extend the enclosed and private area of his home. If he places such a sukkah by the door, the area in which it is permitted to carry objects – private domain – covers not only the space of the house but also the space of the sukkah. That sukkah, erected in connection with Sabbath observance, is compared to the sukkah erected for purposes of keeping the festival. The issue is appropriate here, since the matter concerns the character of the walls of the sukkah built for Sabbath observance. Unit XVI then returns to the Mishnah paragraph. Unit XVIII moves back from the Mishnah's statements and deals with the general principle, taken by some parties, that the sukkah must bear the qualities of a permanent dwelling. That issue intersects with our Mishnah paragraph in connection with Judah's and Simeon's views on the requirement that there be a roof of a certain height and four walls. But the construction as a whole stands independent of the Mishnah paragraph and clearly was put together in its own terms. XVIII takes up XVII.M. Units XIX and XX evidently are miscellaneous – the only such units of discourse in the entire massive construction. I cannot point to a more thorough or satisfying sequence of Babylonian Talmudic units of discourse in which the Mishnah's statements are amplified than the amplifications themselves worked out on their own. The whole is thorough, beautifully articulated, and cogent until the very end.

Since, intersecting in topic and problematic, the Bavli goes over the ground of the Yerushalmi at several points, pursuing essentially the same problem, we have to ask about possible borrowing by the Bavli from the Yerushalmi, not of theses or conventions of interpretation but of whole constructions. To show the points of word-for-word correspondence such as they are, let us now consider side by side one suggestive item, Y. III = B. IV.

Y. 1:1

III

A. [As to the invalidity of a *sukkah* more than twenty cubits high,] R. Ba in the name of Rab: "That applies to a *sukkah* that will hold only the head and the greater part of the body of a person and also his table.

B. "But if it held more than that, it is valid [even at such a height]."

C. [Giving a different reason and qualification,] R. Jacob bar Aha in the name of R. Josiah: "That applies [further] when the walls do not go all the way up with it [to the top, the roofing] but if the walls go all the way up with it to the roofing, it is valid."

D. [Proving that C's reason, not A-B's, is valid, we cite the following:]

E. Lo, the following Tannaite teaching differs [in T.'s version]: Said R. Judah, "MSH B: The *sukkah* of Helene was twenty cubits tall, and sages went in and out, when visiting her, and not one of them said a thing."

F. They said to him, "It was because she is a woman, and a woman is not liable to keep the commandment of sitting in a *sukkah*."

G. He said to them, "Now did she not have seven sons who are disciples of sages, and all of them were dwelling in that same *sukkah!*" [T. Suk. 1:1].

B. 1:1

IV

A. [The specification of the cited authorities, II.A, C, E, on the minimum requirements of the *sukkah*, now comes under discussion in its own terms.] The following objection was raised:

B. A *sukkah* which is taller than twenty cubits is invalid.

C. R. Judah declares it valid [M. 1:1A-B], even up to forty or fifty cubits.

D. Said R. Judah, "M'SH B: The *sukkah* of Helene in Lud was twenty cubits tall, and sages went in and out, when visiting her, and not one of them said a thing."

E. They said to him, "It was because she is a woman, and a woman is not liable to keep the commandment of sitting in a *sukkah.*"

F. He said to them, "Now did she not have seven sons [who are disciples of sages, and all of them were dwelling in that same *sukkah*]" [T. Suk. 1:1A-E].

G. "And furthermore, everything she ever did was done in accord with the instruction of sages."

H. Now what need do I have for this additional reason: "Furthermore, everything she ever did was done in accord with the instructions of sages"?

H. Do you then have the possibility of claiming that the *sukkah* of Helene could not hold more than the head and the greater part of the body and the table of a person? [Surely, someone of her wealth would not build so niggardly a *sukkah*.]

I. Consequently, the operative reason is that the sides of the *sukkah* do not go all the way up [to the *sukkah* roofing at the top, leaving a space].

J. It stands to reason, then, that what R. Josiah has said is so.

K. [And the Tannaite teaching] does not differ [from sages' view], for it is the way of the rich to leave a small bit of the wall out beneath the *sukkah* roofing itself, so that cooling air may pass through.

I. This is the sense of what he said to them: "Now, if you say that the sons were minors, and minors are exempt from the religious duty of dwelling in the *sukkah*, since she had seven sons, it is not possible that among them was not a single one who no longer needed his mother's tending [and so would be required to dwell on his own in the *sukkah*]."

J. "And if, further, you should maintain that a minor who no longer needs his mother's tending is subject to the law only on the authority of rabbis, and that woman paid no attention to rules that rested only on the authority of the rabbis, come and note the following: 'And furthermore, everything she ever did was done in accord with the instructions of sages.'"

K. [We now revert to the issue with which we began, namely, the comparison of the story at hand to the reasons adduced by the authorities at unit III:] Now with reverence to the one who said, the dispute applies to a case in which the walls of the *sukkah* do not touch the *sukkah* roofing, would a queen dwell in a *sukkah*, the walls of which do not touch the *sukkah* roofing?

L. [3A] [Indeed so! The reason is that] the space makes possible good ventilation.

M. But in the view of the one who has said that the dispute pertains to a small *sukkah*, would a queen ever dwell in a small *sukkah*?

N. Said Rabbah bar R. Ada, "At issue in the dispute is solely a case of a *sukkah* which is made with many small cubbies."

O. But would a queen take up residence in a *sukkah* that was subdivided into many small cubbies?

P. Said R. Ashi, "At issue is only [a large *sukkah* which had] such recesses.

Q. "Rabbis take the view that the queen's sons were dwelling in a *sukkah* of absolutely valid traits, while she dwelled in the recesses on account of modesty [i.e., not showing her face among the men], and it was on that account that rabbis said nothing to her [about her dwelling in what was, in fact, an invalid part of the *sukkah*].

R. "And R. Judah maintains the position that her sons were dwelling along with her [in the cubbyholes of the *sukkah*], and even so, the rabbis did not criticize what she was doing [which proves that the small cubbies of the *sukkah* were valid]."

The issue of Y. III.A and B. IV.A is the same. Tosefta's precedent, marked in boldface, is used differently in each Talmud. In the Bavli it makes a point relevant to B. IV.A, the height of the sukkah. It is entirely relevant to the purpose for which it is adduced. The sukkah of the queen was high, so sustaining Judah's view. The secondary issue, IV.K, links the precedent to unit III. The whole is integrated and well composed. By contrast, the Yerushalmi's use of the precedent is odd. The passage is explicit as to the large size of the hut, so Y.III.H is somewhat jarring. It really contradicts Y. III.G. Y. III.I then revises matters to force the precedent to serve Y. III.C. We cannot imagine that Bavli's author has depended on Yerushalmi's composition. He has used the precedent for his own inquiry and in his own way. Where, therefore, Yerushalmi and Bavli share materials, the Bavli's use of those materials – if this case is suggestive – will *not* depend upon the Yerushalmi's. Both refer back to the Mishnah and to the Tosefta, responding to the former in terms (here) of the exegetical program precipitated by the contents available in the latter.

Mishnah-Tractate Sukkah

1:2

A. *[9B] He who makes his sukkah under a tree is as if he made it in [his] house.*

B. *A sukkah on top of a sukkah –*

C. *the one on top is valid.*

D. *And the one on the bottom is invalid.*

E. *R. Judah says, "If there are no residents in the top one, the bottom one is valid."*

Yerushalmi	Bavli
I. Clarification of M. 1:2B-D: How much space defines the separation of the two roofs, so that the upper one is deemed distinct and valid?	I. Clarification of M. 1:2A re character of the tree's foliage.
	II. Scriptural basis of M. 1:2B.
	III. Augmentation of M. 1:2B-D.
II. Clarification of M. 1:2E.	IV. Clarification of M. 1:2B-D: how much space [= Y. I].

Yerushalmi to M. Suk. 1:2. The point is that the roof of the sukkah must be exposed to the firmament and not made up, A, in large part by the boughs of the tree. D follows the same principle, now with reference to a sukkah covered by another. Judah's view is that, without residents, the upper sukkah does not constitute a dwelling, thus excluding A's consideration. Unit I clarifies M. 1:2B's notion of two sukkah roofs near one another by raising a problem independent of M. Unit II amplifies Judah's meaning, M. 1:3E.

Bavli to M. Suk. 1:2. The point is that the roof of the sukkah must be exposed to the firmament and not covered, I.A, in large part by the boughs of the tree. D follows the same principle, now with reference to a sukkah covered by another. Judah's view is that, without residents, the upper sukkah does not constitute a dwelling, thus excluding A's consideration. Unit I then clarifies M. 1:2A. But the real interest is the notion that if invalid and valid forms of sukkah roofing are intertwined, with a greater portion of valid, the whole is valid. That principle, not demanded by the Mishnah's rule, clarifies that rule. Unit II proceeds to the scriptural basis for M. 1:2B. Unit III focuses upon that same rule, making a point that the Talmud's anonymous voice itself calls self-evident. Unit IV clarifies a secondary question – the relationship of the two sukkah constructions, upper and lower – but in so doing also invokes M. 1:2E. Since Y. I and B. IV go over exactly the same question, we shall once more compare the two units of discourse side by side to see how, if at all, they relate:

Yerushalmi	Bavli
I	IV
A. In the case of two sukkah roofs, one on top of the other, in which the upper roofing was such that the light was greater than the shade [and hence invalid], while the lower one was such that the light was not greater than the shade on its own, but, together with the other roof, the shade was greater than the light –	A. And how much space would there be between one sukkah and the other so that the lower sukkah would be invalid [as a sukkah beneath a sukkah]?
	B. Said R. Huna, "A handbreadth. [If the space between the upper-sukkah roofing and the lower-sukkah roofing is less than a handbreadth, the two sets of

B. What is the maximum of space that may be between the two roofs so that they should be deemed joined together [into a single sukkah roofing, hence a valid one for the sukkah beneath]?

C. There were two Amoras. One said, "Ten cubits," and the other said, "Four."

D. The one who maintained that ten cubits distance are permissible objected to the one who said that only four are permissible, "If it is because of the principle of forming a tent [that you want the two so close together], we find that a tent may be no more than a handbreadth [in its principal dimensions, hence also height]. [So you permit too broad a space between the two roofs.]"

roofing are regarded as one. [Then we do not have a case of one sukkah beneath another sukkah at all.]"

C. [Huna continues,] "For so we find that the handbreadth is the standard measure in connection with cases of overshadowing of corpse uncleanness, for we have learned in the Mishnah: *A handbreadth of space by a handbreadth at the height of a handbreadth brings uncleanness [should it be left open in a partition between corpse matter in one otherwise closed room and another such room] or interposes against the passage of the same uncleanness [if such a space is closed off], but a space less than a handbreadth in height neither brings uncleanness [if open] nor interposes [if closed]* [M. Oh. 3:7]. [The operative measure is a handbreadth. If the roof is higher than that distance, it is deemed a separate roof, and if it is lower, it is deemed part of the contained space]."

D. R. Hisda and Rabbah bar R. Huna say, "Four [handbreadths], for we do not find a contained space taken into account if it is less than four handbreadths."

E. And Samuel said, "Ten."

F. What is the reason for the view of Samuel? The requisite measure for rendering the sukkah valid [ten handbreadths above the ground] also operates to render it invalid.

G. Just as the requisite measure of height is ten handbreadths, so the distance that will invalidate likewise is ten handbreadths.

H. [Arguing to the contrary conclusion on the basis of the same principle as F:] We have learned in the Mishnah: *R. Judah says, "If there are no residents in the top one, the bottom one is valid"* [M. 1:2E].

I. What is the sense of "If there are

no residents...valid"?

J. If it is in concrete terms, that is, if the issue is that there really are no occupants, is this the governing criterion? [It is a random fact.]

K. But rather is not the sense of there being no residents to mean, any [upper] sukkah which is not suitable for a dwelling [would leave the lower sukkah valid]?

L. What would be an example of such a case? One which was not ten handbreadths in height.

M. Would this then bear the implication that, in the view of the first [anonymous] authority [vis-à-vis Judah], even one which is not suitable for dwelling [would leave the lower sukkah] invalid? [This would then refute Samuel's position, above].

N. When R. Dimi came, he said, "In the West they say, If the lower [sukkah's roof] cannot hold the weight of the pillows and blankets of the upper one, the lower one is valid. [The upper sukkah then is not sufficiently strong. Its floor, the roof of the lower sukkah, cannot carry the weight.]"

O. Does this then bear the implication that the first of the two authorities takes the view that even if the [lower sukkah] is not suitable to bear [the weight of the upper, the lower one] is invalid?

P. At issue between [Judah and the first authority] is the case of a [lower] sukkah, the floor-roof of which can bear the weight of the upper sukkah only with difficulty.

There is no reason to belabor the obvious. Once more, when the two Talmuds wish to deal with the same issue, the overlap is in conception; but there is no point of verbal contact, let alone of intersection. Each Talmud undertakes its own analysis in its own way. Each Talmud bases its discussion on the common source (the Mishnah, sometimes also the Tosefta), but each one builds its discussion on the basis of points made by its selection of authorities and pursues matters in terms of its own established conventions of rhetoric. The

Bavli has not taken as its task the citation and gloss of the Yerushalmi's treatment of the Mishnah-paragraph before us. Quite to the contrary, the Bavli's authorship has made its own statement, without merely repeating whatever received materials the Yerushalmi's authorship has left as its legacy.

Mishnah-Tractate Sukkah

1:4

A. *[If] one trained a vine, gourd, or ivy over it and then spread sukkah roofing on [one of these], it is invalid.*

B. *But if the sukkah roofing exceeded them,*

C. *or if one cut them [the vines] down,*

D. *it is valid.*

E. *This is the general rule:*

F. *Whatever is susceptible to uncleanness and does not grow from the ground – they do not make sukkah roofing with it.*

G. *And whatever is not susceptible to uncleanness, but does grow from the ground [and has been cut off] – they do make sukkah roofing with it.*

Yerushalmi	Bavli
I. Clarification of M. 1:4C.	I. Clarification of M. 1:4C-D.
II. Illustration of M. 1:4F-G.	II. Expansion on foregoing, with attention to M. 1:4A.
III. Exegetical foundations for M. 1:4E-G about the status, as to cleanness, of what may be used for sukkah roofing.	III. Exegetical foundations for M. 1:4F-G.
	IV. Continuation of foregoing.
	V. Continuation of foregoing.

Yerushalmi to M. 1:4. Unit I complements the rule of M. 1:4A-D. Units II and III take up M. 1:4F-G, what may be used in sukkah roofing. Unit II provides some facts, and unit III, exegetical foundations for M.'s principle.

Bavli to M. 1:4. The Bavli's elaborate discussion, units I-II, accomplishes two things. First, it raises the question of the procedure to be followed in connection with M. 1:4C. Second, it introduces the underlying principle at issue whether the mere act of cutting down the vines also serves to render them suitable for the specific purpose of use as sukkah roofing, or whether some distinct act of designation, thus preparation, is required. The former view is worked out in unit I. Unit II then produces a striking analogy in which a quite different case – making strings into show fringes – is shown to invoke upon the same principle, namely, whether a mere act of destruction – cutting the vines, severing the string – suffices, or whether a clear-cut deed of deliberate and positive validation also is required. It is clear that the issue of show fringes need not involve the matter of the vines for sukkah roofing, but unit II makes a strong argument that the two cases must be worked out in tandem. Units III-V then present the familiar exercise of locating scriptural proof for a Mishnaic proposition.

Because Y. III and B. IV-VI not only go over the same problem, namely, discovering exegetical foundations for the Mishnah's rule, but also resort to the same antecedent materials in constructing their discussions, we have yet again to compare the two compositions side by side.

Yerushalmi

III

A. Said R. Yohanan, "It is written, 'You shall keep the feast of booths seven days, when you make your ingathering from your threshing floor and your wine press' (Deut. 16:13).

B. "From the refuse of your threshing floor and your wine press you may make sukkah roofing for yourself."

C. R. Simeon b. Laqish said, "'But a mist went up from the earth and watered the whole face of the ground' (Gen. 2:6). [The analogy of the covering of the sukkah is to mist, which arises from the ground and is not susceptible to receive uncleanness.]"

D. Said R. Tanhuma, "This one is consistent with opinions held elsewhere, and that one is consistent with opinions held elsewhere.

E. "R. Yohanan has said, 'The clouds came from above,' and so he derives the rule from the reference to 'your ingathering.'

F. "R. Simeon b. Laqish said, 'Clouds come from below,' so he derives the rule from clouds [of mist]."

G. Said R. Abin, "This party is consistent with opinions held elsewhere, and that one is consistent with opinions held elsewhere.

Bavli

III

A. *This is the general rule: Whatever is susceptible to uncleanness, etc.* [M. 1:4F-G]:

B. What is the scriptural basis for this rule?

C. Said R. Simeon b. Laqish, "Scripture has stated, 'And a mist went up from the earth' (Gen. 2:6).

D. "Just as mist is something which is not susceptible to uncleanness and grows from the ground, so a sukkah must be made of some thing which does not receive uncleanness and grows from the ground."

E. That explanation is suitable to the person who holds that the sukkah in which Israel dwelled in the wilderness was clouds of glory.

F. But in the view of him who holds that the sukkah was the genuine article which the Israelites actually made for themselves [and not an analogy to clouds of glory], what sort of proof may one bring?

G. The problem at hand accords with that which has been taught on Tannaite authority:

H. "'For I made the children of Israel dwell in sukkot' (Lev. 23:43), meaning in clouds of glory," the words of R. Eliezer.

H. "R. Yohanan compares the matter to one who sends his fellow a jug of wine, giving him the jug as well as the wine. [Along these same lines God gives the clouds along with the rain from heaven.]

I. "R. Simeon b. Laqish compares the matter to a priest, who said to his fellow, 'Send over your basket and take some grain for yourself.' [Clouds come from below, and God puts rain in them in heaven.]"

I. R. Aqiba says, "They were actually sukkot that people made for themselves."

J. Now [as just noted] the stated proof poses no problems to the view of R. Eliezer, but as to the position of R. Aqiba, what is there to say?

IV

A. When R. Dimi came, [he said that] R. Yohanan said, "Scripture has stated, 'The festal offering of Sukkot you shall prepare' (Deut. 16:13).

B. "The sukkah thus is compared to the festal offering [brought as an animal sacrifice on the festival day].

C. "Just as the festal offering is something that does not receive uncleanness [animals fed from what grows from the ground are, in Yohanan's view, as if they too grow from the ground] and also grows from the ground [as just now explained], so the sukkah must be made of something that does not receive uncleanness and grows from the ground."

D. [12A] But what if you wish to propose a further analogy, just as the festal offering is of an animate being, so the sukkah must be made of an animate being?

V

A. When Rabin came, he said that R. Yohanan said, "Scripture has stated, 'After you have gathered in from your threshing floor and from your winepress...' (Deut. 16:13). Scripture speaks of what is left on the threshing floor and the dregs of the winepress. [These grow from the ground and are not susceptible to uncleanness, so too the sukkah roofing, of which the verse at hand speaks, must conform to the same traits.]"

B. And may I say that Scripture

speaks of the threshing floor itself and the winepress itself? [Perhaps somehow the sukkah must be composed of these objects?]

C. Said R. Zira, "Here it is written, 'Winepress,' and it is hardly possible to make use of a winepress for sukkah roofing!"

D. To this explanation R. Jeremiah objected, "And might I speculate that what is required is use of congealed wine which comes from Senir, like fig cakes? [Perhaps the sense of Scripture is that that is what must be used for sukkah roofing!]"

E. Said R. Zira, "We had a valid proposition in hand, but R. Jeremiah came along and threw an ax at it [and smashed it]!"

F. R. Ashi said, "'From your threshing floor' and not the threshing floor itself, 'from your winepress' and not the winepress itself [is to be the source of materials used for sukkah roofing]."

G. R. Hisda said, "Proof for the desired proposition derives from here: 'Go forth to the mountain and collect olive branches, branches of wild olive, myrtle branches, palm branches, and branches of thick trees' (Neh. 8:15). [All of these are not susceptible to uncleanness and grow from the ground, and, in context, are specified for use as sukkah roofing]."

H. Myrtle branches fall into the category of branches of thick trees [of Lev. 23:40]. [Why specify the same species twice?]

I. Said R. Hisda, "The wild myrtle is for the sukkah roofing, and the branches of thick trees for the lulab."

The composition of the Yerushalmi is in two simple parts: first, the citation of Yohanan and Simeon b. Laqish; second, Tanhuma's and Abin's point that the two parties' explanations are coherent with things each says in another context. The contrast presented by the Bavli is stunning. Now we have an extended composition on Simeon b. Laqish's statement, given verbatim as it appears in the Yerushalmi. The Bavli's discussion, fully worked out in unit III, is totally its own. The interest of the framer is not in setting Yohanan up in a dispute with Simeon b. Laqish. Rather, he has chosen fully to analyze Simeon's proof and then to introduce an available composition on Tannaite authority, III.G-J. Yohanan is introduced on his own at unit IV. The proof is the same; but while the Yerushalmi suffices with a virtually unarticulated citation of proof-texts, the Bavli beautifully articulates what is at issue and then tests matters. In the presentation of Yohanan's proof, the Bavli's framer gives us two complete versions – one at unit IV, the other at unit V.

For our purposes one question now must be settled. Does the Bavli's compositor draw upon the Yerushalmi's version? The answer is decisively negative. The Bavli's author draws upon a shared tradition, known also to the Yerushalmi's writer, that associates Simeon b. Laqish with Gen. 2:6, Yohanan with Deut. 16:13, and both with the present Mishnah paragraph. If the author of the Bavli version had had access to the Yerushalmi's treatment of the matter, he would not have been much impressed, for the point of interest of the Yerushalmi's expansion – the consistency of the two authorities with positions held elsewhere – simply bears no relevance to Bavli's point of entry.

It remains to observe that the two Talmuds come into contact not only through shared access to the Mishnah and to the Tosefta as well as some materials of earlier Amoraic authorities. The two Talmuds meet also in what appears to be a common exegetical program on questions or principles that bear upon a given Mishnah paragraph. But that common program derives over and over again from the contents of the Mishnah paragraph at hand, that is, the principles of law implied by a given rule. It may emerge from the overall task that, linking the Mishnah to Scripture, formed the center of the hermeneutic labor of everyone who received the Mishnah and proposed to deal with it.

The Bavli and the Yerushalmi assuredly stand autonomous from one another. The authorship of the Bavli in its own way works out a singular and independent program of exegesis and amplification of the Mishnah. Word-for-word correspondences are few and, on the whole, peripheral. Where materials are shared, moreover, they derive from either the Mishnah or the Tosefta or some antecedent convention of exegesis.[3] But in all instances of shared language or

---

[3]We shall see the same phenomenon when in Chapter Five we ask how the Bavli intersects with Sifra, Leviticus Rabbah, and Pesiqta deRab Kahana. What we shall see is that all three present in common a treatment of Lev. 23:40, but that the Bavli's authorship in connection with that same verse has an utterly distinct set of questions, out of all relationship with the authorships of Sifra and of Leviticus Rabbah=Pesiqta deRab Kahana. The points in common, which are verbally identical in all the four documents, are minor and peripheral to the foci of each document's authorship. So where we do find intersections, we also uncover evidence of the essential autonomy of the several authorships.

conventional hermeneutics the framers of the Bavli worked things out on their own. They in no way accepted the Yerushalmi as a model for how they said things let alone for the bulk of what they said. What is shared, moreover, derives principally from the Mishnah. It comes, secondarily, from some sort of conventional program (partly encapsulated, also, in the Tosefta). The Tosefta has not dictated to the Bavli's authorship a topical or logical program, it has merely contributed occasional passages for systematic analysis, much as the Mishnah has contributed a much larger volume of passages for systematic analysis. In any event the Bavli's authors developed inherited intellectual conventions in a strikingly independent way. That fact leads us to see the Bavli's authorship's composition as an essentially autonomous statement, standing on its own, borrowing from prior compilations pretty much what suited its purpose – that alone.

On the other hand, the Bavli and the Yerushalmi most certainly do form a cogent part of a larger, continuous statement, that of "the one whole Torah of Moses, our rabbi" or, in modern theological language, a canon, that is, Judaism. That premise of all study of the canon of formative Judaism stands firm. Nothing we have reviewed leads us to doubt its validity for those documents. The particular aspect of continuity at hand, however, requires specification. How is the Bavli continuous with the Yerushalmi? *The Bavli meets the Yerushalmi in the Mishnah.* The two also come together, in markedly diminished measure, in the Tosefta and, still less, in some shared phrases deriving from post-Mishnaic authorities (e.g., those of the third-century masters Yohanan and Simeon b. Laqish). So in one specific way the two documents not only intersect but prove at one with one another and therefore continuous.

In somewhat more general ways, too, they wish to do much the same thing, which is to subject the Mishnah to a process of explanation and amplification. While the authors of the Bavli developed their own principles of hermeneutics, composition, and redaction, still, the upshot of their work, the Bavli as a whole, in the heavenly academy cannot have baffled their predecessors, who had earlier created the Yerushalmi. Apart from disagreements on tertiary details, the later of the two sets of authorities found themselves entirely at home in the conceptions, rhetoric, and documents created by their antecedent counterparts. That seems self-evident proof of the continuity of the Bavli with the Yerushalmi. If the two then turn out to be autonomous as well as continuous with one another, the real problem of nuance and differentiation is presented by matters of connection. These have forthwith to be divided into two parts: first, the connection of one document to the other; second, the connection of both documents to other components of the larger rabbinic canon. Here, once more, we find ourselves making self-evident observations.

To deal with the second question in summary fashion, the two documents are not only connected to one another but also stand essentially autonomous of the rest of the rabbinic canon, except (by definition) for the Mishnah and the

Tosefta, which they serve. How so? In various passages, as we have noticed, we find shared materials in the two Talmuds and a common program of logic and rhetoric. What is shared between them, however, rarely also finds a place in other components of the canon of ancient Judaism. That is to say, while the two Talmuds constantly quote and explain the Mishnah, no other rabbinic document takes so sustained an interest in the Mishnah, or, indeed, much interest at all. So in the rabbinic canon the Talmuds occupy a place entirely their own, secondary to and continuous with the Mishnah-Tosefta. That place turns out to be set apart from the remainder of the canon. Counterparts to the Talmuds' treatment of the Mishnah rarely appear in any other rabbinic composition. The exception to the rule will be Sifra and, to a lesser degree, the two Sifrés. These in places do go over the same matters in much the same way as do the two Talmuds. But the exception proves null when we realize that, where Sifra and the two Sifrés share sizable statements with the two Talmuds (severally or together), it is ordinarily a common interest in the scriptural foundations of a Mishnaic law or, to a markedly diminished degree, one of the Tosefta. So that is hardly an exception since both Talmuds and the exegetical compilations on Leviticus, Numbers, and Deuteronomy meet in a common interest in the Mishnah and Tosefta. Why – to conclude with the obvious – do the two Talmuds stand essentially apart from the remainder of the canon? The two Talmuds form around the Mishnah, while most of the rest of the canon takes shape around books of the Hebrew Scriptures.

The other question – the connection of Bavli to Yerushalmi – brings us back to our main point, the issue of the traditionality of the Bavli, and therefore is the more important of the two. Let me unpack the question at hand. What we want to know concerns the Bavli in particular. The first and most fundamental question is this: Does the Bavli bear a message of its own? Or does the document essentially rest upon, and continue, the work of the Yerushalmi? If the Yerushalmi dictates the program and policy – the hermeneutic and rhetoric – of the Bavli, then we cannot speak of the Bavli as a document on its own. Its logic, its mode of inquiry, its rhetoric, its mode of thought – all these will turn out to belong to its precursors. What would define the Bavli then would be its authors ability to do better or to say at greater length what others had already done and said. In that case the Bavli would have to take its place as a secondary and subordinate component of that sector of the canon of Judaism defined, for all time, by the concerns and the circumstances of the framers of the Yerushalmi. In terms of the choices before us, the Bavli would emerge as traditional and not an essentially fresh systemic construction.

The contrary proposition is that while the Bavli shares with the Yerushalmi a common program and purpose, its authors carry out that program in their own way. By this thesis they should appear to define that purpose in response to interests shaped in their distinct context and framework. Then we may claim that the Bavli presents its own message, a systemic statement of an original character, much as in reshaping and reconstituting received conventions, the composer or the artist accomplishes something fundamentally original. Stated simply, this other proposition will maintain that the authorship of the Bavli accomplishes its own goals. True, its logic, its inquiry, its mode of thought may run parallel to those of the Yerushalmi. But that is only because they derive from sources common to both documents. In terms of this second hypothesis, the Bavli flows not from the Yerushalmi but from the Mishnah. That is the source, also, of the Yerushalmi and hence the cause of the parallel course of both documents. According to this second proposition, the Bavli is not secondary. It is not subordinate to the Yerushalmi in that larger sector of the canon of Judaism defined by the Mishnah.

As between these two propositions, the materials we have examined decisively settle the question in favor of the second. At point after point, we found the two documents connected not only *to* the common source but mainly or solely *through* that source. Where they go over the same problems, it is because the shared source presented these problems to the authors of both documents. In our comparison of the two documents, we found that the rhetoric and literary program of the Bavli owed remarkably little to those of its predecessor. The comparisons of actual texts yielded decisive evidence for several propositions.

First, there is remarkably little verbatim correspondence. The Bavli's authors scarcely ever made use of extensive constructions and only rarely of brief formulations also found in the Yerushalmi. So far as our modest sample suggests, they never did so when it came to detailed expository arguments and analyses. Where there is verbatim sharing, it is a Mishnah paragraph or Tosefta passage that is held in common, on the one side, or a prior, severely abbreviated lemma of an earlier Amoraic authority, on the other. Where the two sets of authors deal with such a shared lemma, however, each group does exactly what it wishes, imputing words to the prior authority (as if the said authority had actually spoken those words) simply not known to the other group.

Second and more important, what the framers of the Bavli wished to do with a saying of an earlier Amoraic authority in no way responded to the policy or program of the Yerushalmi's authors. Quite to the contrary, where both sets of authors shared sayings of Yohanan and Simeon b. Laqish, we noted that each set went its own way. In no aspect did the Yerushalmi's interest in these shared sayings affect the Bavli's treatment of them. The point in common was that prior authorities explained the same passage of the Mishnah. From that simple starting point, the Bavli's authors went in a direction not imagined by the Yerushalmi's. The power and intellectual force of the Bavli's authors in that context vastly overshadowed the capacities of the Yerushalmi's.

What the systematic analysis of a single chapter tells us, therefore, may be stated very briefly. The Yerushalmi and the Bavli are alike in their devotion to the exegesis and amplification of the Mishnah. Viewed as literary constructions, they share, in addition, a basic exegetical program, which flows from the Mishnah and in fundamental ways is defined by the inner logic and cogency of the Mishnah. In relationship to the Yerushalmi, therefore the Bavli's framers pursued their own interests in their own way. They reveal independence of mind and originality of taste. It must follow that the Bavli is sufficiently unlike the Yerushalmi to be judged as an autonomous document, disconnected from and unlike its predecessor in all the ways that matter.

True, in general the Bavli falls into the same classification as does the Yerushalmi. But in detail, it presents its own message in its own way. The genus is the same, the species not. The opening hypothesis has yielded a negative result. When confronting the exegesis of the Mishnah, which is its indicative trait and definitive task, the authorship of the Bavli does not continue and complete the work of antecedents. Quite to the contrary, that authorship made its statement essentially independent of its counterpart and earlier document.

That fact now defines the next stage of our inquiry: the composition of the Bavli in its own terms, in relationship to the other antecedent documents. For at issue is not the general relationship, now established, between the Bavli and the prior systematic exegesis of the same document to which the Bavli is devoted. It is the very specific ties between the Bavli and the *entirety* of the prior writings on the same subject. In this specific inquiry into treatments among diverse authorships of a single topical program, we shall uncover a variety of facts upon the basis of which to reach solid conclusions for the case at hand. For the present purpose, a brief sample must suffice.

VII. The Bavli in Relationship to Other Extant Documents: A Brief Sample

Tradition is supposed to describe a process or a chain of transmission of received materials, refined and corrected but handed on not only unimpaired, but essentially intact. A traditional exegesis of the Mishnah will therefore cite a passage and gloss it, then another and gloss that. Secondary consideration of issues of principle, speculation on larger principles – these will not serve as primary vehicles of exegesis. A systemic reading of the Mishnah-paragraph, by contrast, will bring to bear upon the Mishnah a sustained and cogent program. The Mishnah will dictate topic, but the generative problematic of discourse will derive from the system that prevails and – merely by the way – attends, also, to the Mishnah-paragraph at hand. That choice will guide us in our reading of the first of the three sustained verbatim samples of our tractate, one which shows us how the authorship of the Bavli reads a given Mishnah-paragraph.

I have introduced brief observations on the first ten pericopae, to show the reader why I maintain we deal with well-composed, sustained and cogent propositions, syllogistic discourse with a beginning, middle, and end, following a clear program of inquiry. That program has told the authorship before us how not merely to put together diverse sayings, deriving from various times and persons, into a reasonably coherent statement. On the contrary, we have not a composite but a composition, with sayings all placed so as to serve the larger interests of argument or polemic of the single – and therefore, final – authorship. Beyond the observations on the opening units, I have not continued that mode of commentary, because there is no need to repeat a single, to me self-evident, point. Either we deal with the compositions of authorships capable of making diverse materials over into a single unfolding statement and argument, or we have in hand composites of discrete materials, patched together into a single continuous, but not really coherent and cogent, repertoire. I take the view that, in the aggregate, the Bavli's large scale discourse constitute not composites but compositions, and that in the Bavli we have not a scrapbook but a set of sizable statements of substantial integrity and cogency.

I give the text in my own translation[4] and mark the text to indicate the presence of materials shared with prior documents (excluding the Yerushalmi, for reasons spelled out in Chapter Two). That is the sole purpose of this survey. The Mishnah-passage is given in italics. Then I use bold-face type to indicate that a passage occurs in an earlier compilation. I do not pay attention to the appearance of a passage in another tractate of the Bavli, in the theory that all of the Bavli's thirty-seven tractates came to their present state in more or less the same period of time. It would follow that the appearance of a passage in more than one tractate will tell us nothing about how the same general authorship has made use of materials produced in a prior period. My comments on each passage are limited to some redactional issues and addressed mainly to the question at hand. My sample of Chapter One covers part of the treatment of Mishnah-Tractate Sukkah 1:1 (2a-9a, inclusive).

Bavli to Mishnah-Tractate Sukkah

1:1 A-F

    A. *A sukkah which is taller than twenty cubits is invalid.*

    B. *R. Judah declares it valid.*

    C. *And one which is not ten handbreadths high,*

    D. *one which does not have three walls,*

    E. *or one, the light of which is greater than its shade,*

    F. *is invalid.*

I

    A. We have learned in the Mishnah at another passage: *The crossbeam above an alley-entry which is higher than twenty cubits [is invalid, and one therefore] should diminish it [making it lower]. R. Judah says, "It is not necessary to do so" [M. Er. 1:1A-B].*

    B. What differentiates the case of the sukkah, in which instance the rule is

---

[4]*The Talmud of Babylonia. An American Translation.* VI. *Tractate Sukkah* (Chico, 1984: Scholars Press for Brown Judaic Studies).

formulated in the language of unfitness [without remedy], from the case of the alleyway, in which instance the framer of the Mishnah has specified the remedy [for an improper arrangement]?

C. Since [the religious requirement of building] a sukkah derives [from the authority] of the Torah, the framer of the passage uses the language, "unfit," while, since the arrangement creating an artificial alleyway derives from the authority of rabbis, the framer of the passage has taught the remedy [namely, diminishing the height of the crossbar].

D. If you prefer, I shall propose a different solution:

E. Even in matters deriving from the authority of the Torah one may well teach the required remedy. But in the case of the sukkah, with its numerous rules, the framer of the passage has simply framed matters in terms of unfitness. In the case of the alley-way, without numerous rules and regulations, the framer of the passage taught the remedy [for an improper arrangement].

The issue derives from the Mishnah-passage as it intersects with a counterpart rule elsewhere. No one suggests that the issue at hand derives from a prior tradition, even one of interpretation. The basic proposition at hand maintains that all components of the law join together to make a few utterly cogent and harmonious statements – a premise of exegesis particularly critical to a systemic hermeneutic, but not urgent, I should imagine, for a traditional one. But that proposal surely is subject to argument.

II

A. What is the scriptural source for the rule [that the sukkah may not be taller than twenty cubits]?

B. Said Rabbah, "It is because [Scripture] has stated, 'So that your coming generations may know that I made the children of Israel dwell in sukkot' (Lev. 23:43).

C. "[If the roof is] up to twenty cubits, someone will know that he is dwelling in a sukkah. If it is higher than twenty cubits, one will not know that he is dwelling in a sukkah, because [the roof] will be out of [the ordinary line of] sight."

D. R. Zira said, "The proof derives from here: 'And there shall be a booth [sukkah] for a shadow in the daytime from the heat' (Is. 4:6).

E. "[If the roof is] up to twenty cubits, someone will sit in the shadow of the [roof of the] sukkah. If it is higher than twenty cubits, one will not sit in the shadow of the [roof of the] sukkah [since the shadow will be cast by the walls entirely], but rather, in the shadow of the walls."

F. Said to him Abayye, "But if someone made his sukkah in a glen between two hills [where there is no sun], would you maintain that in such a case it is not a valid sukkah? [Surely not!]"

G. He said to him, "In that case, if one removes the two mountains there will be shade deriving from the roof of the sukkah, but here, if you remove the walls of the sukkah, there will not be any shadow cast by the sukkah at all."

H. And Raba said, "The proof derives from here: 'You shall dwell in sukkot for seven days' (Lev. 23:42), is what the Torah has said. For all seven days, go out of your permanent dwelling and stay in a temporary dwelling.

I. "Now [if the roof is] twenty cubits high, someone will make the sukkah a merely temporary dwelling. If it is higher than that, someone will not make the sukkah a temporary dwelling but a permanent one." [Slotki, p. 2, n. 13: Such a high structure requires firm foundations and walls, and these give it the characteristic of a permanent abode.]

J. Said to him Abayye, "But if so, if one has made the walls of his sukkah out of iron and then made a sukkah-roofing on them, would it be the case that this would not be a valid sukkah? [It certainly is a valid sukkah.]"

K. He said to him, "This is what I was saying to you: If the roof is up to twenty cubits in height, which is the sort of house that a person makes his temporary dwelling, if he makes it his permanent dwelling, he [nevertheless] carries out his obligation. But if the roof is higher than twenty cubits, which is the sort of house that a man makes a permanent dwelling, if one makes it a temporary dwelling, he has not carried out his obligation."

L. [2B] [We now review the proofs of Rabbah, Zira, and Raba, and ask what is at fault that all parties do not concur on any one of the three proposed proof-texts.] All parties do not concur with the proof of Rabbah, for his proof-text depends upon the knowledge of the coming generations.

M. All parties do not concur with the proof-text of R. Zira, for the proof-text he cites refers to the days of the Messiah.

N. But R. Zira [would respond], "If so, the verse should make use of the language of a canopy: 'A canopy will serve for a shade in the daytime.' Why does the verse say, 'A sukkah shall serve for a shade in the daytime'? It serves to make two points [one concerning the proper height of a sukkah, the other concerning matters in the messianic age]."

O. Likewise as to the proof-text adduced by Raba, all parties do not concur, on account of the question raised by Abayye.

The syllogism that underlines the case is that the rules of the Mishnah derive from Scripture. The power of the proof-text then is logically and systematically to link a particular rule to a general, and scriptural, rule. Here too the systemic focus is clear. For I maintain that the issue is not one of mere authority, that is, tradition, but as is clear at L, something more: the cogency of all proof-texts – once again, not a traditional but a systemic question. For a traditional statement can suffice with whatever proof-text comes to hand and has no need to sort out diverse possibilities. A systemic statement must link all the data into a single cogent composition, as is surely accomplished here.

III

A. [With reference to the proof-texts adduced in unit II we turn to the dispute at M. 1:1A-B]: In accord with what authority is the following statement: R. Josiah said Raba said, "The dispute [of the Mishnah at M. 1:1A-B] treats a case in which the walls of the sukkah do not touch the sukkah-roof. But if the walls do touch the sukkah-roof, then even though the roof is higher than twenty cubits, the sukkah is valid."

B. In accord with whose view? It accords with Rabbah, who has said, "The reason is that the roof [if higher] will be out of sight. But since the walls touch the sukkah-roofing, the sukkah-roofing is not out of sight. [The eye will be led up the walls to the sukkah-roofing, which forms a single visual image with the walls.]"

C. In accord with whose view is the following statement that R. Huna made in the name of Rab: "The dispute concerns a case in which the roof is only four cubits by four cubits in area. But if it is larger than four cubits by four cubits in area, then even if the roofing is higher than twenty cubits, the sukkah is valid."

D. In accord with whom? It accords with the view of R. Zira, who has said, "It is because of the need to cast a proper shadow." Now since there is ample space in the sukkah-roofing, the shadow of the sukkah [will be suitable even though the roof is higher than twenty cubits].

E. In accord with which authority is the following statement which R. Hanan bar Rabbah made in the name of Rab: "The dispute concerns a case in which the sukkah can hold only someone's head, the greater part of his body, and his table, then even if the roof is taller than twenty cubits, the sukkah will be valid"?

F. In accord with whom? In accord with none of them [since even if the sukkah can hold more than one's head, etc., the stated reasons still pertain.]

G. Now R. Josiah surely differs from R. Huna and R. Hanan bar Rabbah, for they define a minimum measure for the extent [of the sukkah], while he does not do so.

H. But may we maintain that R. Huna and R. Hanan bar Rabbah differ as to what renders the sukkah valid?

I. The proposed theory will be as follows: one party maintains that what renders the sukkah valid is the four cubits of sukkah-roofing, and the other holds that what renders the sukkah valid is the capacity to contain the head, the greater part of the body, and the table [of a resident].

J. No, that theory is not valid. All parties concur that what renders a sukkah valid is the capacity to hold the head, the greater part of one's body, and the table. But in the present case, this is the point of difference:

K. One party holds that at issue in the Mishnah's dispute is a case of a sukkah which indeed holds one's head, the greater part of one's body, and his table. But if [a sukkah] holds more than one's head, the greater part of one's body, and his table, all parties concur that a sukkah with a roof above twenty cubits remains valid.

L. The other party [Judah, M. 1:1B] maintains the view that at issue in the Mishnah's dispute is a case of a sukkah from a size which suffices to hold one's head, the greater part of one's body, and his table, to a size of four cubits. But if the sukkah is larger than four cubits, all parties concur that the sukkah is valid.

What has been said above applies here without qualification.

IV

A. [The specification of the cited authorities, III A, C, E, on the minimum requirements of the sukkah, now comes under discussion in its own terms.] The following objection was raised:

B. **A Sukkah which is taller than twenty cubits is invalid.**

C. R. Judah declares it valid [M. 1:1A-B], even up to forty or fifty cubits.

D. Said R. Judah, "M'SH B: The sukkah of Helene in Lud was twenty cubits tall, and sages went in and out, when visiting her, and not one of them said a thing."

E. They said to him, "It was because she is a woman, and a woman is not liable to keep the commandment of sitting in a sukkah."

F. He said to them, "Now did she not have seven sons [who are disciples of sages, and all of them were dwelling in that same sukkah!"] [T. Suk. 1:1A-E].

G. "And furthermore, everything she ever did was done in accord with the instruction of sages."

H. Now what need do I have for this additional reason: "Furthermore, everything she ever did was done in accord with the instructions of sages"?

I. This is the sense of what he said to them: "Now, if you say that the sons were minors, and minors are exempt from the religious duty of dwelling in the sukkah, since she had seven sons, it is not possible that among them was not a single one who no longer needed his mother's tending [and so would be required to dwell on his own in the sukkah]."

J. "And if, further, you should maintain that a minor who no longer needs his mother's tending is subject to the law only on the authority of rabbis, and that woman paid no attention to rules that rested only on the authority of the rabbis, come and note the following: 'And furthermore, everything she ever did was done in accord with the instructions of sages.'"

K. [We now revert to the issue with which we began, namely, the comparison of the story at hand to the reasons adduced by the authorities at unit III:] Now with references to one who said, the dispute applies to a case in which the walls of the sukkah do not touch the sukkah-roofing, would a queen dwell in a sukkah, the walls of which do not touch the sukkah-roofing?

L. [3A] [Indeed so! The reason is that] the space makes possible good ventilation.

M. But in the view of the one who has said that the dispute pertains to a small sukkah, would a queen ever dwell in a small sukkah?

N. Said Rabbah bar R. Ada, "At issue in the dispute is solely a case of a sukkah which is made with many small cubbies."

O. But would a queen take up residence in a sukkah that was subdivided into many small cubbies?

P. Said R. Ashi, "At issue is only [a large sukkah which had] such recesses.

Q. "Rabbis take the view that the queen's sons were dwelling in a sukkah of absolutely valid traits, while she dwelled in the recesses on account of modesty [i.e., not showing her face among the men], and it was on that account that rabbis said nothing to her [about her dwelling in what was, in fact, an invalid part of the sukkah].

R. "And R. Judah maintains the position that her sons were dwelling along with her [in the cubbyholes of the sukkah], and even so, the rabbis did not criticize what she was doing [which proves that the small cubbies of the sukkah were valid]."

The unfolding of this discourse shows us the larger traits of our document. The case is not introduced for the sake of preservation or even exemplification of the law. It is subjected to an analysis in terms of the larger program of the framer of the complete discussion. That is a mark of the systemic program, which draws into a single, sustained and on-going discourse the entirety of the received materials chosen for analysis.

V

A. Said R. Samuel bar Isaac, "The law is that a valid sukkah must be able to contain a person's head, the greater part of his body, and his table."

B. Said R. Abba to him, "In accord with which party is this rule? Does it concur with the view of the house of Shammai [at M. 2:7: *He whose head and the greater part of whose body are in the sukkah, but whose table is in the house – the House of Shammai declare invalid. And the House of Hillel declare valid].*"

C. He said to him, "Then in accord with whose opinion [might one allege that this is decided]?"

D. There are those who report [the matter in the following terms:]

E. Said R. Abba, "And who says [that the law is as] you [have stated]?"

F. He said to him, "It is in accord with the House of Shammai, and do not move from that view."

G. R. Nahman bar Isaac objected [to the thesis of Abba, B]: "How [do we know that] the House of Shammai and the House of Hillel debate about a small sukkah, [so that the conclusion drawn at A, B would follow, in line with M. 2:7]? Perhaps the dispute concerns a large sukkah.

H. "It would then involve the case of one who sat at the entrance of the shadowed [part of the large sukkah], with his table in his house.

I. "The House of Shammai then maintain that we rule by decree [that such an arrangement is unacceptable], lest the person be drawn [into the house] after his table.

J. "The House of Hillel take the view that we make no such decree.

K. "From a close reading of the language of the Mishnah itself the same conclusion may be drawn, for it has been taught: *He whose head and the greater part of whose body are in the sukkah, but whose table is in the house – the House of Shammai declare invalid. And the House of Hillel declare valid [M. 2:7].*

L. "Now if matters were [as you say, that is, if the dispute involved a small sukkah, then the framer of the Mishnah should have used the language,] '... holds or does not hold... [one's head, the greater part of the body, etc.].'"

M. Now do they really not dispute concerning the validity of a small sukkah?

N. And has it not been taught on Tannaite authority: [A sukkah that holds one's head, the greater part of his body, and his table is valid. Rabbi says, "It is valid only if it is at least four cubits by four cubits."

O. And it has further been taught on Tannaite authority: Rabbi says, "Any sukkah that is not at least four cubits by four cubits is invalid."

P. And sages say, "Even if it holds only his head, and the greater part of his body, it is valid."

Q. Now note that there is no reference to one's table at all!

R. The cited [teachings on Tannaite authority] present inconsistencies among themselves, so would it not follow that one of them represents the view of the House of Shammai and the other the view of the House of Hillel? [At issue then is the validity of a small sukkah.]

S. Said Mar Zutra, "The Mishnah-paragraph before us also [supports the same view]. Take note that a close reading sustains it: *The House of Shammai declare invalid, and the House of Hillel declare valid.*

T. "Now if [at issue were a large sukkah, used in an improper manner, such as was proposed above,] then it should read, 'The House of Shammai say, "The user has not carried out his obligation,: and the House of Hillel say, "The user has carried out his obligation."' [At issue would be not the character of the sukkah but the use made of it by the owner.]"

U. But there is yet a problem, [since the language at hand is,] He whose head... [etc., as Nahman bar Isaac noted earlier, Gff.].

V. It must follow that there is a dispute on two matters, a dispute first about a small sukkah, second, about a large sukkah. The passage then presents a lacuna, and this is its proper wording:

W. He whose head and the greater part of whose body were in the sukkah, but whose table was in the house –

X. the House of Shammai say, "He has not carried out his obligation."

Y. And the House of Hillel say, "He has carried out his obligation."

Z. And he whose sukkah is able to contain only his head and the greater part of his body alone –

AA. the House of Shammai declare [the sukkah] invalid.

BB. And the House of Hillel declare it valid.

The issue of proof-texts finds its counterpart in the concern for the authorities behind a rule and the consistency of the positions held by those authoritives, respectively. The reason the framer of the discourse asks about authority is not to determine the correct decision of law. It is to ascertain whether and how diverse authorities sustain cogent and consistent positions – once more an inquiry into structure and system, not merely tradition.

VI

A. [Reverting to the discussion of Rabbis' opinion, V N, above:] Who stands behind the following teaching, which our rabbis have taught on Tannaite authority:

B. A building that is not at least four cubits by four cubits [is not truly a "house," and so] is exempt from the requirement of placing a *mezuzah* and of building a parapet [Deut. 22:8], does not contract uncleanness through a *nega* [Lev. 14:34], is not permanently assigned to the ownership of a purchaser in line with the rules governing the transfer of real property in a walled city [Lev. 25:29]; on its account those who are in the battle line do not return from battle [if they have not used the house a requisite period of time, Deut. 20:5]; people do not provide an erub-meal for it [symbolically to create joint ownership among the houses in a given courtyard so as to permit carrying within the entire courtyard in the theory that the whole constitutes a single property] or a *shittuf*-meal for it [so as symbolically to create joint ownership among the courtyards of a single alleyway, for the same purpose as above]; people do not leave an erub-meal in such a house [so as to make it the locus of the symbolic joint meal]; [3B] they do not make of it an extension [outpost] between two towns [regarding such a building as a house equally location in two distinct towns, with the result that the two towns are regarded as one, so that people may walk on the Sabbath from one to the other]; and brothers or partners may not partition it [since it is too small].

C. [Since, in all of the cited matters, Scripture speaks of a house, and Rabbi has said that a sukkah is valid only if it is four cubits by four cubits,] may one say that the cited catalogue represents the views of Rabbi and not those of the rabbis [who would regard a building of smaller size as falling into the category of a house]?

D. You may say that the catalogue represents the views even of the rabbis.

E. They take the views stated there only with reference to a sukkah, which may serve as a random dwelling [not as a permanent house, and hence may be smaller than the normal proportions that would define a house]. But in respect to the definition of a house, which must be able to serve as a permanent dwelling, even rabbis would concur that if a building is four cubits by four cubits, it constitutes a suitable dwelling for people, and if not, it does not constitute a suitable dwelling for people.

F. [Proceeding to the analysis of the passage cited above, B, we move forward:] A master has said, "It is exempt from the requirement of placing a mezuzah and building a parapet, does not contract uncleanness through a nega, is not permanently assigned to the ownership of a purchaser in line with the rules governing the transfer of real property in a walled city; on its account those who are in the battle line do not return from battle."

G. What is the [scriptural] basis for that view?

H. The reason is that in all of these instances, Scripture makes reference to a house. [In no case among those listed is a building of such modest size regarded as a house.]

I. "People do not provide an erub meal for it or a shittuf-meal for it; people do not leave an erub-meal in such a house."

J. What is the reason for that view?

K. It will not serve as [an ordinary] dwelling.

L. [But if that is the operative consideration, then, while] people may not place the erub-meal there for the purpose of joining houses into a single courtyard, a shittuf-meal might well be placed there [since it joins not houses but entire courtyards that open out into a single alleyway. The consideration of whether or not it is a house does not apply.]

M. What is the reason [for such a position]? It is that the building at hand is no worse than a courtyard in an alleyway [and falls into that same category]. For we have learned in a teaching on Tannaite authority: The erub-meals that serve courtyards are placed in a courtyard, and the shittuf-meals serving alleyways are located in alley-ways.

N. And we reflected on that teaching as follows: *"Erub-meals serving courtyards are to be placed in a courtyard." And have we not learned in the Mishnah: He who places his erub in a gate-house, portico, or gallery – it is not a valid erub. And he who lives there [in the gate-house, portico, or gallery, and who does not share in the erub] does not prohibit [another from carrying objects in the courtyard] [M. Er. 8:4A-B].* [Hence these are not regarded as houses in the courtyard for the purposes of the erub-meal.]

O. Accordingly, I must interpret the cited statement [M] as follows: Erub-meals serving courtyards must be placed in a house located in the courtyard, and shittuf-meals serving alleyways must be located in a courtyard in that alley-way.

P. The matter at hand then [the house less than four cubits by four cubits] is no less [a case] than the courtyard in an alleyway [as proposed just now].

Q. "They do not make of it an extension between two towns": for it is not treated even as equivalent to a watchtower. Why not? Watchtowers [however modest] serve their purpose, but this serves no purpose.

R. "And brothers or partners may not partition it": What is the reason? Because it is not in area four cubits by four cubits.

S. But if it were of such an area, would they be able to partition it?

T. And have we not learned in the Mishnah: *People may not divide up a courtyard unless there will be four cubits for one resident and four for another [after the partition] [M. B.B. 1:6]?*

U. Rather, read the matter simply as follows: The law of partition does not apply [to such a house] as it does to a courtyard.

V. For R. Huna has said, "A courtyard is [wholly] divided up in accord with its entryways."

W. And R. Hisda said, "One assigns four cubits to each entryway, and they partition the remainder equally."

X. The stated rules apply to a house, which one plans to keep standing. In such a case one assigns a courtyard [space to such a house]. But as to this building, which is going to be demolished, we do not assign it courtyardspace.

I need not repeat what has already been said; the reader may rapidly identify what I deem to be the systemic traits of this discourse.

VII

A. [If a sukkah] was taller than twenty cubits and one attempted to diminish its height by placing on the ground blankets and pillows, that does not constitute a valid act of diminution [4A], and that is so even though the owner declared the objects to be abandoned [and null, of no value whatsoever] so far as all parties are concerned.

B. The reason is that his intention in the matter is null when measured against the prevailing view of all other people [who will nonetheless regard the blankets and pillows not as abandoned but as objects of value].

C. If he did so with straw and nullified [its value], this does indeed constitute an act of valid diminution, and all the more so if he did it with dirt and nullified [its value].

D. As to the use of straw which the man is not planning to remove later on, and as to dirt of indeterminate condition, there is a dispute between R. Yose and rabbis.

E. For we have learned in the Mishnah: *A house which one wholly filled with dirt or pebbles and which one abandoned is regarded as abandoned [M. Oh. 15:7].*

F. That is the case if one has abandoned the house. If one did not abandon the house, that is not the case.

G. And in this regard there is a Tannaite teaching:

H. **R. Yose says, "Straw which one is not destined to remove, lo, it is in the category of ordinary dirt and is regarded as abandoned and dirt which one is destined to remove, lo, it is in the category of ordinary straw and is not regarded as abandoned [T. Oh. 15:5B] [= D].**

VIII

A. [If a sukkah] was higher than twenty cubits, but palm leaves were hanging down within the twenty cubits, if the shade that they cast is greater than the sunlight they let through, the sukkah is valid, and if not, it is invalid.

B. [If a sukkah] was ten handbreadths high, and palm leaves were hanging down into the space of ten handbreadths,

C. Abayye considered ruling that if the shade that they cast is greater than the sunlight they let through, the sukkah is valid, and if not, it is invalid.

D. [But] Raba said to him, "This really would be a disgraceful sort of dwelling, and no one would live in such a disgraceful dwelling [so the sukkah would be invalid to begin with]."

E. [If] it was higher than twenty cubits, but the owner built a ledge in it across the entire front of the middle [of the three] walls of the sukkah, and [the ledge] has sufficient space to constitute a valid sukkah, it is a valid sukkah.

F. [If the owner] built the ledge on the side wall, if from the edge of the ledge to the [opposite] wall of the sukkah is a space of four cubits [or more], the sukkah is invalid. If the space from the ledge to the wall is less than four cubits, it is a valid sukkah. [Slotki: It is valid because the roof above the area between the ledge and the opposite wall is regarded as a continuation of that wall which thus serves as a third wall for the ledge.]

G. What inference [does the framer of this case] wish to provide for us? Is it that we invoke the principle of the "curved wall" [Slotki]?

H. But we have learned on Tannaite authority: As to a house which is lacking [the middle of its flat roof], and the owner put sukkah-roofing over that empty area, if from the wall to the sukkah-roofing is a distance of four cubits, the area is invalid [to serve as a sukkah].

I. Lo, if the distance is less than that, it is valid. [Accordingly, the principle yielded by the case at hand is not fresh, since it is readily derived from an available teaching.]

J. [No, it was necessary to make the principle explicit in the present case.] What might you have said? In that [available] case, it is valid because [each side] is suitable to serve as a wall [Slotki: it is not higher than the permitted maximum], but here, [where the sukkah is higher than twenty cubits] so that the wall is not suitable to serve as a wall for a sukkah, I might have held that it was not a suitable arrangement.

K. Thus the framer of the case informs us that that is not a consideration.

L. [If a sukkah] was taller than twenty cubits, and the owner built a ledge in the middle of the sukkah, if from the edge of the ledge to the wall is a space of four cubits in all directions, the area is invalid to serve as a sukkah. But if it is less than that space, it is valid.

M. What principle does the framer of the case wish to tell us? Is it that we invoke the principle of the "curved wall"? This is the same [case as the one just reviewed].

N. [No, it was necessary to specify the matter.] What might you have imagined? We invoke the principle of the "curved wall" in the case of a [wall in a] single direction, but we do not invoke that principle in all four directions.

O. Thus the framer informs us that that is not the case. [We invoke the principle for all four directions.]

P. [If a sukkah] was lower than ten handbreadths, and one made a hole in the ground of the sukkah so as to fill out the sukkah ['s requisite space, from ground to roof] up to ten handbreadths, if from the edge of the hole to the wall there is a distance of three or more handbreadths, the sukkah is invalid. If the distance is less than this, [4B] it is valid.

Q. What differentiates the other case, in which you have maintained that the maximum distance may be four cubits, from the present case, in which the maximum acceptable difference is less than three handbreadths?

R. In the earlier case, in which there is a wall, a distance of as much as four cubits will suffice. Here, where the owner has to make a wall, if the distance from the hole to the wall is three handbreadths or less, it is acceptable, and if not, it is not acceptable.

S. If a sukkah was higher than twenty cubits, and the owner built in the sukkah a pillar ten handbreadths in height, with sufficient space [four cubits by four cubits] to constitute a valid sukkah,

T. Abayye considered invoking the principle that the partitions [formed for the sides of the pillar] are [imaginarily] projected upward [Slotki, p. 13, n. 1: As far as the ceiling, and that, since the sides are no less than ten handbreadths high and the distance between the top of the pillar and the roof is less than twenty cubits, the pillar constitutes a valid sukkah].

U. Raba, however, said to him, "To invoke that principle we require partitions that can be recognized, and that condition is not met here."

Has this passage been made up all at once, or has it come into being through a sedimentary process of agglutination and incremental conglomeration? I should maintain that the discourse before us is sustained, smooth, and continuous, rather than a mélange of preserved sayings strung out in some sensible order. There is a beginning, middle, and end; we discern a purpose and an issue that joins the whole. These seem to me marks of deliberation and indications of a program of syllogistic proposition and rigorous argument. I cannot think of a better example of the power of such a program to dictate the composition and proportion of the whole, and I maintain that we do have a proportioned and well composed whole.

IX

A. Our rabbis have taught on Tannaite authority:

B. If a person drove four posts into the ground and spread sukkah-roofing on them,

C. R. Jacob declares the arrangement a valid sukkah.

D. And sages declare it invalid.

E. Said R. Huna, "The dispute concerns an arrangement made at the edge of a roof. R. Jacob takes the view that we invoke the principle that the walls extend upward, and rabbis maintain that we do not invoke that rule.

F. "But if one erected such a contraption in the middle of the roof, all parties concur that the arrangement is invalid [since the sukkah has no walls]."

G. R. Nahman said, "If one erected the arrangement in the middle of the roof, there is a dispute."

H. The following question troubled [the later exegetes of the passage]: Is it true that there is a dispute in the case of such an arrangement built at the middle of the roof, but if it were located on the edge of the roof, all parties would concur that it is valid [in Nahman's view of the matter]? Or is it true that whether the arrangement is in this area [the middle of the roof] or in that [the edge of the roof] [in Nahman's view] there is a dispute?

I. The question stands unanswered.

J. The following objection was raised:

K. If someone drove four poles into the ground and arranged sukkah-roofing on them,

L. R. Jacob declares [the contraption to be a] valid [sukkah].

M. And sages declare it invalid [cf. T. Suk. 1:12-13].

N. Now lo, the ground is equivalent to the middle of the roof, and yet R. Jacob declares it valid.

O. That would constitute a refutation of the theory [F] of R. Huna [on what is at issue], would it not? It indeed constitutes a refutation.

P. Furthermore, there is a dispute as to such a contraption's being located at the middle of the roof, but if it is located at the edge of the roof, all parties concur that it is valid.

Q. Now may I propose that this too constitutes a refutation of R. Huna in both matters?

R. [No, not at all]. R. Huna may reply to you that the dispute pertains to such a contraption in the middle of the roof, and the same rule applies to one constructed at the edge of the roof.

S. And as to the fact that there is a dispute concerning such an arrangement in the middle of the roof, it serves to tell you just how far R. Jacob is prepared to go. For even if we deal with such an arrangement in the middle of the roof, [Jacob] even in such a case would declare it to be valid.

T. Our rabbis have taught on Tannaite authority:

U. If someone dug four [round] poles into the ground and put sukkah-roofing on them,

V. R. Jacob says, "[To determine whether we have valid walls,] we take a perspective such that, if one should cut the pole and plane it, what would result would be a beam with a handbreadth of space on one side and a handbreadth of space on the other. Then the poles are judged to form a rectangular corner piece [and so to constitute a double wall with each surface regarded as a wall unto itself], and if not, they are not required in that way." [If there are two walls, one in each direction, to be imputed to the pillar, we have an adequate sukkah.]

W. For R. Jacob says, "The measure for the assessment of a rectangular corner piece in the case of a sukkah is a handbreadth."

X. And sages say, "The appropriate measure is only if two [of the nearby walls] are fully articulated walls in accord with the law pertaining to them. In that case, then the third wall of the sukkah may be even so small as a handbreadth [in depth]. [So sages reject Jacob's view that we invoke the principle that the estimate, if met, would yield two valid walls for the sukkah, one on each side of the pillar. Sages insist on two fully valid walls, and here there is none.]

The issue comes prior to the citation of cases and opinions. We may readily outline this discourse, with its beginning, middle, and end, and we may discern the points of unfolding logic and reason, the earlier coming first, the later coming last. These seem once more to point toward a plan that, from first to last, has told the composer of the whole where and how to place the received materials in the interest of producing a single and cogent statement.

A survey of the entirety of the chapter at hand, encompassing also materials not given verbatim here, yields a simple result. These units have no counterparts and are made up to serve the interests of the present authorship alone: 1:1A-F: I, II, III, V, VI, VII, VIII, X, XI, XII, XII, XIV, XVI, XVII, XVIII, XIX; 1:1 G-N: I, II. These units are built upon citation and exegesis of a passage of the Tosefta: 1:1A-F: IV, (VII, mere citation), (IX, illustration of a principle, but the passage is not the center of discourse), XIII (continued at XV), (XVII, merely cited), XX; .1:1 G-N: –. Of the 22 units in all, I count 18 entirely automous ones, lacking any point of contact with a prior document. The other four take up passages that occur in the Tosefta, but none appears to intend a systematic inquiry into the Tosefta's materials parallel to the Talmud's systematic study of those in the Mishnah, paragraph by paragraph. On that basis we cannot adduce as evidence of a literary process of tradition the sample before us.

With respect to exegeses of Scripture, we wish to know whether or not available treatments of a biblical verse have guided the formation of any component of our Bavli-passage. Exegetical treatments bearing more than marginal relevance are as follows: Ex. 25:22: Not critical to our passage; in the same category: Ex. 19:20, Zech. 14:4, Ex. 19:3, 25:10-11, 26:16. 33, 1 Kgs. 6:2, 26, 2 Kgs. 2:11, Job 26:9, Ez. 10:14, etc.. These verses supply facts in an inquiry to which they are essentially tangential. No exegetical tradition in the passages in which they occur sets the issue at hand. Note in particular Lev. 23:34: No tradition other than Y. Suk. 2:7, which deals with "the fifteenth of the month" stated with reference to both Passover and Tabernacles; no point of contact with the present issue. The issue is unrelated. Lev. 23:42: Gen. R. 48:10: God paid Abraham's descendants back for his hospitality by having them dwell in booths for seven days. This also will be in the age to come. Pesiqta deRab Kahana 28/a: You shall eat in the sukkah for seven days, not eight days. No point of intersection with our passage at II.H. Y. Suk. 2:7: One is supposed to eat fourteen meals in a Sukkah, in line with Lev. 23:42. Lev. 23:43: Sifré Dt. 140: not relevant to the present passage; Pesiqta deRab Kahana Supplement 2:6 (Braude, pp. 471-2): not relevant. Deut. 16:13: Pesiqta deRab Kahana Supplement 2:6, 7, not relevant; neither passage deals with what is important here. The emphasis in both treatments of PRK deals with the world to come, God's relationship to Israel, the exile and return, and the like.

The upshot may be stated simply. I see no exegetical parallels, no point of intersection between the Bavli's authorship's interest in the key verses, Lev. 23:35ff., and, e.g., the authorship of Pesiqta deRab Kahana. A given verse's point of interest to one authorship bears nothing in common with what, in that same verse, captures the attention of another authorship. Where, elsewhere in this tractate, we do have a biblical verse important both to the authorship of the Bavli-chapter and also to compilers of prior exegetical compilations, we see no material point of intersection whatsoever – and that not in a minor detail but in protracted discourse on the part of several distinct authorships.

I simply did not anticipate how casual and inconsequential would be the points of contact or intersection between and among treatments of verses important in our Bavli passage and the reading of those same verses in other documents. The sole exception to this statement – commonalities of interest in a given verse on the part of the authorships of other tractates of the Bavli or of the Yerushalmi – need not detain us for the reasons already worked out. We come now to the issues we raised at the outset.

Let us in conclusion consider the questions just as we originally asked them.

1. *The topical program* of prior writings on the subject as compared to the topical program of the Bavli on the same subject, with attention to questions such as these: does the Bavli follow the response to the Mishnah characteristic of the authorship of the Tosefta? Not systematically, only episodically. As to the Sifra, Sifré to Numbers or Sifré to Deuteronomy, these documents have little in common with ours. Does the Bavli follow the response to relevant passages of Scripture that have caught the attention of compilers of Midrash-exegeses in Genesis Rabbah, Leviticus Rabbah, Pesiqta deRab Kahana, and other documents generally thought to have come to closure prior to the Bavli? Quite to the contrary, apart from the Yerushalmi and other authorships within the Bavli itself, our authorship turns out to define unique and uncommon points of interest in verses treated both in the Bavli and in some other document.

2. *The Bavli's use or neglect of the available treatments ("sources") in the prior literature*: if the Bavli does make use of available materials, does it impose its own issues upon those materials or does it reproduce those materials as they occur elsewhere? The answer to these questions for the present sample is negative. The Bavli does not make extensive use of available materials. Most of what we have reviewed turns out to be unique to the Bavli. Where there are materials that occur both here and in other documents, they provide mere facts,

not a point of generative discourse. Has the authorship of the Bavli carried forward issues important in prior writings, or has it simply announced and effected its own program of inquiry into the topic at hand? Our authorship has made its own statement in its own way.

3. *The traits of the Bavli's canonical statement, that is, derivative and summary at the end, or essentially fresh and imputed retrospectively?* In consequence of the detailed examination of the Bavli's authorship's use of and response to available sources, for the sample at hand we may characterize the statement of the Bavl as a whole in comparison to prior statements as original, fresh, and self-defined. And, since that statement is canonical by the definition of the entire history of Judaism, we ask about the upshot: the shape and character of a canonical statement on a given subject. The answer, for the sample we have considered, yields a negative finding: the canonical statement does not aim at drawing together available materials and restating a long-term and (assessed in terms of the extent writings) broadly-circulated consensus. Data that constitute evidence for documentary traditionality do not appear to the naked eye – or even to a vision educated to discern literary traits and concerns. Quite to the contrary, the pages of plain type, not the boldface indicative of a passage deriving from a prior compilation, testify to the plain truth that our document does not cite or quote or attempt to summarize and recast available materials, reaching a later authorship out of an earlier and on-going process of tradition. True, individual sayings may have circulated and may have undergone a process of continuous tradition. But the Bavli as we have it, the work of its penultimate and ultimate authorship, makes its own statement in its own way on its own agenda. It gives us not a tradition out of a remote past but a system of its own, composed, quite obviously, in substantial measure from received materials and in accord with received conventions, but, in all and in essence, a singular, autonomous, and, by its nature, unprecedented statement: a system. We shall now survey two more samples of the same tractate, persistently performing the same inquiry and at the end asking exactly the same questions.

VIII.   System or Tradition in Light of Literary Facts

Each document in the corpus of the rabbinic writings of late antiquity bears points in common with others. In their ultimate condition, they did form a tradition, understood in that sense of tradition as a fixed and unchanging essence deriving from an indeterminate past, a truth bearing its own stigmata of authority, e.g., from God at Sinai. Each document in proportion and measure constitutes a partial statement of that complete tradition. But, as we now understand, we have first of all to know whether and how all – or at least some – of them constitute a tradition in that other sense, that is a tradition derived from and formed out of prior sources? This sense of "tradition" refers to the matter of process, specifically, an incremental and linear process that step by step transmits out of the past statements and wordings that bear authority and are subject to study, refinement, preservation and transmission. In that sense, tradition is supposed to describe a process.

The Bavli proves connected with earlier documents and also with some received sayings not written down in a systematic way in prior compilations. But the connections appear episodic and haphazard, not systematic, except in respect to the Mishnah, The Bavli cannot be shown systematically and generally to continue the program and inquiry of predecessors. Therefore with the Bavli a new tradition got underway, but the Bavli does not derive from, and state, a prior tradition in the sense just now spelled out. For in few ways does the Bavli give evidence of taking its place within such a process of tradition, and we cannot appeal to the document to demonstrate that the authorship of the Bavli represented itself as traditional and its work as authoritative *on that account?* The appeal of the authorship of the Bavli is to the ineluctable verity of well-applied logic, practical reason tested and retested against the facts, whether deriving from prior authorities, or emerging from examples and decisions of leading contemporary authorities. We have now tested the hypothesis that the Bavli forms an essentially traditional document, in the sense given in the preface, and the further claim that the reason for the Bavli's traditional – and, by the way, canonical – status lies in its success in completing work begun by the predecessors of the document, for instance, the Yerushalmi. If we can demonstrate a systematic exercise of refinement, completion, summary, we may propose the hypothesis that one definitive trait of a canonical statement is its position at the end of a sustained and continuous process of thought.

True enough, the Bavli contains ample selections from available writings. The authorship of the Bavli leaves no doubt that it makes extensive use of extant materials, sayings and stories. Readers who review the sizable sample before us will see numerous indications – much like footnotes and references – of that fact. For example, the authorship of the Bavli invokes verses of Scripture. It further takes as its task the elucidation of the received code, the Mishnah. More to the point, frequent citations of materials now found in the Tosefta as well as allusions to sayings framed in Tannaite Hebrew and attributed to Tannaite authority – marked, for instance, by TN' – time and again alert us to extensive reference, by our authorship, to a prior corpus of materials. Not only so, but contemporary scholarship has closely read both brief sayings and also extended discourses in light of two or three or more versions and come to the conclusion that a later generation has taken up and made use of available materials.[5] Most

---

[5]I present a sizable sample of these prior exercises in source-criticism in the volumes edited by me, *The Formation of the Babylonian Talmud. Studies on the Achievements of Late Nineteenth and Twentieth Century Historical and Literary-Critical Research* (Leiden: E. J. Brill, 1970) and *The Modern Study of the Mishnah* (Leiden: E. J. Brill, 1973). These two volumes cover the more important contemporary figures, with special attention to David Weiss Halivni. The only figure omitted did his important work afterward, Shamma Friedman, and to a sample of his work I devoted a seminar, the papers of which were then published in William Scott Green, ed., *Law as Literature, Semeia XX* (Chico: Scholars Press, 1984).

strikingly of all, our authorship claims in virtually every line to come at the end of a chain of tradition, since the bulk of the generative sayings – those that form the foundation for sustained inquiry and dialectical discourse – is assigned to named authorities clearly understood to stand prior to the work of the ultimate redactors. Even if we preserve a certain reluctance to take at face value all of these attributions to prior authorities, we have to take full account of the authorship's insistence upon its own traditionality. In all of these ways, the authorship of the Bavli assuredly stands in a line of tradition, taking over and reworking received materials, restating viewpoints that originate in prior ages. And that fact makes all the more striking the fundamental autonomy of discourse displayed by the document at the end. So let us serve as interlocutors for the great authorship at hand and present some pointed questions.

Were we therefore to enter into conversation with the penultimate and ultimate authorship of the Bavli, the first thing we should want to know is simple: what have you made up? And what have you simply repeated out of a long-continuing heritage of formulation and transmission? And why should we believe you? The authorship then would be hard put to demonstrate in detail that its fundamental work of literary selection and ordering, its basic choices on sustained and logical discourse, its essential statement upon the topics it has selected – that anything important in their document derives from long generations past.

Should they say, "Look at the treatment of the Mishnah," we should answer, "But did you continue the Yerushalmi's program or did you make up your own?" And in the total candor we rightly impute to that remarkable authorship, the Bavli's compositors would say, "It is our own – demonstrably so."

And if we were to say, "To what completed documents have you resorted for a ready-made program?" our *soi-disant* traditionalists would direct our attention to Tosefta, their obvious (and sole) candidate. And, if they were to do so, we should open the Tosefta's treatment of, or counterpart to, a given chapter of the Mishnah and look in vain for a systematic, orderly, and encompassing discourse, dictated by the order and plan of the Tosefta, out of which our authorship has composed a sizable and sustained statement.

True, we readily recognize that the Tosefta's materials play their role. But seeing the Tosefta in its terms, noting how slight a portion of a given Tosefta chapter the Mishnah's authorship has found accessible and urgent, we should dismiss out of hand any claim that the Bavli's fundamental structure and plan encompasses systematic and orderly exposition of the Tosefta's structure and plan for a given Mishnah-chapter. The opposite is the case.[6] Tosefta makes its

---

[6]Rabbi Yaakov Elman's study of the impact of Tosefta Pisha upon Bavli Pesahim has shown beyond all doubt the fact that there is no systematic and orderly plan of Tosefta-citation and exegesis at the foundations of the Bavli's inquiry into the matter. Quite to the contrary,

contribution unsystematically and episodically, where and when the authorship of the Bavli, for its reasons (not always obvious to us) has permitted the Tosefta to do so. That is hardly the mark of traditionality, subservience to a received text, such as the counterpart treatment of the Mishnah by the Bavli's authorship – a treatment that is orderly, routine, complete, and systematic – indicates.

And when, finally, we ask our authorship to state its policy in regard to Scripture and inquire whether or not a sustained and on-going tradition of exegesis of Scripture has framed discourse, the reply will prove quite simple. "We looked for what we wanted to seek, and we found it."

That "we" then requires identification, and when we interrogate the "we" of Leviticus Rabbah = Pesiqta deRab Kahana and ask for their program, we meet one community of inquiry, which scarcely has met, though at a few points claims common descent from, the "we" of the Bavli. Distant cousins, each has pursued its own set of questions – no continuities here.

These four loci at which boundaries may have merged, and intersections turned into commonalities, therefore mark walled and sealed borders. A received heritage of sayings and stories may have joined our authorship to its teachers and their teachers – but not to that larger community of sustained learning that stands behind the entirety of the writings received as authoritative, or even a sizable proportion of those writings. The presence, in the ultimate statement of the Bavli, of sayings imputed to prior figures – back to Scripture, back to Sinai – testifies only to the workings of a canon of taste and judgment to begin with defined and accepted as definitive by those who defined it: the authorship at hand itself. The availability, to our authorship, of a systematic exegesis of the same Mishnah-chapter has not made self-evident to our authorship the work of continuation and completion of a prior approach. Quite to the contrary, we deal with an authorship of amazingly independent mind, working independently and in an essentially original way on materials on which others have handed on a quite persuasive and cogent statement. Tosefta on the one side, Scripture and a heritage of conventional reading thereof on the other – neither has defined the program of our document or determined the terms in which it would make its statement, though both, in a subordinated position and in a paltry limited measure, are given some sort of a say. The Bavli is connected to a variety of prior writings but continuous with none of them.

It follows that the Bavli in relationship to its sources is simply not a traditional document, in the plain sense that most of what it says in a cogent and coherent way expresses the well-crafted statement and viewpoint of its authorship. Excluding, of course, the Mishnah, to which the Bavli devotes its sustained and systematic attention, little of what our authorship says derives

---

reference to the Tosefta's materials on the same topic turns out to be casual, episodic, and unpredictable. The sustained research behind his oral report, at the Society of Biblical Literature meeting in Atlanta on November 24, 1986, of this matter will in due course be published in this series.

cogency and force from a received statement, and most does not. But that is only beginning the question: no one (outside the circles of the believers) ever said that the Bavli's authorship has slavishly taken its message merely from the Mishnah, in which its authorship picks and chooses as much as it does in Scripture, first of all deciding to deal with thirty-nine tractates and to ignore twenty-three.

The premise of all learning of an independent order is that the Bavli's authorship has imputed to the Mishnah those meanings that that authorship, on the foundations of its own critical judgment and formidable power of logical reasoning in a dialectical movement, itself chose to impute. That reading of the Mishnah became the substance and center of tradition, that is, the ultimate statement, out of late antiquity, of the Judaism of the dual Torah. We do not know that that reading triumphed because of the persuasive power of applied reason, rationality, cogent discourse resting on acute reasoning that together comprise the hermeneutics of the Bavli. But in an ideal world, that purely intellectual achievement would have accounted for its success. In any event, the Bavli's authorship's cogent, rigorously rational reading of the received heritage has demonstrably emerged *not* from a long process of formulation and transmission of received traditions, in each generation lovingly tended, refined and polished, and handed on essentially as received. Indeed, to revert to the opening question of the preface, I should doubt that it could have, for the literary evidence we have examined hardly suggests that a system of applied reason and sustained, rigorously rational rational inquiry can coexist with a process of tradition. The thought-processes of tradition and those of system-building scarcely cohere. Where applied reason prevails, the one – tradition – feeds the other – the system – materials for sustained reconstruction.

The Bavli's statement has given us such tradition as the Bavli's penultimate and ultimate authorship has chosen and has worked out. This statement we now receive according to the choices dictated by that authorship's sense of order and proportion, priority and importance, and it is generated by the problematic found by that authorship to be acute and urgent and compelling. When confronting the exegesis of the Mishnah, which is its indicative trait and definitive task, the authorship of the Bavli does not continue and complete the work of antecedents. Quite to the contrary, that authorship made its statement essentially independent of its counterpart and earlier document. We revert to the decisive observation, which forms the thesis of this theory of matters.

The system comes first. In the present context, that means that the logic and principle of orderly inquiry take precedence over the preservation and repetition of received materials, however holy. The mode of thought defined, the work of applied reason and practical rationality may get underway.

To state matters in more general terms, first in place is the system that the Bavli as a whole expresses and serves in stupefying detail to define. Only then comes that selection, out of the received materials of the past, of topics and even concrete judgments, facts that serve the Bavli's authorship in the articulation of its system. Nothing out of the past can be shown to have dictated the Bavli's program, which is essentially the work of its authorship. In this context, the Mishnah forms no exception, for the work of the Bavli's authorship began with the selection of tractates to study and designation of those to ignore. I cannot think of a more innovative or decisive – reforming – judgment than one simply to bypass fully a third of what is allegedly to be "the Tradition." No one to our knowledge rejected the ignored tractates; but everyone concurred on ignoring them.[7]

So Judaism – the Judaism of the dual Torah that appeals for its ultimate encyclopaedic statement of law and theology to the Bavli – really is the making of the authorship of the Bavli, not principally the accumulation, in the Bavli, of the sifted-over detritus of prior authorships. The upshot as to theory may be stated very simply, and in a way to be tested in the study of the history of other religions as well:

The system begins exactly where and when it ends.

In the example of the Judaism of the dual Torah come to full expression in the Bavli, such tradition as the authorship at hand has received ends when the system that receives that tradition begins. So I conclude that where reason reigns, its inexorable logic and order, proportion and syllogistic reasoning govern supreme and alone, revising the received materials and restating into a compelling statement, in reason's own encompassing, powerful and rigorous logic, the entirety of the prior heritage of information and thought. That restatement is the Bavli.

I therefore claim that the canonical documents of formative Judaism constitute, each on its own, statements at the end of a sustained process of rigorous thought and logical inquiry, applied logic and practical reason. The only way to read a reasoned and systematic statement of a system is defined by the rules of general intelligibility, the laws of reasoned and syllogistic discourse about rules and principles. The way to read a traditional and sedimentary document by contrast lies through the ad hoc and episodic display of instances

---

[7]Many years ago Jacob Sussman, professor of Talmud at the Hebrew University, completed his dissertation on whether the authorship of the Bavli studied the orders, Agriculture and Purities, to which no Talmud-tractates are devoted. Hearsay has it that he concluded that it did not, though materials were available for the construction of an appropriate set of tractates. But to my knowledge the dissertation has not been published, so we do not have the advantage of what appears to have been ground-breaking and painstaking research. The possibilities of a Talmud Bavli to Purities were fully exploited by the brilliant work on Kelim and Ohalot by Gerson Enoch Leiner, in Sifré Tohorot (1873, repr. N.Y.: 1960). I. Kelim. II. Ohalot. Leiner created the Talmud for those two tractates out of the available materials of Tosefta and scattered Tannaite sayings, as well as Amoraic discourse on those sayings found in the extant writings. He then wrote a commentary on whatever he had assembled. Abraham J. Heschel, who called Leiner's work to my attention, told me that he understood Leiner had done the same for all of the tractates of Mishnah's Division of Purities, but that, when accused of trying to write a new Talmud, Leiner had burned his manuscripts. I cannot vouch for the accuracy of the story, but Heschel spoke, so he told me, from first-hand knowledge of the matter.

and examples, layers of meaning and eccentricities of confluence, intersection, and congruence. That is why, for my part I maintain that tradition and system cannot share a single crown, and that, the formative documents of Judaism demonstrate, Judaism constitutes not a traditional but a systemic religious statement, with a hermeneutics of order, proportion, above all, reasoned context, to tell us how to read each document. We cannot read these writings in accord with two incompatible hermeneutical programs, and, for reasons amply stated, I argue in favor of the philosophical and systemic, rather than the agglutinative and traditional, hermeneutics.

At stake in the present debate therefore is the fundamental issue of hermeneutics. For claims as to the character of the literature of Judaism entail judgments on the correct hermeneutics, down to the interpretation of words and phrases. We can read everything only in light of everything else, fore and aft. That is how today nearly everyone interested in these writings claims to read them – citing the Bavli as proof for that hermeneutics. Or we can read each item first of all on its own, a document as an autonomous and cogent and utterly rational, syllogistic statement, a unit of discourse as a complete and whole composition, entire unto itself, taking account, to be sure, of how, in the larger context imposed from without, meanings change(d). That is how – and not solely on the basis of the sample we have surveyed – I maintain any writing must be read: in its own context, entirely on its own, not only in the one imposed by the audience and community that preserved it.

For whatever happens to thought, in the mind of the thinker ideas come to birth cogent, whole, complete – and on their own. Extrinsic considerations of context and circumstance play their role, but logic, cogent discourse, rhetoric, – these enjoy an existence, an integrity too. If sentences bear meaning on their own, then to insist that sentences bear meaning only in line with friends, companions, partners in meaning contradicts the inner logic of syntax that, on its own, imparts sense to sentences. These are the choices: everything imputed, as against an inner integrity of logic and the syntax of syllogistic thought.[8]

We therefore conclude by recalling and reaffirming for the Bavli the second sense of the word tradition: a fixed and unchanging essence deriving from an indeterminate past, a truth bearing its own stigmata of authority, from God at Sinai. Because of its compelling and, in terms now defined, secular demonstration of the reasoned and rational character of all of created existence, the authorship of the Bavli created what assuredly became a profoundly traditional and, again in defined terms, religious and theological document, laying forth in its authorship's terms and language the complete and authoritative

---

[8] No one can maintain that the meanings of words and phrases, the uses of syntax, bear meanings wholly integral to discrete occasions. Syntax works because it joins mind to mind, and no mind invents language. But that begs the question and may be dismissed as impertinent, since the contrary view claims far more than the social foundation of the language.

statement of the Torah, oral and written, that is the world-creating statement, made by Judaism, of that reasoned and orderly world that God had by rule created and by rule now sustains, world without end until by God's will and reasoned rule, the Messiah comes – an eternity of perfect rationality.

Chapter Six

Literary Studies of Aggadic Narrative
A Bibliography

Joseph M. Davis

Harvard University

Introduction

Aggadic narratives have, over the generations, both excited and perplexed their readers; their problematic nature has made them subject, at different times and places, to broad neglect or to intense study. This bibliography lists modern literary studies of aggadic narrative. The list is by no means comprehensive, but it is widely representative of the scholars who have worked in the field and of the types of studies that have been written, and it includes most of the more important and repercussive studies of the last century.

Several types of works have been excluded from the list. Most historical studies of the early rabbis have been based very largely on aggadic narratives; such studies necessarily interpret those narratives; but this bibliography does not in general list studies whose primary purpose is historical. Neither does it list either traditional or scholarly collections, indices, translations of, or commentaries on, aggadic narratives.

Finally, the *Jewish Encyclopedia,* the German *Encyclopaedia Judaica* (A-Lyra; never completed) and the English language *Encyclopedia Judaica* all have many articles on the aggadah and aggadic narrative. These are particularly rich in the field of aggadic treatments of Biblical narratives and the parallel Christian and Muslim traditions; this bibliography does not, however, list them.

I would like to thank Mr. Daniel Dyckman for his very gracious assistance. The bibliography is organized in the following categories:

I. Bibliographies and Surveys of Secondary Literature

II. Aggadah with Reference to Narrative

III. Folk-Narrative with Reference to Aggadah

IV. Aggadic Narrative in General

V.   Personalities and Events
    i.   General
    ii.   Martyrs and Martyrdom
    iii. Miracles, Miracle-Workers, and Pietists
    iv.   R. Yohanan ben Zakkai and Mysticism
    v.   Disputations and Roman Emperors
    vi.   Alexander of Macedon
    vii. Jesus and Christians
    viii. Other

VI.   Themes and Motifs
    i.   General
    ii.   Folkloristic Motifs
    iii. Responses to Catastrophe
    iv.   Angels and Devils
    v.   Heaven and Hell
    vi.   Messiah and Apocalypse
    vii. Miscellaneous Motifs and Themes

VII. Aggadic Retellings of Biblical Narratives
    i.   General
    ii.   Antediluvians
    iii. The Binding of Isaac
    iv.   Moses and Aaron
    v.   Elijah
    vi.   Other

VIII. Parables and Fables

IX.   Court Cases and Legal Precedents

X.   Sources and Parallels of Aggadic Narratives
    i.   General
    ii.   Jewish Writings
    iii. Greek and Roman Authors
    iv.   Christian Traditions
    v.   Muslim Traditions
    vi.   Other

XI.   Interpretations and Retellings of Aggadic Narratives
    i.   Medieval and Early Modern
   ii.   Modern

Abbreviations

ANRW	Austieg und Niedergang der Römischen Welt
FRCS	Folklore Research Center Studies (Mehkerei ha-Merkaz le-heker ha-folklor)
HThR	Harvard Theological Review
HUCA	Hebrew Union College Annual
JBL	Journal of Biblical Literature
JJS	Journal of Jewish Studies
JQR o. s.	Jewish Quarterly Review, original series
JQR	Jewish Quarterly Review, new series
JStJ	Journal for the Study of Judaism in the Persian, Hellenistic and Roman Period
JSHL	Jerusalem Studies in Hebrew Literature (Mehkerei Yerushalayim be-sifrut Yisra'el)
JSJF	Jerusalem Studies in Jewish Folklore (Mehkerei Yerushalayim be-folklor Yehudi)
MGWJ	Monatsschrift für Geschichte und Wissenschaft des Judentums
PAAJR	Proceedings of the American Academy for Jewish Research
REJ	Révue des Études Juives
SBL	Society of Biblical Literature
SH	Scripta Hierosolymitana
WCJS	World Congress of Jewish Studies
ZDMG	Zeitschrift der Deutschen Morgenländischen Gesellschaft
Fischel, *Essays*	Henry A. Fischel ed., *Essays in Greco-Roman and Related Talmudic Literature* (New York: 1977)
Shinan, *Mikra'ah*	Avigdor Shinan ed., *Mikra'ah be-sifrut ha-agadah: mehkarim u-mekorot* (Jerusalem: 1983) (Likutei *Tarbiz*, 4)

I. Bibliographies and Surveys of Secondary Literature

1. Barth, Lewis M. "Recent Studies in Aggadah," *Prooftexts* 4 (1984), pp. 204-213.

2. Fischel, Henry A. "Selected Annotated Bibliography ... on Greco-Roman Philosophical and Rhetorical Literature and Talmudic-Midrashic Writings 1850-1975," in Fischel, *Essays*, pp. xxi-lxxii.

3. Haas, Lee. "Bibliography on Midrash," *The Study of Ancient Judaism I: Mishnah, Midrash, Siddur*, ed. Jacob Neusner (New York: 1981), pp. 55-92.

4. Heller, Bernard. "Neuere Literatur zur jüdischen Sagenkunde," MGWJ 70 (1926), pp. 385-410, 476-497; 71 (1927), pp. 13-38.

5. Jellinek, Adolph. *Kuntres ha-magid: sofer u-moneh ma'amarim u-sefarim 'al darkhei ha-agadah veha-midrashim* (Vienna, 1878).

6. Miller, Merrill P. "Targum, Midrash, and the Use of the Old Testament in the New Testament," JStJ 2 (1971), pp. 29-82.

7. Scheiber, Alexander [Sándor]. "Le folklore juif dans la *Révue des Études Juives*," REJ 139 (1980), pp. 19-37.

8. Shinan, Avigdor. "Mavo," in Shinan, *Mikra'ah*, pp. vii-x.

9. Valfish, Dov. *Ishei ha-Mikra ba-sifrut ha-batar-Mikra'it: bibliyografiyah nivheret* (Jerusalem: 1976).

10. Yassif, Eli. *Jewish Folklore: An Annotated Bibliography* (New York: 1986).

II. Aggadah with Reference to Narrative

11. Abrahams, Israel, "The Midrash and its poetry," in *A Short History of Jewish Literature* (London: 1906), pp. 28-36 (= *Understanding the Talmud*, ed. Alan Corré (New York: 1975), pp. 27-32).

12. Bacher, Wilhelm. *Die Agada der babylonischen Amoräer* (Strassburg: 1878).

13. _____. *Die Agada der Tannaiten*, 2 vol. (Strassburg: 1884-1890) (tr. A. Z. Rabinovits, *Agadot ha-Tana'im*, 3 vol. [Jaffa: 1920-1923]).

14. _____. *Die Agada der palästinensischen Amoräer*, 3 vol. (Strassburg, 1892-1899) (tr. A. Z. Rabinovits, *Agadat Amora'ei erets Yisra'el*, 7 vol. [Tel Aviv: 1925-1937]).

15. Bamberger, Bernard J. "The Dating of Aggadic Materials," JBL 82 (1963), pp. 169-176.

16. Ben Amos, Dan. "Generic Distinctions in the Aggadah," in *Studies in Jewish Folklore: Proceedings of a Regional Conference of the Association for Jewish Studies Held at the Spertus College of Judaica, Chicago, May 1-3, 1977*, ed. Frank Talmage (Cambridge, Mass.: 1980), pp. 45-71.

17. Bergmann, Juda. "Die runden und hyperbolischen Zahlen in der Agada," MGWJ 82 (1938), pp. 361-376.

18. Bialik, Hayim Nahman, "Halakhah ve-agadah," in *Kitvei H. N. Bialik* (Tel Aviv, 1926), vol. 2, pp. 244-257, and frequently reprinted (tr. "Halakhah

and Aggadah," in *Modern Jewish Thought*, ed. Nahum Glatzer [New York: 1977], pp. 55-64).

19. Brown, Ronald. "Midrashim as Oral Traditions," HUCA 39 (1968), pp. 91-116.

20. De Vries, Benjamin. "ha-Sugim ha-sifrutiyim shel ha-agadah," in *Mehkarim be-sifrut ha-Talmud* (Jerusalem: 1968), pp. 290-299.

21. Dunski, Shimshon. "Midrash agadah: mahatsavto u-derakhav," *Molad* 250 (1980), pp. 160-175.

22. Feldman, Emanuel. "The Rabbinic Lament," JQR 63 (1972), pp. 51-75.

23. Finkelstein, Louis. "The Sources of the Tannaitic Midrashim," JQR 31 (1940-41), pp. 211-244.

24. Fishler, Bracha. "Pitgam aligori – mai ka mashma' lan?" JSJF 7 (1984), pp. 7-21.

25. Gerhardsson, Birger. *Memory and Manuscript: Oral Tradition and Written Transmission in Rabbinic Judaism and Early Christianity*, tr. Eric Sharpe (Copenhagen: 1964), esp. "The Narrative Tradition *(ma'asim)*," pp. 181-189.

26. Hagai, S. "Sha'ashu'ei lashon be-sifrut Yisra'el," *Mahanayim* 67 (1962), pp. 25-27.

27. Hakohen, Mordekhai, "Humor satirah u-vedihah be-fi Hazal," *Mahanayim* 67 (1962), pp. 8-19.

28. Hazan-Rokem, Galit. "ha-Pasuk ha-Mikra'i ke-fitgam ukhe-tsitat," JSHL 1 (1981), pp. 155-166.

29. Heinemann, Isaak. *Altjüdische Allegoristik* (Breslau: 1936).

30. _____. *Darkhei ha-agadah* (Jerusalem: 1950).

31. Heinemann, Joseph. *Agadot ve-toldotehen: 'iyunim be-hishtalshelutan shel mesorot* (Jerusalem: 1974).

32. Heschel, Abraham J. *Torah min ha-shamayim be-aspeklaryah shel ha-dorot*, 2 vol. (Jerusalem: 1962-1965).

33. Loewe, Heinrich. *Reste von altem jüdischen Volkshumor* (Berlin: 1912).

34. _____. *Alter jüdischer Volkshumor aus Talmud und Midrasch* (Reichenberg: 1931).

35. Neusner, Jacob. "History and Midrash," *Judaism* 19 (1960), pp. 47-54 (= Neusner, *History and Torah: Essays in Jewish Learning* (London: 1965), pp. 17-29).

36. Noy, Dov. *Mavo le-sifrut ha-agadah*, ed. M. Ganan (Jerusalem: 1966).

37. _____. "Yesodot humor be-midrash Ester Rabah," *Mahanayim* 87 (1963), pp. 88-93.

38. Porton, Gary, "Defining Midrash," in *The Study of Ancient Judaism I: Mishnah, Midrash, Siddur*, ed. Jacob Neusner (New York: 1981), pp. 55-92 (= "Midrash: Palestinian Jews and the Hebrew Bible in the Greco-Roman Period," ANRW II.19.2 (1979), pp. 103-138).

39. Saldarini, Anthony J. *Scholastic Rabbinism: a Literary Study of the Fathers according to Rabbi Nathan* (Chico, Calif.: 1982).

40. Schechter, Joseph. *Mavo le-agadah* (Tel Aviv: 1950).

41. Shinan, Avigdor. "Sifrut agadah: ben higud 'al peh u-masoret ketuvah," JSJF 1 (1981), pp. 44-60.

42. Spiegel, Shalom. "Introduction," to Louis Ginzberg, *Legends of the Bible* (Philadelphia: 1956), pp. xi-xxxix (= *The Jewish Expression*, ed. Judah Goldin [New York: 1970], pp. 134-162).

43. Towner, Wayne Sibley. *The Rabbinic Enumeration of Scriptural Examples* (Leiden: 1973).

44. Urbach, Ephraim E. "Halakhah u-nevu'ah," *Tarbiz* 18 (1946-47), pp. 1-27.

45. _____. "Halakhah and History," in *Jews, Greeks and Christians: Religious Cultures in Late Antiquity: Essays in Honor of William David Davies*, ed. Robert Hamerton Kelly and Robin Scroggs (Leiden: 1976), pp. 112-128.

46. Visotsky, Burton. "Introduction," to "Midrash Mishle: a critical edition," (Ph.D. thesis, J.T.S.: 1982), pp. 3-125; esp. "Style," pp. 56-77.

47. Wachten, Johannes. *Midrasch-Analyse: Strukturen im Midrasch Qohelet Rabba* (Hildesheim: 1978), esp. "Nichtbiblische Aggadot," pp. 214-263.

48. Yerushalmi, Yosef Hayim. "Biblical and Rabbinic Foundations," in *Zakhor: Jewish History and Jewish Memory* (Seattle: 1982), pp. 5-26.

49. Zunz, Leopold. *Die gottesdienstliche Vörtrage der Juden: historisch entwickelt*, 2nd ed. (Frankfurt a. M.: 1892) (tr. and ed. Chanoch Albeck, *ha-Derashot be-Yisra'el ve-hishtalshelutan ha-historit*, (Jerusalem: 1947)).

III. Folk-Narrative with Reference to Aggadah

50. Ben Amos, Dan. "The Haggadah in Socio-Linguistic Perspectives," 6th WCJS *Abstracts* (Jerusalem: 1973), p. D-42.

51. Bergmann, Juda. *Die Legenden der Juden* (Berlin: 1919).

52. _____. "Sitten und Sagen," MGWJ 74 (1930), pp. 161-172.

53. _____. "Folkloristische Beiträge," MGWJ 79 (1935), pp. 322-334.

54. _____. *ha-Folklor ha-Yehudi* (Jerusalem: 1951).

55. Gaster, Moses. *Beiträge zur Vergleichenden Sagen- und Marchenkunde* (Bucharest: 1883); also appeared in 12 parts in MGWJ 29-30 (1880 - 1881); and as revised by Bernard Heller in MGWJ 77 (1933), pp. 431-

435; 78 (1934), pp. 273-278, 324-342; 80 (1936), pp. 32-52, 127-128; and see Gaster, "Beiträge zur Vergleichenden Sagen- und Marchenkunde zu Paulis Schimpf und Ernst," in *Jubilee Volume in honour of Prof. Bernhard Heller,* ed. Alexander Scheiber (Budapest: 1941), pp. 149-156.

56. Ginzberg, Louis. "Jewish Folklore: East and West," in *On Jewish Law and Lore* (Philadelphia: 1955), pp. 59-73 (tr. "Agadot 'am Yehudiyot: mizrah u-ma'arav," in Ginzberg, *'Al halakhah ve-agadah: mehkar u-masah* [Tel Aviv: 1960], pp. 251-262).

57. Grünbaum, Max. *Gesammelte Aufsätze zur Sprach und Sagenkunde* (Berlin: 1901), esp. "Beiträge zur vergleichenden Mythologie aus der Hagada," pp. 1-237 (= ZDMG 31 [1877], pp. 183-359).

58. Heller, Bernard. "Devarim ahadim 'al hokhmat ha-agadot (folklor)," *ha-Tsofeh le-hokhmat Yisra'el* 9 (1925), pp. 162-170.

59. Jason, Heda. *Studies in Jewish Ethnopoetry* (Taipei: 1975), esp. "Conflict and Resolution in the Sacred Legend," pp. 63-176.

60. Neusner, Jacob. "Does Midrash fall into the Category of Folklore?" in *Formative Judaism: Religious, Historical and Literary Studies: Fourth Series* (Chico, Calif.: 1984), pp. 55-63.

61. Noy, Dov. *ha-Sipur ha-'amami ba-Talmud uva-Midrash,* ed. Y. Barlev (Jerusalem: 1960).

62. _____. "Shelakh lahmekha 'al penei ha-mayim," *Mahanayim* 99 (1965), pp. 164-176.

63. _____. "Sipurei-'am Galiliyim," *Mahanayim* 101 (1965), pp. 18-25.

64. _____. *Mavo le-sifrut 'amamit,* ed. Ziporah Kagan (Jerusalem: 1967).

65. Rappaport, Angelo S. *The Folklore of the Jews* (London: 1937).

66. Rubinstein, Gilbert. "The Role of the Folktale in Post-Biblical Jewish Culture," *Midwest Folklore* 3 (1953), pp. 85-97.

67. Schwarzbaum, Haim. *Studies in Jewish and World Folklore* (Berlin: 1968).

IV. Aggadic Narrative in General

68. Aderet, Avraham. "Agadot Hazal ke-sifrut petuhah," *'Alei Sefer* 2 (1975), pp. 78-89.

69. _____. "Ha-sipur be-ma'arekhet midrash Hazal," *'Alei Sefer* 7-8 (1979), pp. 101-115.

70. Avery-Peck, Alan. "Classifying Early Rabbinic Pronouncement Stories," SBL *Seminar Papers* (1983) pp. 223-244.

71. Ben Amos, Dan, "Narrative Forms in the Haggadah: Structural Analysis," (Ph.D. thesis, Indiana Univ.: 1966)

72. _____. " 'Iyun tsurani u-mivni be-agadot ha-Talmud veha-Midrash," 4th WCJS (Jerusalem: 1969), vol. 2, Heb. sect. pp. 352-359.

73. Bergmann, Juda. "Geschichte und Legende," in *Festschrift Adolf Schwarz*, ed. S. Krauss (Berlin: 1917), pp. 89-108.

74. Fraenkel, Jonah. "Bible Verses Quoted in the Tales of the Sages," SH 22 (1971), pp. 80-99.

75. _____. " She'elot hermenoitiyot be-heker sipur ha-agadah," *Tarbiz* 47 (1977-78), pp. 139-172 (= Shinan, *Mikra'ah*, pp. 325-358; and see E. E. Halevi, " 'Od 'al 'genre' hadash be-sipurei ha-agadah," *Tarbiz* 49 [1980], pp. 424-428, and Fraenkel, "Teshuvah," p. 429).

76. _____. "Paronomasia in Aggadic Narratives," SH 27 (1978), pp. 27-51.

77. _____. "ha-Zeman ve-'itsuvo be-sipurei ha-agadah," in *Mehkarim be-agadah, Targumim u-tefilat Yisra'el le-zekher Yosef Heinemann*, ed. Ezra Fleischer and Jakob J. Petuchowski (Jerusalem: 1981), Heb. sect., pp. 133-162.

78. _____. "Kavim boltim be-toldot masoret ha-tekst shel sipurei ha-agadah," 8th WCJS (Jerusalem: 1981), vol. 3, Heb. sect. pp. 45-69.

79. _____. "ha-Tavniyot shel sipurei ha-agadah ha-Talmudit," FRCS 7 (1983), Heb. sect., pp. 45-97.

80. Gaster, Moses. *Exempla of the Rabbis*, (London: 1924; repr. New York: 1968, with a "Prolegomenon" by William G. Braude, pp. xix-xxxii); and see Bernard Heller, "Quelques problèmes relatifs aux légendes juives: à propos des *Exempla of the Rabbis* publiés par M. Gaster," REJ 81 (1925), pp. 1-26, and B. Heller, "Sefer ha-Ma'asiyot," *ha-Tsofeh le-hokhmat Yisra'el* 9 (1925), pp. 171-176.

81. Gereboff, Joel. "To Speak, How to Speak, and When Not to Speak: Answers from Early Rabbinic Stories," *Semeia* 34 (1985), pp. 29-51; and see Jack N. Lightstone, "Response to Joel Gereboff: When Speech is No Speech: the Problem of Early Rabbinic Rhetoric as Discourse," *ibid.*, pp. 53-57.

82. Goldenberg, Robert. "History and Ideology in Talmudic Narrative," in *Approaches to Ancient Judaism IV: Studies in Liturgy, Exegesis, and Talmudic Narrative*, ed. William Scott Green (Chico: Calif., 1983), pp. 159-172.

83. Halévy, J. "Traces d'aggadot saducéenes dans le Talmud," REJ 8 (1883), pp. 38-56.

84. Jacobs, Louis. "Further Evidence of Literary Device in the Babylonian Talmud," JJS 9 (1958), pp. 138-147 (= Jacobs, *Studies in Talmudic Logic and Methodology* [London: 1961], pp. 60-69).

85. Kagan, Ziporah. "Divergent Tendencies and their Literary Molding in the Aggadah," SH 22 (1971), pp. 151-170.

86. Karlin, A. "Darkhei ha-sipur bi-shenei ha-Talmudim," *Moznayim* 10 (1939-40), pp. 407-414, 11 (1940), pp. 399-408 (= *Divrei sefer: masot* [Tel Aviv: 1952], pp. 5-42).

87. _____. "Sipurim historiyim ba-Talmud," *Sinai* 15 (1944-45), pp. 217-225.

88. Meir, Ofra, "ha-Demuyot ha-po'alot be-sipurei ha-Talmud veha-Midrash ('al pi midgam)" (Ph.D. thesis, Hebrew Univ.: 1977).

89. _____. "The Narrator in the Stories of the Talmud and the Midrash," *Fabula* 22 (1981), pp. 79-83.

90. _____. "Li-she'elat amot ha-midah ba-'arikhat mafteah sipurim le-midreshei Hazal," 8th WCJS (Jerusalem: 1981), vol. 3, Heb. sect., pp. 17.

91. _____. "ha-Demut ha-mishtaneh veha-demut ha-mitgaleh be-sipurei Hazal," JSHL 6 (1984), pp. 61-77.

92. Neusner, Jacob. "Story as History in Ancient Judaism: Formulating Fresh Questions," in *History of Judaism: the Next Ten Years,* ed. Baruch M. Bokser (Chico, Calif.: 1980), pp. 3-29.

93. _____. "From Exegesis to Fable," in *Method and Meaning in Ancient Judaism: Third Series* (Chico, Calif.: 1981), pp. 129-135.

94. _____. "Beyond Historicism, After Structuralism: Story as History in Ancient Judaism," in *Method and Meaning in Ancient Judaism: Third Series* (Chico, Calif.: 1981), pp. 217-238.

95. _____. "Story and Tradition in Judaism," in *Judaism: The Evidence of the Mishnah* (Chicago: 1981), pp. 307-328.

96. _____. "History in Formative Judaism: the Age of the Tannaim and Amoraim," in *Major Trends in Formative Judaism: Second Series* (Chico, Calif.: 1984), pp. 49-71.

97. _____. "Is the Talmud a Historical Document ?" in *Formative Judaism: Religious, Historical and Literary Studies: Fourth Series* (Chico, Calif.: 1984), pp. 73-82.

98. _____. "When Tales Travel: the Interpretation of Multiple Appearances of a Single Saying or Story in Talmudic Literature," in *Formative Judaism: Religious, Historical and Literary Studies: Fifth Series* (Chico, Calif.: 1985), pp. 87-103.

99. Safrai, Shmuel. "Tales of the Sages in the Palestinian Tradition and the Babylonian Talmud," SH 22 (1971), pp. 209-232.

100. Saldarini, Anthony J. "Last Words and Deathbed Scenes in Rabbinic Literature," JQR 68 (1977), pp. 28-75.

V. Personalities and Events

i. General

101. Green, William Scott. "What's in a Name ? – The Problematic of Rabbinic 'Biography'", in *Approaches to Ancient Judaism: Theory and Practice,* ed. William Scott Green (Missoula, Mont.: 1978).

ii. Martyrs and Martyrdom

102. Cohen, Gerson D. "Ma'aseh Hanah ve-shiv'ah baneha ba-sifrut ha-'Ivrit," in *Mordecai M. Kaplan Jubilee Volume* (New York: 1953), Heb. sect., pp. 109-122.

103. Lévi, Israel. "Le Martyre des Sept Macchabées dans la Pesikta Rabbati," REJ 54 (1907), pp. 138-141.

104. Lieberman, Saul. "Roman Legal Institutions in Early Rabbinics and in the Acta Martyrum," JQR 35 (1944-45), pp. 1-57 (= Lieberman, *Texts and Studies* (New York: 1974), pp. 57-111).

105. _____. "'Al hata'im ve-'onsham," in *Louis Ginzberg Jubilee Volume* (New York: 1945), Heb. sect., pp. 249-270 (tr. "On Sins and their Punishment," *Texts and Studies,* pp. 29-56).

106. _____. "The Martyrs of Caesarea," *Annuaire de l'Institut de Philologie et d'Histoire Orientales and Slaves* 7 (1939-44), pp. 395-446 (revised version published as "Redifat dat Yisra'el," in *Salo Baron Jubilee Volume,* ed. S. Lieberman et al. (Jerusalem: 1975), Heb. sect. pp. 213-245).

107. Piron, Mordechai. "Gevurat ha-em ha-'Ivriyah," *Mahanayim* 87 (1963), pp. 88-93.

108. Zeitlin, Solomon. "The Legend of the Ten Martyrs and its Apocalyptic Origins" and "A Note on the Legend of the Ten Martyrs," JQR 36 (1945-6), pp. 1-16 , 209.

iii. Miracles, Miracle-Workers, and Pietists

109. Baumgarten, A. I. "Miracles and Halakhah in Rabbinic Judaism," JQR 73 (1982-83), pp. 238-253.

110. Berman, Dennis. "Hasidism in Rabbinic Traditions," SBL *Seminar Papers* (1979), vol. 2, pp. 15-33.

111. Bokser, Baruch M. "Hanina ben Dosa and the Lizard: the Treatment of Charismatic Figures in Rabbinic Literature," 8th WCJS (Jerusalem: 1981) vol. 3, Eng. sect. pp. 1-6.

112. _____. "Wonder-working and the Rabbinic Tradition: The Case of Hanina ben Dosa," JStJ 16 (1985), pp. 42-92.

113. Fiebig, Paul. *Jüdische Wundergeschichten des neutestamentlichen Zeitalters* (Tübingen: 1911).

114. Goldin, Judah. "On Honi the Circle-Maker: a Demanding Prayer," HThR 56 (1963), pp. 232-237.

115. Green, William Scott, "Palestinian Holy Men: Charismatic Leadership and Rabbinic Tradition," ANRW II.19.2 (1979), pp. 619-647.

116. Guttmann, Alexander. "The Significance of Miracles for Talmudic Judaism," HUCA 20 (1947), pp. 363-406 (= Guttman, *Studies in Rabbinic Judaism* [New York: 1976], pp. 47-90).

117. Heinemann, Isaak. "Die Kontroverse über das Wunder im Judentum der Hellenistischen Zeit," in *Jubilee Volume in honour of Prof. Bernhard Heller,* ed. Alexander Scheiber (Budapest: 1941), pp. 149-156.

118. Kolenkow, Anitra Bingham. "A Problem of Power: How Miracle Doers Counter Charges of Magic in the Hellenistic World," SBL *Seminar Papers* (1976), pp. 105-110.

119. Mach, R. *Der Zaddik in Talmud und Midrash* (Leiden: 1957).

120. Nisim, Rahel. "Demut *ha-hasid:* 'imut ben R. Hanina ben Dosa le-ven R. Pinhas ben Ya'ir le-or 'emdat Hazal bi-ve'ayat ha-gemul ('al pi mekorot Tana'iyim ve-erets Yisra'eliyim mukdamim)," *'Alei Sefer* 12-14 (1982), pp. 135-154.

121. Patai, Raphael. "Control of Rain in Ancient Palestine," HUCA 14 (1939), pp. 251-286.

122. Safrai, Shmuel. "Teaching of Pietists in Mishnaic Literature," JJS 16 (1963), pp. 15-33.

123. Sarfatti, G. B. "Hasidim ve-anshei ma'aseh veha-nevi'im ha-rishonim," *Tarbiz* 26 (1956-7), pp. 126-153 (= Shinan, *Mikra'ah,* pp. 289-316).

124. Vermes, Geza. "Hanina ben Dosa," in *Post-Biblical Jewish Studies* (Leiden: 1975), pp. 178 -214 (= JJS 23 [1972], pp. 28-50; 24 [1973], pp. 51-64).

iv. R. Yohanan ben Zakkai and Mysticism

125. Chernus, Ira. *Mysticism in Rabbinic Judaism: Studies in the History of Midrash* (Berlin: 1982).

126. Gruenwald, Ithamar. *Apocalyptic and Merkabah Mysticism* (Leiden: 1980).

127. Halperin, David. *The Merkabah in Rabbinic Literature* (New Haven: 1980) (American Oriental Series, vol. 62).

128. Neusner, Jacob. "In Quest of the Historical Rabban Yohanan ben Zakkai," HThR 59 (1966), pp. 391-413.

129. _____. *Development of a Legend: Studies on the Traditions Concerning Yohanan ben Zakkai* (Leiden: 1970).

130. _____. "The Traditions Concerning Yohanan ben Zakkai: Reconsiderations," JJS 24 (1973), pp. 65-73.

131. _____. "History of a Biography: Yohanan ben Zakkai in the Canonical Literature of Formative Judaism," in *Formative Judaism: Religious, Historical and Literary Studies: Fifth Series* (Chico, Calif.: 1985), pp. 79-86.

132. Saldarini, Anthony J. "Johanan ben Zakkai's Escape from Jerusalem: Origin and Development of a Rabbinic Story," JStJ 6 (1975), pp. 189-204.

133. Schäfer, Peter. "Johanan b. Zakkai und Jabne," ANRW II.19.2 (1979), pp. 43-101.

134. Schalit, Abraham. "Nevu'otehem shel Yosef ben Matityahu ve-Rabi Yohanan ben Zakai 'al 'aliyat Espasianus la-shilton," in *Salo W. Baron Jubilee Volume* (Jerusalem: 1975), Heb. sect. pp. 397-432.

135. Scholem, Gershom G. *Jewish Gnosticism, Merkabah Mysticism, and Talmudic Tradition* (New York: 1960).

136. Urbach, Ephraim E. "ha-Mesorot 'al torat ha-sod bi-tekufat ha-Tana'im," in *Studies in Mysticism and Religion presented to Gershom G. Scholem*, ed. E. E. Urbach et al. (Jerusalem: 1967), Heb. sect. pp. 1-28.

v. Disputations and Roman Emperors

137. Bastomsky, S. J. "The Emperor Nero in Talmudic Legend," JQR 59 (1968-69), pp. 321-325.

138. Bergmann, Juda. "Die Schicksalserforschung der römischen Kaiser in der Agada," MGWJ 81 (1937), pp. 478-481.

139. Böhl, Felix. "Die Matronenfragen im Midrasch," *Frankfurter Judaistische Beiträge* 3 (1975), pp. 29-64.

140. Gershenzon, Rosalie and Eliezer Slomovic. "A Second-Century Jewish-Gnostic Debate: Rabbi Jose ben Halafta and the Matrona," JStJ 16 (1985), pp. 1-41.

141. Kagan, Ziporah. "ha-Matronita me-Tsipori," *Mahanayim* 101 (1965), pp. 30-37.

142. Krauss, Samuel. *Antoninus und Rabbi* (Frankfort a. M.: 1910).

143. Lévi, Israel. "La mort de Titus," REJ 11 (1885), pp. 209-234.

144. Marmorstein, Arthur. "The Background of the Haggadah," HUCA 6 (1929), pp. 141-204.

145. _____. "R. Josué b. Hanania et la sagesse grecque," REJ 87 (1929), pp. 200-208.

146. Piron, Mordechai. "Hadei ha-vikuhim 'al ha-Shabat ba-Talmud uva-Midrashim," *Mahanayim* 85-86 (1963), pp. 64-71.

147. Rieger, Paul. "The Foundation of Rome in the Talmud: A Contribution to the Folklore of Antiquity," JQR 16 (1925-26), pp. 227-235.

148. Wallach, Luitpold. "The Colloquy of Marcus Aurelius with the Patriarch Judah I," JQR 31 (1940-41), pp. 259-286.

vi. Alexander of Macedonia

149. Donath, L. *Die Alexandersage in Talmud und Midrasch* (Fulda: 1873).

150. Friedländer, Israel. *Die Chadhirlegende und der Alexanderroman: eine sagengeschichtliche und literarhistorische Untersuchung* (Berlin: 1913), esp. "Der babylonische Talmud," pp. 42-50.

151. Kazis, Israel J. "Introduction," to Kazis ed., *The Book of the Gests of Alexander of Macedon* ... (Cambridge, Mass.: 1962), pp. 1-55; and "Notes to the Introduction," pp. 181-201.

152. Lévi, Israel. "La légende d'Alexandre dans le Talmud," REJ 2 (1881), pp. 293-309.

153. _____. "Les traductions hebraïques de l'histoire légendaire d'Alexandre," REJ 3 (1881), pp. 238-265.

154. _____. "La légende d'Alexandre dans le Talmud et le Midrasch," REJ 7 (1883), pp. 78-93.

155. _____. "Alexandre et les Juifs d'après les sources rabbiniques," in *Gedenkbuch zur Erinnerung an David Kaufmann,* ed. M. Brann and F. Rosenthal (Breslau: 1900), pp. 346-354.

156. _____. "La dispute entre les Égyptiens et les Juifs devant Alexandre: écho des polémiques antijuives à Alexandrie," REJ 63 (1912), pp. 211-215.

157. Reich, Rosalie, "Introduction," to *Tales of Alexander the Macedonian* ... : *A Medieval Hebrew Manuscript* ..., ed. and tr. R. Reich (New York: 1972), pp. 1-20.

158. Wallach, Luitpold. "Alexander the Great and the Indian Gymnosophists in Hebrew Tradition," PAAJR 11 (1941), pp. 47-83.

vii. Jesus and Christians

159. Gero, Stephen. "Jewish Polemic in the Martyrium Pionii and a 'Jesus Passage' from the Talmud," JJS 29 (1978), pp. 164-168.

160. Halévy, J. "Ben-Thymélion et Bartholomée," REJ 10 (1884), pp. 60-65; and see Israel Lévi, "Encore un mot sur la légende de Bartalmion," *ibid.,* pp. 66-73, and Wilhelm Bacher, "La language de l'exorcisme d'un démon par R. Simon b. Yohai," REJ 35 (1897), pp. 285-287.

161. Herford, Robert Travers. *Christianity in Talmud and Midrash* (London: 1903).

162. Lachs, Samuel Tobias. "A 'Jesus Passage' in the Talmud Re-examined," JQR 59 (1968-69), pp. 321-325.

163. Lauterbach, Jacob. "Jesus in the Talmud," in *Rabbinic Essays* (Cincinnati: 1951), pp. 473-570.

164. Maier, Johann. *Jesus von Nazareth in der talmudischen Überlieferung* (Darmstadt: 1978) (and see review by Robert Goldenberg in JQR 73 (1982-83), pp. 78-86).

165. Rokeah, David. "Ben Stara Ben Pantera hu," *Tarbiz* 39 (1969), pp. 9-18.

166. Schoeps, Hans Joachim. "Simon Magus in der Haggada?" HUCA 21 (1948), pp. 257-274.

167. Zeitlin, Solomon. "Jesus in the Early Tannaitic Literature," in *Abhandlungen zur Erinnerung an Hirsch Perez Chajes* (Vienna: 1933), pp. 295-308.

viii. Other

168. Bacher, Wilhelm. "Étude critique sur quelques traditions étranges relatives à Rabbi Méir," REJ 5 (1882), pp. 178-187.

169. Ben Amos, Dan, "Talmudic Tall Tales," in *Folklore in Context: Essays* (New Delhi, 1982), pp. 88-110 (= *Folklore Today: a Festschrift for Richard M. Dorson*, ed. Linda Dégh et al. (Bloomington, Indiana: 1976), pp. 25-44).

170. Elbaum, Jacob. "Tavniyot lashon ve-'inyan be-ma'asei hakhamim: le-tivan shel ha-'eduyot 'al Rabi 'Akiva be-Avot de-Rabi Natan," 8th WCJS (Jerusalem: 1981), vol. 3, Heb. sect. pp. 71-77.

171. Fraenkel, Jonah, "Ma'aseh be-Rabi Shila (Bavli Berakhot 58a)," *Tarbiz* 40 (1970-71), pp. 33-40 (= Shinan, *Mikra'ah*, pp. 317-324).

172. _____. "Demuto shel R. Yehoshu'a ben Levi be-sipurei ha-Talmud ha-Bavli," 6th WCJS (Jerusalem: 1973), vol. 3, Heb. sect. pp. 403-417.

173. Gafni, Isaiah. "ha-Yeshivah ha-Bavlit le-or sugyat B. K. 117a," *Tarbiz* 49 (1980), pp. 292-301.

174. Gereboff, Joel. *Rabbi Tarfon: the Tradition, the Man, and Early Rabbinic Judaism* (Missoula, Mont.: 1979).

175. Goldenberg, Robert. "The Deposition of Rabban Gamaliel II: An Examination of the Sources," in *Persons and Institutions in Early Rabbinic Judaism*, ed. William Scott Green (Missoula, Mont.:1977), pp. 9-48 (= JJS 23 [1972], pp. 167-190).

176. Goodblatt, David. "The Beruriah Traditions," in *Persons and Institutions in Early Judaism*, ed. Green, pp. 207-236 (= JJS 26 [1975], pp. 68-85).

177. Hazan-Rokem, Galit. "ha-Meser ha-idi'ologi veha-meser ha-psikhologi be-Ma'aseh bi-shenei benei Tsadok ha-kohen – kavim le-farshanut ha-sipur be-midrash ha-agadah," JSHL 3 (1983), pp. 122-139.

178. Karlin, A. "Sipurei pela'ot shel Rabah bar Bar Hana," *Sinai* 20 (1946-47), pp. 56-61.

179. Levine, Lee. "R. Simeon b. Yohai and the Purification of Tiberias: History and Tradition," HUCA 49 (1975), pp. 143-185.

180. Licht, Hayim. "Ma'aseh ha-ishah ba-shuk (Avot de-Rabi Natan nusha alef 3:8)," *'Alei Sefer* 15-16 (1982), pp. 237-246.

181. _____. "ha-Agadah 'al ha-haver veha-prakmatoten (Midrash Tanhuma parashat Terumah)," *'Alei Sefer* 19-20 (1983), pp. 230-238.

182. Marks, Richard. "Dangerous Hero: Rabbinic Attitudes Toward Legendary Warriors," HUCA 54 (1983), pp. 181-194.

183. Meir, Ofra. "'Al Rabi Yohanan be-yahaso el talmidav," *'Alei Sefer* 15-16 (1982), pp. 224-236.

184. _____. "Hamorato shel R. Pinhas ben Ya'ir," FRCS 7 (1983), pp. 117-137.

185. Neusner, Jacob. "From Exegesis to Fable in Rabbinic Traditions About the Pharisees," JJS 25 (1974), pp. 262-269.

186. _____. "When Tales Travel: Shammai and Jonathan Ben 'Uzziel," in *Method and Meaning in Ancient Judaism: Third Series* (Chico, Calif.: 1981), pp. 137-141.

187. _____. *In Search of Talmudic Biography: The Problem of the Attributed Saying* (Chico, Calif.: 1984).

188. Neusner, Jacob and Alan Avery-Peck. "The Quest for the Historical Hillel: Theory and Practice," in *Formative Judaism: Religious, Historical and Literary Studies* (Chico, Calif.: 1982), pp. 45-64; and "Literature and Society: the Unfolding Literary Conventions of Hillel," *ibid.* pp. 87-97.

189. Saldarini, Anthony J. "The Adoption of a Dissident: Akabya ben Mahalaleel in Rabbinic Tradition," JJS 33 (1982), pp. 517-525.

190. Schwarzbaum, Haim, "Eliyahu ha-Navi ve-Rabi Yehoshu'a ben Levi," *Yeda' 'Am* 7 (1962) pp. 22-31.

191. Shenhar, Aliza, "Le-'amamiyutah shel agadat Beruriyah, eshet Rabi Me'ir," FRCS 3 (1972), Heb. sect. pp. 223-227.

192. _____. "Li-demuto shel R. Me'ir ve-'itsuvah be-sifrut ha-agadah," in *Heker ve-'iyun be-mad'ei ha-Yahadut: sifrut, Mikra, lashon,* ed. Jacob Bahat et al. (Haifa: 1976), pp. 259-266.

193. Shinan, Avigdor. "Ahiv shel Rabi Me'ir," JSHL 2 (1983), pp. 7-20.

194. Wiesenberg, E. "The Nicanor Gate," JJS 3 (1952), pp. 14-29.

VI. Themes and Motifs

i. General

195. Bin Gorion, Emanuel. *Shevilei ha-agadah* (Jerusalem: 1949).

196. Fraenkel, Jonah, "Tsurot hitsoniyot le'umat 'arakhim penimiyim," in *Mikhtam le-David: sefer zikaron ha-rav David Ochs,* ed. Y.D. Gilat and Eliezer Stern (Ramat Gan: 1978), pp. 120-137.

197. _____. *'Iyunim be-'olamo ha-ruhani shel sipur ha-agadah* (Tel Aviv: 1981) (and see review by Avigdor Shinan, "A New Approach to the Study of Aggadic Narratives," *Immanuel* 16 [1983], pp. 65-69).

198. Kadushin, Max. *The Theology of Seder Eliahu: A Study in Organic Thinking* (New York: 1932).

199. _____. *A Conceptual Approach to the Mekilta* (New York: 1969).

199A. Kariv, Abraham. "'Arkhei musar u-midot ba-agadah," *Molad* 245-6 (1975), pp. 103-111.

200. _____. *Mi-sod hakhamim: bi-netivei agadot Hazal* (Jerusalem: 1976).

201. Marmorstein, Arthur [Avraham]. "Re'ayonot ha-agadah ve-korot ha-zeman," *Tarbiz* 5 (1933-34), pp. 134-147 (= Shinan, *Mikra'ah,* pp. 99-112).

202. _____. "Ma'amar 'al 'erkah ha-histori shel ha-agadah," *Sefer ha-Yovel li-Profesor Shmu'el Krauss,* ed. S. Klein (Jerusalem: 1936), pp. 55-68.

203. Piron, Mordechai. *Bi-netivei agadot Hazal: 'iyunim be-mishnatam shel kadmonim* (Tel Aviv: 1970).

204. _____. *Be-sha'arei ha-agadah: halikhot ve-'arakhim be-midreshei Hazal* (Tel Aviv: 1974).

205. Schechter, Solomon. *Aspects of Rabbinic Theology* (New York, 1909; repr. New York: 1961).

206. Urbach, Ephraim E. *Hazal: pirkei emunot ve-de'ot* (Jerusalem: 1969) (tr. Israel Abrahams, *The Sages: their Concepts and Beliefs,* 2 vol. [Jerusalem: 1979]).

ii. Folkloristic Motifs

207. Aptowitzer, Viktor. "The Rewarding and Punishing of Animals and Inanimate Objects: On the Aggadic View of the World," *HUCA* 3 (1926), pp. 117-155.

208. Englard, Izhak. "Kanya de-Rava, ha-mizbeah shel Nikolaus veha-shalshelet shel David ha-Melekh: li-ve'ayat ha-ha'aramah bi-shevu'ah," *Tarbiz* 52 (1982-83), pp. 591-609.

209. Heller, Bernard. "L'epée gardienne de chasteté dans la litérature juive," REJ 52 (1906), pp. 169-176.

210. Kagan, Ziporah. "ha-Ishah ha-ne'emanah be-sipur ha-'amami," *Mahanayim* 98 (1965), pp. 132-143

211. _____. "Mei hayim ve-tal hayim," *Mahanayim* 99 (1965), pp. 146-153.

212. Lachs, Samuel Tobias, "Serpent Folklore in Rabbinic Literature," *Jewish Social Studies* 28 (1965), pp. 168-184.

213. Lévi, Israel. "Le lait de la mère et le coffre flottant," REJ 59 (1910), pp. 1-15.

214. _____. "Le conte du *Diable dupé* dans le folklore juif," REJ 85 (1928), pp. 137-163.

215. Meir, Ofra. "ha-Nusha'ot ha-Yehudiyot shel ha-tipus ha-sipuri AT 875," *Yeda' 'Am* 19 (1979), pp. 55-61; cf. Meir, "The Jewish Versions of AT 875 'The Clever Girl'," 6th WCJS *Abstracts* (Jerusalem: 1973), p. D-70.

216. Niditch, Susan, "Father-Son Folktale Patterns and Tyrant Typologies in Josephus' Ant. 12:160-222," JJS 32 (1981), pp. 47-55.

217. Noy, Dov. *Motif-Index of Talmudic-Midrashic Literature* (Ph.D. thesis, Indiana University: 1954)

218. _____. *ha-Sipur ha-'amami ba-Talmud uva-Midrash,* ed. Yosef Tovi (Jerusalem: 1968)

219. _____. "The Jewish Versions of the 'Animal Languages' Folktale (AT 670)," SH 22 (1971), pp. 171-208.

220. _____. "ha-Tsadik ha-nistar be-sipurei tsiduk ha-din," *Yeda' 'Am* 18 (1976), pp. 32-40.

221. Patai, Raphael. *Adam va-adamah,* 2 vol. (Jerusalem: 1943).

222. _____. *Man and Temple in Ancient Jewish Myth and Ritual,* 2nd ed., (New York: 1967).

223. Schnitzler, Otto. "A Yiddish-Canadian Version of Motif K 814 (woman in disguise wooed by her faithless husband) from Toronto," 6th WCJS *Abstracts* (Jerusalem: 1973), pp. D-6, D-7.

224. Schoenfeld, Elisheva. "Adam ha-domeh le-hamor," *Yeda' 'Am* 12 (1967), pp. 83-87.

225. Schwarzbaum, Haim. "The Hero Predestined to Die on his Wedding Day (AT 934 B)," FRCS 4 (1974), Eng. sect., pp. 223-252.

226. _____. "Lamed-vav tsadikim be-folklor ha-Yehudi (le-heker ha-tipusim ha-sipuriyim D 756; B 759; A 809) mi-yesodam shel ha-hokrim Aarne-Thompson," *Yeda' 'Am* 18 (1976), pp. 20-28.

227. _____. "Kotser re'uto shel malakh ha-mavet: le-heker ha-mekorot ha-Yehudiyim veha-Islamiyim shel ha-tipus ha-sipuri AT 795," FRCS 1 (1970), Heb. sect., pp. 323-337.

228. Shenhar, Aliza. "Concerning the Nature of the Motif 'Death by a Kiss' (Mot. A 185.6.1.1)," *Fabula* 19 (1978), pp. 62-73.

229. _____. "Motiv retsah-ah ba-agadah uve-sipurei ha-'am shel 'edot Yisra'el (Motiv S 573.1)," *Yeda' 'Am* 21 (1982), pp. 52-57; cf. Shenhar, "Fratricide (Motif 573.1) in Jewish Agada and Folktales," 6th WCJS *Abstracts* (Jerusalem: 1973), p. D-82.

230. _____. "The Jewish Oicotype of the *Predestined Marriage* Folktale: AaTh 930 *E (IFA)," *Fabula* 24 (1983), pp. 43-55.

iii. Responses to Catastrophe

231. Aderet, Avraham, "Mavo le-agadot ha-hurban," *'Alei Sefer* 1 (1974), pp. 40-42.

232. Bokser, Baruch M. "Rabbinic Responses to Catastrophe: from Continuity to Discontinuity," PAAJR 50 (1983), pp. 37-63.

233. Cohen, Norman J. "Shekhinta ba-Galuta: a midrashic response to destruction and persecution," JStJ 13 (1982), pp. 147-159.

234. Cohen, Shaye J. D. "The Destruction: From Scripture to Midrash," *Prooftexts* 2 (1982), pp. 18-39.

235. Goldenberg, Robert. "Early Rabbinic Explanations for the Destruction of Jerusalem," JJS 33 (1982), pp. 517-525.

236. Hammer, Reuven. "A Rabbinic Response to the post-Bar Kochba Era: the Sifra to Ha'azinu," PAAJR 52 (1983), pp. 37-62.

237. Heinemann, Joseph. "A Homily on Jeremiah and the fall of Jerusalem (Pesiqta Rabbati, Pisqa 26)" in *The Biblical Mosaic: Changing Perspectives,* ed. Robert Polzin and Eugene Rothman (Philadelphia: 1982), pp. 27-44.

238. Mintz, Alan. "Midrash and the Destruction," in *Hurban: Responses to Catastrophe in Hebrew Literature* (New York: 1984), pp. 48-83.

239. Saldarini, Anthony J. "Varieties of Rabbinic Response to the Destruction of the Temple," SBL *Seminar Papers* (1982), pp. 437-458.

iv. Angels and Devils

240. Bamberger, Bernard. *Fallen Angels* (Philadelphia: 1952), esp. "Talmud and Midrash," pp. 89-111.

241. Jung, Leo, "Fallen Angels in Jewish, Christian and Mohammedan Literature: A Study in Comparative Folklore," JQR 15 (1924-25), pp. 467-502; 16 (1925-26) pp. 45-88, 171-205, 287-336.

242. Kaminka, Armand. "The Origin of the Ashmedai Legend in the Babylonian Talmud," JQR 13 (1922-23), pp. 221-224.

243. Kohut, Alexander. *Ueber die jüdische Angelogie und Daemonologie in ihrer Abhängigkeit vom Parsismus* (Leipzig: 1866).

244. Marmorstein, Arthur. "Anges et hommes dans l'Agada," REJ 84 (1927), pp. 37-50; and "Notes complementaires à anges et hommes dans l'Agada," pp. 138-140.

245. _____. "Vikuhei ha-malakhim 'im ha-bore," *Melilah* 3-4 (1950), pp. 93-102.

246. Schäfer, Peter. *Rivalität zwischen Engeln und Menschen: Untersuchungen zur rabbinischen Engelvorstellung* (Berlin: 1975).

247. Schultz, Joseph P. "Angelic Opposition to the Ascension of Moses and the Revelation of the Law," JQR 61 (1970-71), pp. 282-307.

248. Schwarzbaum, Haim. "Malakh ha-mavet be-folklor ha-Yehudi veha-Muslami," 5th WCJS (Jerusalem: 1969), vol. 4, pp. 29-33.

v. Heaven and Hell

249. Aptowitzer, Viktor. "Bet ha-Mikdash shel ma'alah le-fi ha-agadah," *Tarbiz* 2 (1930-31), pp. 137-153, 257-287 (= Shinan, *Mikra'ah,* pp. 51-98).

250. Castelli, David. "The Future Life in Rabbinical Literature," JQR 1 (1889), pp. 314-352.

251. Elbaum, Jacob. "Nashim she-nikhnesu hayim le-Gan 'Eden," *Mahanayim* 98 (1965), pp. 124-131.

252. Fox, Samuel J. *Hell in Jewish Literature* (Northbrook, Ill.: 1972).

253. Kagan, Ziporah. "Ba'al melakhah ke-shakhen be-Gan 'Eden," *Mahanayim* 91 (1964), pp. 42-47.

254. Lévi, Israel. "Si les morts ont conscience de ce qui se passe ici-bas," REJ 26 (1893) pp. 69-74.

255. _____. "Le repos sabbatique des ames damnées," REJ 25 (1892), pp. 1-13; "Notes complementaires sur le repos sabbatique des ames damnées," 26 (1893), pp. 131-135.

256. Lieberman, Saul. "Some Aspects of After Life in Early Rabbinic Literature," in *Harry Austryn Wolfson Jubilee Volume,* ed. Saul Lieberman et al., (Jerusalem: 1965), Eng. sect., pp. 495-532 (= Lieberman, *Texts and Studies,* pp. 235-272; Fischel, *Essays,* pp. 387-424).

257. Marmorstein, Arthur. " La participation à la vie éternelle dans la théologie rabbinique et dans la légende," REJ 89 (1930), pp. 305-320.

258. Maswari-Caspi, Mishael. "Gilgul shel neshamot – gilgulo shel motiv," *Yeda' 'Am* 22 (1984), pp. 82-93.

vi. Messiah and Apocalypse

259. Aberbach, Moshe, "Hizkiyahu melekh Yehudah ve-Rabi Yehudah ha-Nasi: heksherim meshihiyim," *Tarbiz* 53 (1984), pp. 353-371.

260. Berger, Abraham. "Captive at the Gate of Rome: the Story of a Messianic Motif," PAAJR 44 (1977), pp. 1-17.

261. Heinemann, Joseph, " Mashiah ben Efrayim vi-yetsi'at Mitsrayim shel benei Efrayim be-terem kets," *Tarbiz* 40 (1970-71), pp. 450-461 (= Heinemann, *Agadot ve-Toldotehen*, pp. 131-142; Shinan, *Mikra'ah*, pp. 162-173; = "The Messiah of Ephraim and the Premature Exodus of the Tribe of Ephraim," HThR 68 (1975), pp. 1-16.)

262. Lévi, Israel. "Apocalypses dans le Talmud," REJ 1 (1880), pp. 108-114.

263. _____. "Les morts et l'avènement de l'ère messianique," REJ 69 (1919), pp. 122-128.

264. Neusner, Jacob. *Messiah in Context: Israel's history and destiny in formative Judaism* (Philadelphia: 1984).

265. Noy, Dov. "ha-Esh ke-ot be-midreshei ge'ulah," *Mahanayim* 80 (1963), pp. 105-114.

266. _____. "Demut ha-Mashiah ke-gibor 'amami," *Mahanayim* 124 (1970), pp. 114-125

vii. Miscellaneous Motifs and Themes

267. Abrahams, Israel. "Marriages are made in Heaven," JQR o.s. 2 (1890), pp. 172-177 (= Abrahams, *The Book of Delight and other Papers* [Philadelphia: 1912; repr. New York: 1980], pp. 172-183).

268. Aderet, Avraham. "Tahlikhei 'ilui ve-dildul be-sipurei ha-agadah," *'Alei Sefer* 6 (1978), pp. 156-177.

269. Aptowitzer, Viktor. "Die Seele als Vogel," MGWJ 69 (1925), pp. 150-168.

270. _____. "Spuren des Matriarchats in Juedischen Schrifttum," HUCA 4 (1927), pp. 207-240; 5 (1928), pp. 261-297.

271. Goldberg, Arnold M. *Untersuchungen über die Vorstellung von der Schekhinah in der frühen rabbinischen Literatur* (Berlin: 1969).

272. Hurwitz, Solomon. "Pygmy-legends in Jewish Literature," JQR 6 (1915-16), pp. 339-358.

273. Krauss, Samuel. "Jewish Giants in the Gentile Folklore," JQR 38 (1947-48), pp. 135-149.

274. Lauterbach, Jacob. "Tashlik: a Study in Jewish Ceremonies," HUCA 11 (1936), pp. 207-340 (= *Rabbinic Essays* [Cincinnati: 1951], pp. 299-433).

275. _____. "Belief in the Power of the Word, " HUCA 14 (1939), pp. 287-302.

276. Lévi, Israel. "Signes de danger et de malheur," REJ 17 (1888), pp. 202-209.

277. Meir, Ofra. " 'Iyun nosaf bi-shetayim me-agadot Hazal," 'Alei Sefer 7-8 (1979), pp. 89-100 (on Aderet, "Tahlikhei 'ilui..." and Shenhar "'Ve-yashov he-'afar ...").

278. Meyer, Rudolf. "Geschichte eines orientalischen Märchenmotiv in der rabbinischen Literatur," Festschrift Alfred Bertholet (Tübingen: 1950), pp. 365-378.

279. Nacht, Jacob. Simlei ishah bi-mekorotenu ha-'atikim ... (Tel Aviv: 1959).

280. Noy, Dov. "Luz: ha-'ir ha-agadit shebe-erets Yehudah," Mahanayim 102 (1966), pp. 42-49.

281. _____. "Sipurei-'am 'al ha-Kotel ha-Ma'aravi," Mahanayim 107 (1966), pp. 44-55 (= Mahanayim 107 [1967], pp. 64-83; cf. "ha-Kotel ha-Ma'aravi be-sipurenu ha-'amamiyim," Mahanayim 71 [1962], pp. 46-48).

282. _____. "Yahas ha-agadah li-refu'ah," Mahanayim 122 (1969), pp. 68-93.

283. Patai, Raphael. "Some Hebrew Sea Legends," in Jubilee Volume in honor of Edward Mahler (Budapest: 1937), pp. 488-493.

284. _____. "Jewish Seafaring in Ancient Times," JQR 32 (1941-42), pp. 1-26.

285. Rubin, Salomon. Kabbala und Agada in mythologischer, symbolischer und mystischer Personification in der Natur (Vienna: 1895).

286. Saban, Yitshak, "ha-Emunah be-tsiduk ha-din be-agadat Hazal," Mahanayim 109 (1967), pp. 49-52.

287. Schäfer, Peter. Die Vorstellung vom heiligen Geist in der rabbinischen Literatur (Munich: 1972).

288. Scholem, Gershom G. "The Idea of the Golem," in On the Kabbalah and its Symbolism, tr. Ralph Manheim, (pbk. New York: 1969), pp. 158-204.

289. Schwarzbaum, Haim. "Bet ha-keneset be-agadot ha-'am," Mahanayim 95 (1964), pp. 58-65.

290. Shenhar, Aliza. "Ve-yashov he-'afar 'al ha-arets keshe-hayah (Kohelet 12:7): 'iyun bi-shetei me-agadot Hazal," 'Alei Sefer 4-5 (1977), pp. 113-121.

291. Yaniv, Shelomoh. "ha-Hevrah ha-utopit me-'ever la-Sambatyon," Karmelit 20-21 (1977-78), pp. 277-291.

292. Zimmerman, David. "Sipur ahavah min ha-midrash," 'Alei Sefer 7-8 (1979), pp. 84-88.

293. _____. *Shemonah sipurei ahavah min ha-Talmud veha-Midrash* (Tel Aviv: 1981).

VII.　Aggadic Retellings of Biblical Narratives

i. General

294. Ginzberg, Louis. *Legends of the Jews,* 7 vol. (New York: 1909-1938); and see Bernard Heller, "Ginzberg's *Legends of the Jews,*" JQR 24 (1933-34), pp. 51-66, 165-190, 281-307, 393-418; 25 (1934-35), pp. 29-52.

295. Grünbaum, Max. Neue Beiträge zur semitischen Sagenkunde (Leiden: 1893).

296. Margaliot, Eliezer. *ha-Hayavim be-Mikra ve-zaka'im ba-Talmud uva-Midrashim* (London: 1949).

297. Shinan, Avigdor. "Mi-derashat ha-pasuk el ha-agadah ha-hofshit: perek be-toldot ha-sipur ha-Mikra'i ha-murhav," JSHL 5 (1984), pp. 203-220.

298. Vermes, Geza. *Scripture and Tradition in Judaism: Haggadic Studies,* 2nd ed. (Leiden: 1973); and see review by Joseph Heinemann in *Tarbiz* 35 (1965-66), pp. 84-94.

ii. Antediluvians

299. Altmann, Alexander. "The Gnostic Background of the Rabbinic Adam Legends," JQR 35 (1944-45), pp. 371-391.

300. Aptowitzer, Viktor. *Kain und Abel in der Agada, den Apokryphen, der hellenistischen, christlichen und muhammedanischen Literatur* (Vienna: 1922).

301. Fraade, Steven D. *Enosh and His Generation: Pre-Israelite Hero and History in Postbiblical Interpretation* (Chico, Calif.: 1984).

302. Ginzberg, Louis. "Mabul shel esh," *ha-Goren* 8 (1912), pp. 11-23 (= Ginzberg, *'Al halakhah ve-agadah: mehkar u-masah* [Tel Aviv: 1960], pp. 205-219).

303. Himmelfarb, Martha. "A Report on Enoch in Rabbinic Literature," SBL *Seminar Papers* (1978), vol. 1, pp. 259-269.

304. Klijn, A. F. J. *Seth in Jewish, Christian and Gnostic Literature* (Leiden: 1977).

305. Lewinski, Yom Tov. "Hanokh-Metatron tofer man'alim," *Yeda' 'Am* 12 (1967), pp. 17-22.

306. Lewis, Jack P. *A Study of the Interpretation of Noah and the Flood in Jewish and Christian Literature* (Leiden: 1968).

iii. The Binding of Isaac

307. Elbaum, Jacob. "From Sermon to Story: the Transformation of the Akedah," *Prooftexts* 6 (1986), pp. 97-116.

308. Lévi, Israel. "Le sacrifice d'Isaac et la mort de Jésus," REJ 64 (1912), pp. 161-184.

309. Noy, Dov. "ha-'Akedah ke-avtipus shel kidush ha-Shem," *Mahanayim* 60 (1961), pp. 140-144.

310. Saldarini, Anthony J. "Interpretations of the *Akedah* in Rabbinic Literature," in *The Biblical Mosaic: Changing Perspectives,* ed. Robert Polzin and Eugene Rothman (Philadelphia: 1982), pp. 149-165; and Dan Ben Amos, "A Folklorist's Response," *ibid.,* pp. 166-7

311. Spiegel, Shalom. "Me-agadot ha-'akedah ...," in *Alexander Marx Jubilee Volume,* ed. S. Lieberman et al. (New York: 1950), Heb. sect., pp. 471-547 (tr. Judah Goldin, *The Last Trial* [New York: 1967]).

iv. Moses and Aaron

312. Beer, Moshe, " 'Oshro shel Mosheh be-agadat Hazal," *Tarbiz* 43 (1973), pp. 70-87 (= Shinan, *Mikra'ah,* pp. 188-205).

313. Bloch, Renée, ed. *Moïse: l'homme de l'alliance* in *Cahiers Sioniens* 8 (1954), pp. 120-405; (tr. *Moses in Schrift und Überlieferung* (Düsseldorf, 1963)); esp. R. Bloch, "Quelques aspects de la figure de Moïse dans la tradition rabbinique," *Cahiers,* pp. 211-285.

314. Ish-Shalom, Michael. "Me'arat ha-Makhpelah u-kevurato shel Mosheh – le-gilgulah shel mesoret agadah," *Tarbiz* 41 (1972), pp. 203-210.

315. Krauss, Samuel. "Mosheh, safra rava de-Yisra'el," *ha-Goren* 7 (1908), pp. 29-34.

316. _____. "A Moses Legend," JQR 2 (1911-12), pp. 339-364; and Israel Friedländer, "Note on 'A Moses Legend'," 3 (1912-13), pp. 179-180.

317. _____. "Ma'aseh 'al ha-dor ha-'asiri," *ha-Goren* 8 (1912), pp. 11-23.

318. Rosmarin, Aaron. *Moses im Lichte der Agada (inaugural-dissertation ... Wurzburg ...)* (New York: 1932).

319. Schäfer, Peter and Klaus Haacker, "Nachbiblische Traditionen vom Tod des Mose," in *Josephus-Studien ... Otto Michel ... gewidmet,* ed. Otto Betz et al. (Gottingen: 1974), pp. 147-174.

320. Schwarzbaum, Haim. "Jewish, Christian and Falasha Legends of the Death of Aaron the High Priest," *Fabula* 5 (1962), pp. 185-237.

v. Elijah

321. Guttmann, Joshua. "Eliyahu ha-Navi be-agadot Yisra'el," *ha-Atid* 5 (1913; repr. 1923), pp. 14-46.

322. Levinsohn, Moses Wolf. *Der Prophet Elia nach den Talmudim und Midraschimquellen* ... (New York: 1929).

323. Margaliot, Elizer. *Eliyahu ha-Navi be-sifrut Yisra'el* (Jerusalem: 1960).

324. S. K. "Der Prophet Elia in der Legende," MGWJ 12 (1863), pp. 241-255, 281-296.

325. Wiener, Aharon. *The Prophet Elijah in the Development of Judaism: a Depth-Psychological Study* (London: 1978).

vi. Other

326. Aberbach, Moshe. "ha-Yehasim ben 'Ira ha-Ya'iri ve-David ha-melekh le-fi ha-agadah ha-Talmudit," *Tarbiz* 33 (1964), pp. 358-361 (= Shinan, *Mikra'ah*, pp. 233-236).

327. Aberbach, Moshe and Leivy Smolar. "Jeroboam and Solomon: Rabbinic Interpretations," JQR 59 (1968-69), pp. 118-132.

328. Amaru, Betsy Halpern. "The Killing of the Prophets: Unraveling a Midrash," HUCA 54 (1983), pp. 153-180.

329. Aptowitzer, Viktor. "Asenath, the wife of Joseph: a Haggadic Literary-Historical Study," HUCA 1 (1924), pp. 239-306.

330. _____. "Malkizedek zu den Sagen der Agada," MGWJ 70 (1926), pp. 93-113.

331. Beer, Moshe. "Yissakhar u-Zevulun: li-she'elat kiyumam ha-kalkali shel Amora'ei erets Yisra'el," *Bar Ilan: sefer ha-shanah...* 6 (1968), pp. 167-180.

332. _____. "Banav shel 'Eli be-agadat Hazal: minuyim shel banim 'al yedei avotehem le-mishrot tsiburiyot," *Bar Ilan: sefer ha-shanah...* 14-15 (1977), pp. 79-93.

333. Blank, Sheldon H. "The Death of Zechariah in Rabbinic Literature," HUCA 12-13 (1937-38), pp 327-346.

334. Elbaum, Jacob. "Rabi El'azar ha-Moda'i ve-Rabi Yehoshu'a 'al parashat 'Amalek," FRCS 7 (1983), Heb. sect., pp. 99-116.

335. Goldenberg, Robert. "The Problem of False Prophecy: Talmudic Interpretations of Jeremiah 28 and I Kings 22," in *The Biblical Mosaic: Changing Perspectives,* ed. Robert Polzin and Eugene Rothman (Philadelphia: 1982), pp. 87-104.

336. _____. "Ma'asei yadai tov'in ba-yam ...," *Bar Ilan: sefer ha-shanah* 7-8 (1970), pp. 80-84.

337. Lévi, Israel. "L'orgueil de Salomon," REJ 15 (1888), pp. 58-65.

338. Lewinski, Yom Tov. "He'akh nikba' mekom Bet ha-Mikdash," *Yeda' 'Am* 13 (68), pp. 24-40; cf. Haim Schwarzbaum, "Li-mekoroteha shel ha-

agadah 'al makom mat'im le-vinyan Bet ha-Mikdash bi-Yerushalayim," *ibid.,* pp. 41-45.

339. Meir, Ofra. "Sipur mahalat Hizkiyahu be-agadat Hazal," *ha-Sifrut* 9 (1981), pp. 109-130.

340. Murmelstein, B. "ha-Agadah 'al damo shel Zekharyah ha-navi: shorshah ve-'anafah," *Sefer Yovel li-Profesor Shmu'el Krauss,* ed. S. Klein (Jerusalem: 1936), pp. 161-168.

341. Perles, Joseph. "La légende d'Asnath, fille de Dina et femme de Joseph," REJ 23 (1891), pp. 87-92.

342. Rabinowitz, L. I. "The Study of a Midrash," JQR 58 (1967-8), pp. 143-161 [on the courtship of Rebekah].

343. Shinan, Avigdor. "Hata'ehem shel Nadav ve-Avihu be-agadat Hazal," *Tarbiz* 48 (1978-79), pp. 201-214 (= Shinan, *Mikra'ah,* pp. 174-187).

344. Steinsalz, Adin. "Khil'av ben David be-midreshei Hazal," *Sinai* 62 (1967-68), pp. 79-80.

345. Uffenheimer, Benjamin. "Hakdashat Yesha'yahu ve-gilguleha be-masoret Hazal," in *ha-Mikra ve-toldot Yisra'el: mehkarim le-zikhro shel Ya'akov Liver,* ed. B. Uffenheimer (Tel Aviv: 1972), pp. 18-50.

346. Urbach, Ephraim E. "Teshuvat anshei Ninveh veha-vikuah ha-Yehudi-Notsri," *Tarbiz* 20 (1949), pp. 118-122 (= Shinan, *Mikra'ah,* pp. 237-244).

347. _____. "Derashot Hazal 'al nevi'ei umot ha-'olam ve-'al parashat Bil'am le-or ha-vikuah ha-Yehudi-ha-Notsri," *Tarbiz* 25 (1956), pp. 272-289 (= Shinan, *Mikra'ah,* pp. 206-223).

348. Wieder, Arnold Aaron. *Jeremiah in Aggadic Literature* (Ph.D. thesis, Brandeis Univ.: 1962).

VIII. Parables and Fables

349. Abrahams, Israel, "The Fox's Heart," in *The Book of Delights and Other Papers* (Philadelphia: 1912; repr. New York: 1980), pp. 159-171 (= JQR o.s. 1 [1889], pp. 216-222).

350. Back, Samuel. "Die Fabel in Talmud und Midrasch," appeared in 22 parts in MGWJ 24-33 (1874-1881).

351. Crossan, John Dominic. "Hidden Treasure Parables in Late Antiquity," SBL *Seminar Papers* (1976), pp. 359-379.

352. Daube, David. "Ancient Hebrew Fables," (lecture, Oxford Univ.: 1973).

353. Feldman, Asher. *The Parables and Similes of the Rabbis: Agricultural and Pastoral* (Cambridge: 1927).

354. Goldberg, Arnold. "Das Schriftauslegende Gleichnis im Midrasch," *Frankfurter Judaistische Beiträge* 9 (1981), pp. 1-90.

355. Guttman, Theodor. *ha-Mashal bi-tekufat ha-Tana'im*, 2nd. ed. (Jerusalem: 1949).

356. Heller, Bernard. "Ein Homerisches Gleichnis im Midrasch," MGWJ 76 (1932), pp. 330-334.

357. Johnston, Robert M. "Parables among the Pharisees and Early Rabbis," in Jacob Neusner, *A History of the Mishnaic Law of Purities*, vol. 13 (Leiden: 1976), pp. 224-226.

358. _____. "The Study of Rabbinic Parables: Some Preliminary Observations," SBL *Seminar Papers* (1976), pp. 337-357.

359. Levi, Israel. "L'aveugle et le cul-de-jatte," REJ 23 (1891), pp. 199-205.

360. Meir, Ofra. "Nose ha-hatunah be-mishlei ha-melakhim be-agadat Hazal," FRCS 4 (1974), Heb. sect. pp. 9-51.

361. _____. "Mashal ha-hitim," in *Heker ve-'Iyun be-Mad'ei ha-Yahadut: sifrut, Mikra, lashon*, ed. Jacob Bahat et al. (Haifa: 1976), pp. 259-266.

362. Noy, Dov. "ha-Koves u-*meshalot kovsim*," *Mahanayim* 91 (1964), p. 34-40.

363. Schwarzbaum, Haim. "The Vision of Eternal Peace in the Animal Kingdom (AaTh 62)," *Fabula* 10 (1969), pp. 107-131.

364. _____. *The Mishle Shu'alim (Fox Fables) of Rabbi Berechiah ha-Nakdan: A study in comparative folklore and fable lore* (Tel Aviv: 1979).

365. Singer, Aharon M. " 'Iyun be-mishlei shu'alim be-sifrut Hazal," JSJF 4 (1983), pp. 79-91.

366. Stern, David. "Interpreting in Parables: The Mashal in Midrash, with Special Reference to Lamentations Rabba," (Ph.D. thesis, Harvard Univ.: 1981).

367. _____. "Rhetoric and Midrash: The Case of the Mashal," *Prooftexts* 1 (1981), pp. 262-291.

368. _____. "Tafkido shel ha-mashal be-sifrut Hazal," JSHL 7 (1985), pp. 90-102.

369. Wallach, Luitpold. "The Parable of the Blind and the Lame: A study of comparative literature," JBL 62 (1943), pp. 333-339.

370. Ziegler, Ignaz. *Der Königsgleichnisse der Midrasch* (Breslau: 1903).

IX.   Court Cases and Legal Precedents

371. Gafni, Isaiah. "Ma'asei bet din ba-Talmud ha-Bavli: tsurot sifrutiyot ve-hashlakhot historiyot," PAAJR 49 (1982), Heb. sect., pp. 22-40.

372. Goldberg, Arnold. "Form und Funktion des Ma'ase in der Mischna, " *Frankfurter Judaistische Beiträge* 2 (1974), pp. 1-38.

373. Goodblatt, David. *Rabbinic Instruction in Sasanian Babylonia* (Leiden: 1975).

374. Kaminka, Armand. "ha-Ma'aseh be-tor mekor ha-halakhah," in *Mehkarim be-Mikra ve-Talmud uva-sifrut ha-rabanit*, vol. 2 (Tel Aviv: 1951), pp. 142.

375. Melamed, Ezra Zion. "ha-Ma'aseh ki-mekor le-halakhah," *Sinai* 46 (1959-60) pp. 152-166.

376. _____. "Kovtsei ma'asim shel Tana'im," 8th WCJS (Jerusalem: 1981), vol. 3, Heb. sect., pp. 45-69.

377. Neusner, Jacob. *A History of the Jews in Babylonia*, 5 vol. (Leiden: 1965-70).

378. Segal, Eliezer Lorne. "The Use of the Formula *ki ha de* in the Citation of Cases in the Babylonian Talmud," HUCA 50 (1979), pp. 199-218.

379. _____. "Variant Traditions of Cases *('uvda)* in the Babylonian Talmud," JQR 70 (1979), pp. 1-27.

380. Wachholder, Ben Zion. "ha-Ma'asim veha-sipurim shel Raban Gamliel ba-Mishnah uva-Tosefta," 4th WCJS (Jerusalem: 1967), pp. 143-144.

X. Sources and Parallels of Aggadic Narratives

i. General

381. Halevi, E. E. "Ben hashpa'ah le-hakbalah," *Tarbiz* 51 (1981-82), pp. 310-311, and Avigdor Shinan, "Teshuvah," pp. 311-312.

ii. Jewish Writings

382. Albeck, Chanoch. "Agadot im Lichte der Pseudepigraphen," MGWJ 83 (1939), pp. 162-169.

383. Braun, Martin. *History and Romance in Graeco-Oriental Literature* (Oxford: 1938).

384. Feldman, Louis H. "Josephus' Portrait of Saul," HUCA 53 (1982), pp. 4599.

385. Heller, Bernard. "Die Scheu vor Unbekanntem, Unbenanntem in Agada und Apokryphen," MGWJ 83 (1939), pp. 170-184.

386. Kirschner, Robert. "The Rabbinic and Philonic Exegeses of the Nadab and Abihu Incident (Lev. 10:1-6)," JQR 73 (1982-83), pp. 375-393.

387. Kohler, K. "The Pre-Talmudic Haggada," JQR 5 (1893), pp. 399-419; 7 (1895), pp. 581-606.

388. Loftus, Francis. "The Martyrdom of the Galilean Troglodytes (B.J. i. 312-3; A. xiv. 429-30): a suggested *traditionsgeschichte*," JQR 66 (1976), pp. 212-223.

389. Rappaport, Salomo. *Agada und Exegese bei Flavius Josephus* (Vienna: 1930).

390. Sandmel, Samuel. "Philo's Place in Judaism: A Study in Conceptions of Abraham in Jewish Literature," HUCA 25 (1954), pp. 209-238; 26 (1955), pp. 151-332.

391. Sigal, Phillip. "Manifestations of Hellenistic Historiography in Select Judaic Literature," SBL *Seminar Papers* (1984), pp. 161-185.

392. Smolar, Leivy and Moshe Aberbach. "The Golden Calf Episode in Post-Biblical Literature," HUCA 39 (1968), pp. 91-116.

iii. Greek and Roman Authors

393. Aptowitzer, Viktor. "Eine interessante griechische Parallele zu einem merkwürdigen Ausspruch der Agada," MGWJ 69 (1925), pp. 355-357.

394. Cohen, Shaye J. D. "Patriarchs and Scholarchs," PAAJR 48 (1981), pp. 57-85.

395. Elbaum, Jacob. "Ma'asim be-shikor u-mekho'ar be-agadatenu uve-agadat Yavan," *Mahanayim* 112 (1967), pp. 122-129.

396. Finkel, Joshua. "A Link betwen Hasidism and Hellenistic and Patristic Literature," PAAJR 26 (1957), pp. 1-24; 27 (1958), pp. 19-42.

397. _____. "The Guises and Vicissitudes of a Universal Folk-belief in Jewish and Greek Tradition," in *Harry Austryn Wolfson Jubilee Volume*, ed. Saul Lieberman et al. (Jerusalem: 1965), pp. 233-255 (=Fischel, *Essays*, pp. 344-365).

398. Fischel, Henry A. "Studies in Cynicism and the Ancient Near East: The Transformation of a *chria*," in *Religions in Antiquity: Essays in Memory of Erwin Ramsdell Goodenough*, ed. Jacob Neusner (Leiden: 1968), pp. 372-411.

399. _____. "Story and History: Observations on Greco-Roman Rhetoric and Pharisaism," *American Oriental Society, Middle West Branch, Semi-Centennial Volume*, ed. Dennis Sinor (Bloomington, Indiana: 1969), pp. 59-88 (= Fischel, *Essays*, pp. 443-472).

400. _____. "Literary Forms of Midrash in their Relations to Greco-Roman Rhetoric," 6th WCJS *Abstracts* (Jerusalem: 1973), p. C-36.

401. _____. *Rabbinic Literature and Greco-Roman Philosophy: a study of Epicurea and Rhetorica in Early Midrashic Writings* (Leiden: 1973).

402. _____, ed. *Essays in Greco-Roman and Related Talmudic Literature* (New York: 1977).

403. Hadas, Moses. "Rabbinic Parallels to *Scriptores Historiae Augustae*," *Classical Philology* 24 (1929), pp. 258-262 (= Fischel, *Essays*, pp. 43-47).

404. Halevi, E. E. *Sha'arei ha-agadah: 'al mahut ha-agadah, sugeha, derakheha, mataroteha ve-zikatah le-tarbut zemanah* (Tel Aviv: 1963).

405. _____. "Me-agadot ha-hurban veha-nehamah," *Moznayim* 21 (1965), pp. 270-273.

406. _____. "Kinoro shel David," *Moznayim* 22 (1965-66), pp. 334-336.

407. _____. "Lo yetse adam le-huts la-arets," *Moznayim* 23 (1966), pp. 72-73.

408. _____. "Aharei mot ...," in *Sefer zikaron le-Vinyamin De Vries*, ed. E. Z. Melamed (Jerusalem: 1969), pp. 94-100.

409. _____. "Motivim Yevanim ba-agadah," *Tarbiz* 40 (1970-71), pp. 293-300.

410. _____. *'Olamah shel ha-agadah: ha-agadah le-or mekorot Yevanim* (Tel Aviv: 1972).

411. _____. *Parshiyot ba-agadah le-or mekorot Yevanim* (Haifa: 1973).

412. _____. *ha-Agadah ha-historit-biografit: me-anshei Keneset ha-gedolah 'ad Rabi Yehudah ha-Nasi: le-or mekorot Yevanim ve-Latiniyim* (Tel Aviv: 1975).

413. _____. *Agadot ha-amora'im: ha-agadah ha-biografit shel amora'ei Erets Yisra'el u-Vavel le-or mekorot Yevanim ve-Latiniyim* (Tel Aviv: 1977).

414. Kagan, Ziporah. "Tevat Pandorah ba-mitus ha-Yevani uve-agadat Yisra'el," *Mahanayim* 112 (1967), pp. 130-135.

415. Kaminka, Armand. "Hillel's Life and Work," JQR 30 (1939), pp. 107-122 (= Fischel, *Essays*, pp. 78-93)

416. Lachs, Samuel Tobias. "The Pandora-Eve Motif in Rabbinic Literature," HThR 67 (1974), pp. 341-345.

417. Reinach, Theodore. "Hérodote et la Talmud," REJ 54 (1907), pp. 271-273.

418. Scheiber, Alexander, *Essays on Jewish Folklore and Comparative Literature* (Budapest, 1985) (parts appeared in "Aggada und Antike" and other articles in *Acta Antiqua* 9- 26 [1961-1978]).

419. Schwarzbaum, Haim. "Mishlei Esopus etsel Hazal," *Yeda' 'Am* 8 (1963), pp. 54-56.

420. _____. "Talmudic-Midrashic Affinities of Some Aesopic Fables," *Laographia* 22 (1965), pp. 466-483 (= Fischel, *Essays*, pp. 425-442).

421. Wallach, Luitpold. "A Palestinian Polemic against Idolatry: A Study in Rabbinic Literary Forms," HUCA 19 (1946), pp. 389-404 (= Fischel, *Essays*, pp. 111-126).

iv. Christian Traditions

422. Abrahams, Israel. *Studies in Pharisaism and the Gospels: First and Second Series* (2 vol., Cambridge: 1917-1924; repr. 1 vol., New York: 1967).

423. Aptowitzer, Viktor. "Les éléments juives dans la légende du Golgotha," REJ 79 (1924), pp. 144-162.

424. Bultmann, Rudolf. *Die Geschichte der synoptischer Tradition*, 2nd ed. (Gottingen: 1931) (tr. John Marsh, *The History of the Synoptic Tradition* [Oxford: 1968]).

425. Fiebig, Paul. *Altjüdische Gleichnisse und die Gleichnisse Jesu* (Tübingen: 1904).

426. Flusser, David. "Ha-ra'ita mi-yamekha ari sabal?" in *ha-Mikra ve-toldot Yisra'el: mehkarim le-zikhro shel Ya'akov Liver*, ed. Benjamin Uffenheimer (Tel Aviv: 1972), pp. 330-340.

427. _____. *Die rabbinischen Gleichnisse und der Gleichniserzähler Jesus* (Bern: 1981).

428. Ginzberg, Louis. *Die Haggada bei den Kirchvätern* 2 vol. (Amsterdam: 1899; Berlin: 1900); sections published in ten parts MGWJ 42-43 (1898-1899); other sections published in *Sefer zikaron li-khevod Dr. Shmu'el Poznanski* (Warsaw: 1927), Eng. sect. pp. 199-216; *Studies in Jewish Bibliography and Related Subjects in Memory of Abraham Solomon Freidus* (New York: 1929), pp. 503-518; *Abhandlungen zur Erinnerung an Hirsch Perez Chajes* (Vienna: 1933), Eng. sect. pp. 22-50; *Studies in Memory of George A. Kohut*, ed. Salo W. Baron and Alexander Marx (New York: 1935), pp. 279-314.

429. Heller, Bernard. "Éléments, paralleles et origine de la légende des sept dormants," REJ 49 (1904), pp. 190-208; and "Encore un mot sur la légende des sept dormants," REJ 53 (1907), pp. 111-114.

430. _____. "La légende judéo-chrétienne du compagnon au paradis," REJ 56 (1908), pp. 198-221.

431. Lévi, Israel. "La légende de l'ange et l'ermite dans les écrits juifs," REJ 8 (1883), pp. 64-73; and "Nouvelle note sur la légende de l'ange et l'ermite," REJ 48 (1904), pp. 275-277.

432. _____. "Légendes judéo-chrétiennes," REJ 8 (1883), pp. 197-205.

433. Mirsky, Aaron. "Mi-derashot Hazal be-shirei ha-Mikra shel ha-Anglo-Saksim," in *Sefer Hayim Schirmann: kovets mehkarim*, ed. Aaron Mirsky and Shraga Abramson (Jerusalem: 1970), pp. 179-194.

434. Neusner, Jacob, "Types and Forms in Ancient Jewish Literature: Some Comparisons," *History of Religions* 11 (1971-72), pp. 354-390.

435. Oesterley, W. O. E. *The Gospel Parables in the Light of their Jewish Background* (New York: 1936).

436. Porton, Gary G. "The Pronouncement Story in Tannaitic Literature: A Review of Bultmann's Theory," *Semeia* 20 (1981), pp. 81-100.

437. Smith, Morton. *Makbilot ben ha-Besorot le-sifrut ha-Tana'im* (Ph.D. thesis, Heb. Univ.: 1945) (tr. *Tannaitic Parallels to the Gospels* (Philadelphia: 1951)).

438. _____. "A Comparison of Early Christian and Early Rabbinic Tradition," *JBL* 82 (1963), pp. 169-176.

v. Muslim Traditions

439. Goitein, Shlomo Dov. *Jews and Arabs: Their Contacts Through the Ages*, 3rd ed. (pbk., New York: 1974), esp. "Folk Literature and Art," pp. 192-211.

440. Heller, Bernard. "La chute des anges: Schemhazai, Ouzza et Azaël," *REJ* 60 (1910), pp. 202-212.

441. Perles, Joseph. "Rabbinische Agada's in 1001 Nacht: ein Beitrag zur Geschichte der Wanderung orientalischer Märchen," *MGWJ* 22 (1873), pp. 14-34, 61-85, 116-125.

442. Schapiro, Israel. *Die haggadischen Elementen im erzählenden Teil des Korans* (Berlin: 1907).

443. Schussman, Aviva. "Mekoro ha-Yehudi shel sipurei bikurei Avraham etsel Yishma'el," *Tarbiz* 49 (1980), pp. 325-345 (= Shinan, *Mikra'ah*, pp. 266-288).

444. Schwarzbaum, Haim. "The Jewish and Moslem Versions of Some Theodicy Legends," *Fabula* 3 (1959), pp. 119-169.

445. _____. *Mi-mekor Yisra'el ve-Yishma'el: Yahadut ve-Islam be-aspeklaryat ha-folklor* (Tel Aviv: 1975).

vi. Other

446. Darmesteter, James. "Les six feux dans le Talmud et dans le Bundehesh," *REJ* 1 (1880), pp. 186-196.

447. _____. "David et Rama," *REJ* 2 (1880), pp. 300-302.

448. Heller, Bernard. "Egyiptomi elemek az aggádában" in *Jubilee Volume in honour of Edward Mahler* (Budapest: 1937), pp. 436-441 (tr. "Egyptian Elements in the Haggadah," in *Ignace Goldziher Memorial Volume:* Part I, ed. Samuel Löwinger and Joseph Somogyi [Budapest: 1948], pp. 412-

418; "Yesodot Mitsriyim ba-agadah," in *Arba'ah ma'amarim 'al ha-agadah*, ed. Dov Noy [Jerusalem: 1956], pp. 9-15).

449. Kohut, Alexander. "Parsic and Jewish Legends of the First Man," JQR 3 (1891), pp. 231-250.

450. Krappe, Alexander Hagerty, "An Indian Tale in the Midrash Tanhuma," in *Papers and Transactions of the Jubilee Congress of the Folklore Society* (London: 1929), pp. 278-283 (tr. "Ma'asiyah Hodit be-Midrash Tanhuma," in *Arba'ah ma'amarim 'al ha-agadah*, ed. Noy [Jerusalem: 1956], pp. 42-46).

451. Marmorstein, Arthur. "Egyptian Mythology and Babylonian Magic in Bible and Talmud," in *Jubilee Volume in Honour of Edward Mahler* (Budapest: 1937), pp. 469-487.

452. Schwarzbaum, Haim. "Me-otsar ha-folklor ha-Mitsri ha-'atik," *Mahanayim* 105 (1966), p. 112-127.

453. Spiegel, Shalom. "Noah, Danel and Job: touching on Canaanite Relics in the Legends of the Jews," in *Louis Ginzberg Jubilee Volume* (New York: 1945), Eng. sect., pp. 305-356 (esp. "Heyyin and his Brother in Rabbinic and Moslem Legend," pp. 341-356).

XI.   Interpretations and Retellings of Aggadic Narratives

i. Medieval and Early Modern

454. Bacher, Wilhelm. "Die Agada in Maimunis Werken," in *Moses ben Maimon: sein Leben, seine Werke, und sein Einfluss*, ed. J. Guttmann (Leipzig: 1914), vol. 2, pp. 131-197.

455. Bergmann, Juda. "Abrabanels Stellung zur Agada," MGWJ 81 (1931), pp. 270-280.

456. Braude, William G. "Maimonides' Attitude to Midrash," in *Studies in Jewish Bibliography, History and Literature in Honor of I. Edward Kiev*, ed. Charles Berlin (New York: 1971), pp. 75-82.

457. Dan, Joseph. *ha-Sipur ha-'Ivri bi-yemei ha-benayim* (Jerusalem: 1974).

458. Elbaum, Jacob. "R. Judah Loew and his Attitude to the Aggadah," SH 22 (1971), pp. 28-47.

459. _____. "Ben midrash le-sefer musar: 'iyun bi-ferakim 1-6 be-Tana de-ve Eliyahu," JSHL 1 (1981), pp. 144-154.

460. Falk, Felix. "Di Talmudishe agadah fun Shelomoh ha-melekh mitn Ashmeday un dem shamir in tsvay altyidishe nusha'ot," *Yivobleter* 13 (1938), pp. 246-274.

461. Gaster, Moses. "Introduction," to *Ma'aseh Book: Book of Jewish Tales and Legends*, tr. M. Gaster (Philadelphia: 1934).

462. Heinemann, Joseph. "'Ibudei agadot kedumot be-ruah ha-zeman be-Firkei Rabi Eli'ezer," in *Sefer ha-Yovel le-Shim'on Halkin*, ed. Boaz Shahevitch and Menahem Peri (Jerusalem: 1975), pp. 321-343.

463. Landau, Luis. "ha-Transformatsyah shel ha-sipur ha-Talmudi be-*Me-'am lo'ez*," *Pe'amim* 7 (1981), pp. 35-49.

464. Lévi, Israel. "Contes Juifs," REJ 11 (1885), pp. 209-234.

465. Mirsky, Aaron. "Tsurot noi u-samemanei piyut shebe-midreshei ha-agadah: avot tsurot la-piyut ha-erets Yisra'eli," (Ph.D. thesis, Hebrew Univ.: 1954).

466. Rabinowitz, Zvi Meir. *Halakhah ve-agadah be-fiyutei Yanai* (Tel Aviv: 1965).

467. Saperstein, Marc. "R. Isaac b. Yeda'ya: a Forgotten Commentator on the Aggada," REJ 138 (1979), pp. 17-45.

468. _____. "The Earliest Commentary on the Midrash Rabbah," in *Studies in Medieval Jewish History and Literature*, ed. Isadore Twersky (Cambridge, Mass.: 1979), pp. 283-306.

469. _____. *Decoding the Rabbis: A Thirteenth Century Commentary on the Aggadah* (Cambridge, Mass.: 1980) (and see review by Jacob Elbaum, "'Al parshanut ha-agadah," *Tarbiz* 52 [1982-83], pp. 669-679).

470._____. "Yedaiah Bedersi's Commentary on the Midrashim," 8th WCJS (Jerusalem: 1981), vol. 3, Eng. sect., pp. 59-65.

471. _____. "Selected Passages from Yedaiah Bedersi's Commentary on the Midrashim," in *Studies in Medieval Jewish History and Literature II*, ed. Isadore Twersky (Cambridge, Mass.: 1984), pp. 423-440.

472. Schirmann, Hayim [Jefim]. "The Battle Between Behemoth and Leviathan according to an Ancient Hebrew *Piyyut*," *Proceedings of the Israel Academy of Sciences and Humanities* 4 (1969-70), pp. 327-369.

473. Twersky, Isadore, "R. Yeda'yah ha-Penini u-ferusho la-agadah," in *Studies in Jewish Religious and Intellectual History Presented to Alexander Altmann*, ed. Siegfried Stein and Raphael Loewe (University of Alabama: 1979), Heb. sect., pp. 63-82.

474. Yassif, Eli. "*Sefer Ma'asim*: le-ofyav, mekorotav ve-hashpa'ato shel kovets sipurim mi-zemanam shel Ba'alei ha-Tosafot," *Tarbiz* 53 (1984), pp. 409-429.

ii. Modern

475. Aderet, Avraham. "ha-Sipur be-*Sefer ha-agadah*," *'Alei Sefer* 3 (1976), pp. 170-181; 4-5 (1977), pp. 122-139 (and see David Corona, "'Al ha-ma'amar ha-Sipur be-*Sefer ha-agadah*," and Aderet, "Teshuvah," *'Alei Sefer* 6 (1978), pp. 241-246.

476. Bin Gorion, Emanuel and Dan Ben Amos. "Introduction," to Micha Joseph Bin Gorion, *Mimekor Yisrael: Classical Jewish Folktales,* tr. I. M. Lask (Bloomington: 1976), pp. 15-65.

477. Guttman, Joshua. "Bialik ba'al ha-agadah," *Keneset* 5 (1940), pp. 62-71.

478. Halevi, E. E. "ha-Kompositsiyah shel ha-agadah ('al *Sefer ha-agadah*)," *Keneset* 10 (1945-46), pp. 41-58.

479. Heller, Bernard. "Di Talmudishe agadah vegn Ashmeday in Tolstoys a folksma'aseh," *Yivobleter* 13 (1938), pp. 29-35.

480. Kagan, Ziporah. "ha-Agadah bi-yetsirato shel M. Y. Berdichevski (Bin Gorion)" (Ph.D. thesis, Hebrew Univ.: 1972).

481. _____. "Me-agadah le-novelah: metamorfozah sifrutit bi-yetsirato shel M. Y. Berdichevski," *ha-Sifrut* 3 (1971), pp. 242-254 (= "From Folktale to Novella: Literary Metamorphosis in a work of M. Y. Berdichevski," *Genre* 7 [1974], pp. 362-391).

482. _____. "Darkhei shiluvah shel ha-agadah be-*Miryam* le-Mikhah Yosef Berdichevski (Bin Gorion)," *ha-Sifrut* 4 (1973), pp. 519-545.

484. _____. "Ugat-Honi: darkah shel strukturah mitit me-sifrut ha-agadah el sifrut ha-'Ivrit ha-hadashah," *Sefer ha-Yovel le-Shim'on Halkin,* ed. Boaz Shahevitch and Menahem Peri (Jerusalem: 1975), pp. 489-501.

485. _____. "Sefat ha-mar'ot: gesher ben sifrut ha-agadah le-ven ha-sifrut ha-'Ivrit ha-hadashah 'al pi *Bayit tivneh* le-M. Y. Berdichevski (Bin Gorion)," *Karmelit* 20-21 (1977-78), pp. 292-308.

486. _____. "ha-Zikah ben defusei ha-sipur ha-agadi ha-mesorati li-defusei ha-sipur ha-moderni shel M. Y. Berditshevski 'al pi sipuro *Ben ha-hayim veha-metim," in Heker ve-'iyun be-mad'ei ha-Yahadut: sifrut, Mikra, lashon* (Haifa: 1976), ed. Jacob Bahat et al., pp. 259-266.

487. _____. *Me-agadah le-siporet modernit bi-yetsirat Berdichevski* (Tel Aviv: 1983).

488. Shenhar, Aliza. "Li-mekoroteha ha-'amamiyim shel *Agadat sheloshah ve-arba'ah* (nusah A)," *Yeda' 'Am* 17 (1974), pp. 28-32.

489. Werses, Samuel. "Motivim demonologiyim be-*Susati* le-Mendele u-mekorotehem," *Tarbiz* 50 (1981), pp. 515-531.

490. Yassif, Eli. "ha-Siporet ha-'Ivrit be-artsot ha-mizrah: hitgabshutah bi-yemei ha-benayim u-ma'avarah la-'et ha-hadashah," *Pe'amim* 26 (1986), pp. 53-70; and see Galit Hazan-Rokem, "Teguvah," pp. 71-74.